Desegregating
America's Colleges and Universities
TITLE VI REGULATION OF HIGHER EDUCATION

Desegregating
America's Colleges and Universities
TITLE VI REGULATION OF HIGHER EDUCATION

John B. Williams, III
Editor

Teachers College, Columbia University
New York and London

Published by Teachers College Press, 1234 Amsterdam Avenue,
New York, NY 10027

Library of Congress Cataloging-in-Publication Data

Desegregating America's colleges and universities.

   Essays presented at the Colloquium on Title VI Regulation of Higher Education,
held at the Harvard Graduate School of Education, 1985.
   Bibliography: p.
   Includes index.
   1. Segregation in higher education—United States—Congresses. 2. Afro-Amer-
icans—Education (Higher)—United States—Congresses. 3. Educational law and
legislation—United States—Congresses. I. Williams, John B., 1944-   . II. Colloquium on Title VI Regulation of Higher Education (1985 : Harvard Graduate School
of Education) III. Title.
LC212.72.D47   1987   370.19′342   87-19082
ISBN 0-8077-2870-5

Manufactured in the United States of America

93 92 91 90 89 88   1 2 3 4 5 6

Contents

Acknowledgments

A grant from the Ford Foundation enabled me to organize the Colloquium on Title VI Regulation of Higher Education at the Harvard Graduate School of Education in spring 1985. The essays included in the
volume were presented at the colloquium, and their preparation is in large
measure due to the generosity of the Ford Foundation.

I would also like to acknowledge the advice and guidance of colloquium participants who read and offered enlightening comments about
the essays presented. As a result of their thoughtful participation many
improvements were made and new materials were added.

I would like to offer a special note of appreciation to four individuals
who played vital roles in the colloquium project. Patricia A. Graham,
Dean of the Harvard Graduate School of Education, encouraged me to
organize the colloquium and provided an opportunity to edit and prepare
the essays for publication. Professor Charles Willie, also at Harvard, in-
troduced me to the study of Title VI regulation of higher education. Jean
Fairfax, formerly of the NAACP Legal Defense Fund, has over the years
exemplified the kind of effective leadership needed to accomplish improved minority participation in higher education. And finally, Beatrice
Dambreville provided expert preparation of the manuscript for publication. The participation and essential support of these individuals is acknowledged and deeply appreciated.

J.B.W.

Introduction

JOHN B. WILLIAMS, III

This book addresses the issue of black Americans' limited access to higher education. Despite attempts to remedy this problem since the mid-1960s, blacks remain underrepresented within the nation's system of colleges and universities. Perhaps more notably, their participation is declining. Between 1976 and 1982 the black proportion of total higher education enrollment nationwide declined from 9.4 to 8.9%. It declined an additional 3.2% between 1980 and 1984. This change occurred despite the fact that black 18- to 24-year-olds constituted an increasingly larger proportion of this total age cohort, a trend that will continue for the next two or three decades.

Evidence also exists that some of the limited gains in employment of black faculty during the last two decades have been reversed. Where faculty are concerned, data are less certain, but best estimates are that about 1% of today's college faculty at four-year, predominantly white institutions are black, representing a reduction of about 1% from about a decade earlier. Between 1977 and 1983, black faculty declined from 4.4% of total faculty nationwide, to 4.0%.

The increase in black enrollment that began in the mid-1960s and peaked in 1976 is attributed by many educators and policy analysts to government action. In particular, the federal government's student financial aid programs for low-income college aspirants are credited with having accelerated black enrollment, since so many black students require financial assistance in order to afford the costs of college attendance. But federal and state governments since 1976 have dealt with this problem perhaps less successfully on other fronts.

This volume is concerned with a little known but potentially significant set of public policy interventions aimed at correcting the problem of underrepresentation of blacks in public higher education in a cross-section of states. More specifically, the chapters that follow address continued failure to comply, in a legal sense, with the provisions of Title VI of the 1964 Civil Rights Law. Title VI prohibits the distribution of federal funds to colleges and universities that discriminate on the basis of race, color, or national origin. Through a combination of action by the US Department of Education, the federal courts, and public interest groups like the NAACP Legal Defense Fund, 19 states have been found guilty of operating *de jure* segregated higher education facilities. Government officials and educators in each of these states have planned remedies for the lingering effects of past laws that denied access to higher education on the basis of race, but no previously segregated state college or university system has achieved full compliance with Title VI.

Over 53% of all blacks in college are affected, and over 46% of all public colleges and universities in the country are directly involved. The 19 states are: Alabama, Arkansas, Delaware, Florida, Georgia, Kentucky, Louisiana, Maryland, Mississippi, Missouri, Ohio, Oklahoma, Pennsylvania, North Carolina, South Carolina, Tennessee, Texas, Virginia, and West Virginia.

The contributors to this volume explore the manner in which compliance with Title VI has been undertaken. Through formal research and others forms of inquiry, the authors describe: (1) the federal-state-local regulatory process; (2) state and local desegregation remedies; and (3) problems directly and indirectly associated with the implementation of desegregation remedies.

Perhaps more than any other salient fact, the evidence contained in this book shows convincingly that little progress has been made in improving black participation in the 19 affected state higher education systems despite the fact that Title VI regulatory activities have been taking place since 1969. According to most recent data, black enrollment declined between 1980 and 1984 in 13 of the 19 states involved in Title VI regulation, and only small increases or no change occurred in the remaining six.

In view of these results, it will come as no surprise that the process of achieving compliance with the law has not been a popular one. Stated reservations about Title VI programs do not center upon the goal of improved participation by blacks. Critics instead question: (1) the appropriateness of offering remedial instruction and the consequences, for the regular academic program of a college or university, of doing so on a large scale; (2) financially and politically competitive pressures surrounding special efforts to train, recruit, and promote black faculty and administrators; (3) disappearance of traditionally black colleges and universities; (4) greater control over campus affairs by state and federal government; and (5) higher college budgets resulting from increased student aid programs, new faculty recruitment and development opportunities, and black college enhancement.

On one level this book is about failure by government to address these fears and to remedy the problem of unequal college opportunities for blacks in states that in the past legally denied access by race. At least in the 19 states affected by Title VI, the information presented refutes the widely held notion that equity problems in higher education have disappeared—that anyone can attend these days who has the ability and will to do so.

On another level Title VI exemplifies a particular kind of public policy attempt to resolve what most would regard as an important broad-based social problem. If only by implication, this book also discusses the difficulties involved in implementing certain kinds of government policies within public-sector institutions. Title VI is a redistributive regulatory policy, the sort perhaps most difficult to implement. It aims at redistributing college resources so that blacks obtain their lawful share, and it attempts to do so by threatening to apply sanctions—the withdrawal of federal funds—if colleges and university systems do not reach compliance. Such policies inevitably meet with great resistance from those groups that previously benefited from the lion's share of public resources, and from other participants who feel directly threatened by the application of sanctions. From previous attempts to undertake such policy implementations, it is clear that policy officials must somehow deal with this type of resistance if policy goals are to be attained. The chapters explore reasons for failure of Title VI regulation from a public administration perspective as well.

The contributions to this volume were prepared for the Research Colloquium on Title VI Regulation of Higher Education, which took place at the Harvard Graduate School of Education in April, 1985. The Ford Foundation generously provided funding for the colloquium. The papers are presented in two parts. Chapters in Part I use policy analysis methods to offer a portrait of progress toward Title VI goals including increased black student enrollment and increased employment of black faculty and administrators. The writers assume both the broad perspective of measuring progress on a statewide basis and, on a smaller scale, the tasks of changing enrollment and employment in a single state system or a single campus. The chapters making up Part II address issues and problems raised by Part I's portrayal of limited success with demonstrable pockets of progress.

To begin Part I, the first chapter, "Title VI Regulation of Higher Education," briefly provides a survey of court decisions and other important policy events surrounding Title VI regulation. This discussion highlights important problems associated with achieving improved black participation in higher education through government regulatory means. This paper presents data from public sources describing changes in employment and enrollment, initiating the major theme of the entire volume—that little progress has been achieved. The author relies upon standards for measuring progress and assessments by the federal government to illustrate this finding, and also speculates about the reasons for slow progress, drawing upon prior public policy implementation research.

The next chapter, "The Production of Black Doctoral Recipients: A Description of Five States' Progress," looks in more detail at a specific element of the federal government's Title VI compliance program. This provision of the 1964 Civil Rights Law requires an increase at all levels in black student participation, but the authors determine whether public systems have successfully increased a specific sector of enrollment, the Ph.D. sector. They are concerned with whether the states involved have successfully increased the number of Ph.D.s awarded to blacks by providing student financial aid. The authors report and analyze current attempts in this direction.

The third chapter, "Title VI Issues as Viewed from a Chancellor's Office," offers a discussion of what takes place in a state system once Title VI regulatory activities begin. In particular, from the perspective of a chancellor, interactions between Title VI regulation and related state higher education policy are explored. The author discusses ways in which emerging state reforms aimed at improving the quality of higher education sometimes interact with achievement of Title VI goals.

The fourth chapter, "*Adams* Litigation: One State's Unique Response for the Enhancement of Its Historically Black University," provides an account of what takes place at a black college campus once Title VI implementation begins. From the perspective of a college president, this chapter conveys the reality of undertaking the tasks involved in desegregation at the campus level. The author's views "from the bottom up" complement, clarify, and contradict some of the assertions made "from the top down" in the earlier chapters.

Similar to the two previous chapters, the last in Part I, "Desegregation of Higher Education: A Private/Public Cooperative Alternative," presents a personalized view of the resources and amount of effort that may actually be needed to accomplish a very small portion of Title VI goals. The current director of a new scholarship program for postgraduate education describes his experience leading to involvement in the new program and the manner in which he has undertaken responsibility to organize it. The program exemplifies a substantial long-range approach to the problem of the absence of a pool of black faculty for employment in public higher education in Title VI states.

As already mentioned, Part II contains chapters that further explore Title VI implementation and progress by providing information about the context in which these events occur. The first chapter, "Initiation of Desegregation Litigation: A Majority or Minority Responsibility," explores assumptions upon which Title VI as a public policy is based. The author's concern is primarily whether the manner of implementation is dependent upon how Title VI implementation came about. More specifically, he asks whether blacks might have pushed for a different and perhaps more thorough implementation process if they, the aggrieved parties, had played a leading role in court litigation leading up to forced implementation. This discussion offers a different perspective on the decisions reached about the requirements and process of implementing the Title VI policy.

The second chapter, "Trends in Black Enrollment and Degree Attainment in Higher Education," suggests changes in the overall picture of college and university enrollment in the states involved in Title VI regulation. Unlike the chapters of Part I, this chapter explores enrollment trends without any attempt to attribute them to a particular source. It therefore suggests changes that would have occurred even if Title VI intervention had not taken place. Including data for all states involved, the authors illustrate the magnitude of the tasks involved in achieving heightened black participation.

The third chapter in Part II, "The Educational Attainment Process among Black Youth," also explores important aspects of black students' college participation under circumstances not particularly affected by Title VI. The authors hypothesize that social-psychological factors play a smaller role in blacks' educational attainment than similar factors play for whites; comparatively, quality of schooling seems more important among blacks than among whites. One implication is that remedies for higher education desegregation should consist of long-term interventions that provide better preparatory schooling, rather than short-term incentives that may change black students' aspirations once they reach high school.

The results of the fourth chapter, "Black and White Students' Academic Performance in Majority White and Majority Black College Settings," hold similar advice for revising the current Title VI regulatory approach. The reported research assesses how well students who constitute a racial minority perform at both majority white and majority black institutions. This study probes the controversial issue of whether attendance at a white college is beneficial for blacks, and vice versa. The implication might be that Title VI ought to emphasize the attainment of equal academic achievement between blacks and whites, even if doing so requires maintaining racially distinct institutions.

The fifth chapter of Part II, "Determining Financial Inequities in Previously Segregated Public Systems of Higher Education," presents a method for determining and then eliminating disparities in funding black and white institutions within the same system. This task is especially difficult for judicial and administrative decision-makers. Moreover, financial equity is fundamental to other Title VI goals. Although bringing black institutions up to parity with white ones constitutes a major element of Title VI regulation, few states have done so effectively. On the assumption that failure to do so results from lack of knowledge, this chapter aims at offering useful advice.

The sixth chapter, "A Research Agenda in Support of Desegregation in Higher Education," suggests areas for research that can contribute to improvements in Title VI regulation. Very little research has been undertaken on this topic for the same reason as with almost any public policy topic: (1) the problems confronted by policy-makers and implementors are complex and not conducive to short-term research and inquiry approaches, (2) academic and professional theory does not match the complexity of the problem involved, (3) political support for Title VI regulation is not substantial, and (4) appropriate research and inquiry is expensive. These difficulties notwithstanding, the author of the final chapter, based on his experience with Title VI as a researcher, advisor, and administrator, identifies useful areas of inquiry and suggests their relationship to salient aspects of the Title VI implementation and policy-making effort.

In the final chapter, I attempt to suggest what will happen in the future with Title VI regulation of higher education. A risky undertaking, at best, the essay draws upon the findings and views expressed in the preceding chapters.

PART I

Implementation and Progress

1
Title VI Regulation of Higher Education

JOHN B. WILLIAMS, III
Harvard University

The nation's unsuccessful pursuit of remedies for *de jure* racial segregation in public college and university systems since 1969 is a largely unknown public policy event. Despite its long history and its broad scope, federal regulation of higher education aimed at achieving compliance with Title VI of the 1964 Civil Rights Law goes unnoticed for at least two reasons. First of all, the news and sports media present an image of higher education characterized by widespread racial diversity—even in states like Mississippi and Alabama where violent racial confrontations against admitting black youth to college occurred on campus in the recent past. The public impression is that problems of racial segregation in higher education have ended. Other problems, such as drug abuse in college sports, have captured the public's attention.

Indeed, improvement in desegregation has occurred over the past two decades: Virtually all colleges and universities today espouse race-neutral student admission and personnel policies, and substantial increases in black student enrollment have taken place. Between 1965 and 1970, total black student enrollment at predominantly white colleges and universities increased 308%, and increased again by 148% between 1970 and 1976 (NCES, 1976). Voluntary action taken by colleges and universities, availability of federal student financial aid, and affirmative action regulations all led to these changes (Mingle, 1981; Peterson et al., 1978). But this dramatic upsurge in total black participation leads educators to overlook the lingering effects of legally sanctioned racial segregation.

The segregation problem still exists. As a recent American Council on Education study showed, the following problems offer evidence of its persistence:

1. Blacks . . . continue to be underrepresented in enrollments in four-year institutions.

3

2. Blacks experienced proportional enrollment declines at all postsecondary levels, though they have registered slight increases in absolute numbers since 1976.

3. Blacks experienced losses in their proportional share of degrees earned at every level between 1976 and 1981.

4. Black men registered significant decreases in degrees received at all levels between 1976 and 1981.

5. [B]lacks experienced increases in the number of high school graduates from 1975 to 1980, but the percentage of high school graduates enrolling in college . . . declined. (American Council on Education, 1986, p. 4)

These data not only confirm the continued existence of racial segregation as a problem but illustrate why government officials, educators, students, and the public at large overlook Title VI compliance efforts. The record of achievement of federal regulatory goals and therefore the success of Title VI regulatory activities has not been outstanding. Consequently, the courts have repeatedly admonished the several parties involved to pursue desegregation with more determination and commitment (*Adams v. Weinberger*, 1975; *Adams v. Califano*, 1977).

A third reason that Title VI regulation is a little-known policy, despite the considerable implications of full compliance, is that other civil rights policies are often confused with Title VI regulation. Desegregation changes also come about as a result of federal regulation of college and university systems not based upon findings of *de jure* segregation, or segregation caused by statutes requiring colleges and universities to separate students on the basis of race. The distinction between *de jure* and *de facto* segregation emerged in the Birmingham, Alabama, school desegregation court decision *US v. Jefferson County Board of Education* (1966).

In addition, voluntary action by private colleges to recruit and enroll larger numbers of minority students at times resembles campus-level strategies mandated under Title VI. Implementation of "affirmative action" policies is also confused with Title VI implementation even though several statutes independent of Title VI give rise to affirmative action remedies, and are implemented in different ways (Carnegie Council, 1975).

Several elements of Title VI regulation distinguish it from other federal interventions that share the goal of increased racial equity. Among these elements are the following:

1. Title VI regulation, where higher education is concerned, holds state governments accountable for proposing and implementing desegregation remedies. In other instances individual institutions are cited for failure to comply.

2. Since 1969 the District Court of the District of Columbia has been al-

most exclusively involved in judicial oversight, rendering judgments about compliance requirements and results in public higher education, even though courts in Mississippi, Alabama, Tennessee, Louisiana, Maryland, and North Carolina have in recent years become actively involved. Judicial oversight for civil rights cases involving individuals or individual institutions is spread throughout the nation's judiciary system.

3. Within the federal *executive* branch, the Office for Civil Rights (OCR) at the Department of Education holds responsibility for Title VI regulation. Where other civil rights laws are concerned, responsibility for implementation is shared among numerous administrative units.

4. In most states where a finding has been rendered, only one set of administrative guidelines is used to prescribe remedies. Exceptions occur in instances where the Justice Department has pursued litigation to force compliance either on its own or by joining with private cases as in North Carolina, Mississippi, and Louisiana.

5. Except in Texas, only black Americans are considered plaintiffs in class action litigation under Title VI.

The following analysis explores continued noncompliance with Title VI of the 1964 Civil Rights Law. It is concerned with three issues: (1) the extent to which Title VI remedies have been undertaken with success; (2) the reasons why full compliance, relying upon the judgments of the courts, has not been achieved; and (3) whether remediable barriers to compliance might yet be removed.

HISTORY OF TITLE VI REGULATION OF HIGHER EDUCATION

Federal legislators intended Title VI of the Civil Rights Act of 1964 to enhance implementation of the well-known *Brown v. Board of Education* (1954) decision. The then existing US Department of Health, Education and Welfare (DHEW) assumed responsibility for conducting desegregation compliance reviews at colleges and universities. Based upon reviews of public higher education in 1968 and 1969—federal expeditions never previously undertaken—DHEW sent letters to the governors of 10 states informing them that their systems of higher education stood in violation of Title VI and thus ran the risk of losing federal funds. The letters of finding described desegregation problems in the 10 systems and requested formal plans for addressing the problems (*Adams v. Richardson*, 1973).

In a brief space, it is difficult to generalize about the contents of these initial letters of finding, since the standards for judging segregation and the nature of the federal government's responsibility under Title VI was substantially unclear at the time they were written. Some letters emphasize findings of persistently low black enrollment at predominantly white institutions, while others seem more concerned with the continued existence of predominantly black institutions in the states where compliance reviews took place. Nonetheless, a December 2, 1969 letter to then-Governor Mills E. Godwin of the Commonwealth of Virginia describes in typical fashion elements leading to findings of segregation in Virginia's public college system.

Honorable Mills E. Godwin   December 2, 1969
Governor of Virginia
Richmond, VA 23219

Dear Governor Godwin:

The Office for Civil Rights of the Department of Health, Education, and Welfare has required that all institutions of higher education receiving Federal financial assistance submit a compliance report indicating the racial enrollment at these institutions. Based on these reports, particular colleges are visited to determine their compliance with Title VI of the Civil Rights Acts of 1964. These visits, together with the reports received from the four-year State colleges and universities in Virginia, indicate that the State of Virginia is operating a non-unitary system of higher education.

Specifically, the predominantly white State institutions providing four or more years of higher education have an enrollment which is approximately 99 percent white. The predominantly black institutions have an enrollment which is predominantly black in similar proportions. In addition to this situation which prevails in individual institutions throughout the State, the two land grant colleges, Virginia Polytechnic Institute and Virginia State College, originally devised as separate agricultural and technical colleges, one for blacks and one for whites, remain structurally separate and predominantly of one race, the latter black and the former white. Another manifestation of the State's racially dual system of higher education is evident in the City of Norfolk in which are situated two large institutions, predominantly white Old Dominion University and predominantly black Norfolk State, the enrollment of which is 98 percent Negro.

Educational institutions which have previously been legally segregated have an affirmative duty to adopt measures to overcome the effect of the past segregation. To fulfill the purposes and intent of the Civil Rights Act of 1964, it is not sufficient that an institution maintain a nondiscriminatory admissions policy if the student population continues to reflect the formerly *de jure* racial identification of that institution.

This appears to be the situation at nearly all of the State institutions in

Virginia; therefore, these institutions must discharge their affirmative duty by adopting measures that will result in desegregation as soon as administratively possible.

We are aware that the scope of authority of each individual institution is not broad enough to effect the necessary changes and achieve the desired objectives. However, this legal disability does not relieve responsible State officials of the duty to make whatever cooperative arrangements are needed to continue the eligibility of the institutions for Federal financial assistance. Accordingly, I am directing to you the request that a desegregation plan for the public institutions of higher education in Virginia which are under State control be submitted for comment to this office in outline form 120 days from receipt of this letter, and that a final desegregation plan be submitted for our approval no later than 90 days after you have received comments on the outline of the plan.

While I do not wish to stipulate the form which a desegregation plan should take, I would suggest that a system-wide plan of cooperation between institutions involving consolidation of degree offerings, faculty exchange, student exchange, and general institutional sharing of resources would seem to offer a constructive approach. The Southern Regional Education Board, established by the Governors of the Southern and Border States, has available the programs and the results of inter-institutional cooperation and no doubt the Board would be willing to work with you, members of your staff, the State college presidents, and other Virginia State education officials in order to formulate an appropriate plan. In addition, officials of the Bureau of Higher Education in Washington and the Regional Office of Education have had considerable experience in this area, and these officials would be available to assist appropriate State education officials.

Needless to say, our staff will be available to offer whatever services may be appropriate. Dr. Eloise Severinson, Regional Civil Rights Director, Office for Civil Rights, Department of Health, Education and Welfare, 220 Seventh Street, N.E. Charlottesville, Virginia 22901, would be the person to contact for any information and assistance.

We look forward to working with you to bring about a desegregated system of State higher education in Virginia.

Sincerely yours,

Leon E. Panetta
Director, Office for Civil Rights
(Panetta to Godwin, 1969)

After receiving letters similar to this one, the states of Pennsylvania, Maryland, Georgia, and Arkansas joined Virginia in submitting plans which DHEW subsequently held to be unacceptable. Florida, Louisiana, Mississippi, North Carolina, and Oklahoma simply failed to submit plans. DHEW did little during 1970 to require the guilty states to submit plans or to require revisions of the unacceptable plans already submitted (*Adams v. Richardson*, 1973). This was the case because, upon election, President Richard M. Nixon inaugurated a new policy of nonenforcement of federal desegregation laws and policies. Evidence of nonaction extended to the primary and secondary arenas as well. Between 1964 and 1970, DHEW initiated about 600 compliance proceedings against local public school districts that refused to comply with Title VI desegregation requirements. About 100 enforcement proceedings were initiated in both 1968 and 1969, but between March 1970, when President Nixon's newly appointed director of the DHEW Office of Civil Rights took office, and February 1971, OCR initiated no enforcement proceedings (*Adams v. Richardson*, 1973).

Displeased by this course of events, the NAACP Legal Defense Fund inaugurated a class action suit aimed at eliciting a change in Nixon's policy. Where higher education was concerned, *Adams v. Richardson* (1973) aimed at forcing DHEW officials to (1) respond to the plans that had been received two to three years earlier, (2) institute enforcement proceedings where necessary, (3) monitor progress, and (4) conduct additional compliance reviews in other states.

Judge Henry Pratt of the US District Court of the District of Columbia found in favor of the plaintiffs. The court held that "continuation of HEW financial assistance to the segregated systems of higher education in the ten states violated the rights of plaintiffs and others similarly situated and protected by Title VI of the Civil Rights Act of 1964" (*Adams v. Richardson*, 1973). Judge Pratt ordered DHEW to begin within 120 days enforcement proceedings against states that failed to comply. DHEW appealed the decision, but the US Court of Appeals for the District of Columbia affirmed the district court ruling. The appeals court also allowed an additional 180 days after the submission of the state's desegregation plans for inauguration of enforcement proceedings (*Adams v. Richardson*, 1973).

Based upon the 1973 appeals court ruling, DHEW notified the 10 states to submit new desegregation plans, and by June 1974 eight of the 10 had done so and obtained DHEW approval. Louisiana again refused to submit a plan, and Mississippi's was deemed unacceptable. Both states were then referred to the Justice Department, but since private desegregation suits were pending in both states, the district courts asked the Justice Department to desist and join with plaintiffs in the private litigation. A settlement was not reached in Louisiana until 1981. Since the court ruled that individual agreements had to be reached with the boards of trustees at each two-year college in Mississippi (*Adams v. Califano*, 1977), negotiations have not been completed.

The original plaintiffs in *Adams v. Richardson* (1973) reviewed the eight approved plans during 1974 and the progress reports submitted to DHEW in 1975. Judging the plans to be inadequate and the reports to show little progress, plaintiffs petitioned for further relief. The district court in *Adams v. Califano* (1977) granted plaintiff's motion and ordered DHEW to devise specific criteria for construction of a desegregation plan and to require the states to submit new plans.

During the court's deliberation, Maryland and Pennsylvania filed separate actions removing them from consideration in *Adams v. Califano*. Maryland sought relief from further regulation by DHEW on the basis that the department had failed to adequately seek voluntary compliance before instituting enforcement proceedings. On August 9, 1977 the court ordered DHEW to discontinue the proceedings against the state of Maryland and to submit to state officials guidelines for the establishment of a new desegregation plan. Pennsylvania chose to negotiate a settlement with plaintiffs, but failed to do so until 1983 (*Chronicle of Higher Education*, July 27, 1983).

As a result of the *Adams v. Califano* decision, DHEW issued desegregation guidelines in July, 1977 and received court approval of them in February, 1978 (*Federal Register*, 1977). The Title VI guidelines identify four major elements that must be reflected in state higher education desegregation plans: (1) restructuring dual systems; (2) increasing black enrollments at predominantly white institutions and increasing white enrollment at traditionally black institutions; (3) increasing "other race" faculty, administrators, nonprofessional staff, and trustees; and (4) reporting and monitoring requirements.

In order to "disestablish the structure of the dual systems," the Office of Civil Rights' guidelines require in each state desegregation plan: (1) "definitions of the mission of each state college and university on a basis other than race"; (2) "specific steps to eliminate educationally unnecessary program duplication among traditionally black and traditionally white institutions in the same service arena"; (3) "steps . . . to strengthen the role of traditionally black institutions in the state system"; and (4) "prior consideration to placing . . . new . . . degree programs . . . at traditionally black institutions." The guidelines also suggest specific actions. These include reassigning duplicative instructional programs from one institution to another, mounting jointly conducted academic programs, adding new "high demand" programs at traditionally black institutions, and merging institutions or branches of colleges and universities.

Secondly, the guidelines require state systems to adopt strategies for increasing black student enrollment at traditionally white institutions. More specifically, the proportion of black high school graduates in a state who enter the state college and university system should at least equal the percentage of whites who graduate and similarly matriculate. At each traditionally white, four-year institution and the system as a whole, specified annual increases in the proportion of black undergraduate enrollment should occur. By the 1982–83 school year, such yearly increase should have resulted in a reduction by 50 percent of the disparity between the percentage of black and white high school graduates entering public institutions, but no state need increase its current black student enrollment by more than 150 percent over the enrollment for the 1976–77 school year.

Where graduate enrollment is concerned, the guidelines require goals for equalizing the proportion of white and black bachelor's degree recipients who enroll in graduate and professional programs in the state system. Separate annual and total goals must be established for each major field of study at the graduate and professional levels.

According to the guidelines, numerical goals for increasing the percentage of white students at traditionally black institutions should only take place when: (1) increase in black student enrollment at traditionally white institutions is demonstrably improved; (2) specific steps to enhance traditionally black institutions are successfully undertaken; (3) competing instructional programs at geographically proximate black and white institutions within the same system are eliminated; and (4) a complete assortment of new instructional programs has been assembled at traditionally black institutions. Goals for white enrollment at traditionally black institutions were required on September 1, 1979, assuming that the aforementioned changes had occurred.

The third substantive area addressed in the guidelines is the desegregation of faculty, administration, nonprofessional staff, and governing boards within the affected state systems. They call for an across-the-board increase in the number of blacks in all positions of employment and all fiduciary roles. More specifically:

1. The proportion of black faculty and of administrators at each institution and on the staffs of each governing board or any other state higher education entity, in positions not requiring the doctoral degree, shall at least equal the proportion of black students graduating with masters degrees from institutions within the state system, or the proportion of black individuals with the required credentials for such positions in the relevant labor market area, whichever is greater.
2. The proportion of black faculty and of administrators at each institution and on the staffs of each governing board or any other state higher education entity, in positions requiring the doctoral degree, shall at least equal the proportion of black individuals with the credentials required for such positions in the relevant labor market area.

3. The proportion of black non-academic personnel (by job category) at each institution and on the staffs of each governing board or any other state higher educational entity, shall at least equal the proportion of black persons in the relevant labor market area.

4. Until the foregoing goals are met that for the traditionally white institutions as a whole, the proportion of blacks hired to fill faculty and administrative vacancies shall not be less than the proportion of black individuals with the credentials required for such positions in the relevant labor market area. (*Federal Register*, 1978)

Where systemwide and institutional governing boards are concerned, the racial composition of the state or area served must be reflected in their composition. Timetables are required for accomplishing all the above outcomes. The fourth area of the guidelines specifies requirements for the submission of plans, deadlines, and timetables for monitoring progress.

Using these guidelines, six states—Arkansas, Florida, Georgia, Oklahoma, Virginia, and North Carolina—submitted new plans to DHEW. Five were approved for the 1978–79 school year after negotiation and revision, but North Carolina's was rejected, and DHEW inaugurated compliance proceedings. DHEW notified an additional eight states of *de jure* segregation violations in January, 1981, and asked them, using the guidelines, to assemble desegregation plans. The additional states were Alabama, Delaware, Kentucky, Missouri, South Carolina, Ohio, Texas, and West Virginia (Brown to White, 1981; Dodds to Rockefeller, 1981; Thomas to James, 1981; Dodds to Brown, 1981; High to Bond, 1981).

Interestingly, most states affected by *Adams v. Bell* (1973) did not publicly challenge DHEW's findings that effects of past *de jure* segregation still existed and that failure to institute remedies persisted. States that did engage in active resistance through the courts instead objected to the extent of the remedy required, including the range of institutions within their system that had to be affected. Mississippi argued, for example, that its community colleges founded after the *Brown* decision never were governed in a *de jure* discriminatory manner and, therefore, need not be included in the state desegregation plan (*Adams v. Califano*, 1977). In other states, face-saving postures emerged. Many used language in their plans that obfuscated the need to admit the existence of past *de jure* segregation as an unrecognized problem. Some state plans suggested the need to push further some of the remedies the states had themselves already undertaken.

The *Plan for the Further Desegregation of the University System of Georgia* begins, for example, with the following assertion of innocent acquiescence to the federal mandate:

All materials submitted in this document are prefaced by the specific observation that the University System is neither now nor has been in recent years
operated in a manner discriminatory toward any minority group. . . . [G]ood
faith has been, and is being practiced, in all aspects of the operations of the
University System of Georgia. (Georgia State Board of Regents, 1977,
pp. 2–3)

Similarly, Florida's desegregation plan begins with a resolution pleading
earlier compliance with the DHEW requirements:

WHEREAS the State Board of Education, the State's system of universities and
community colleges, and the Florida Legislature have taken positive actions
to provide equality of education and equality of educational opportunities for
all the citizens of Florida, and . . .

BE IT RESOLVED by the Board of Education, State of Florida that the Board
adopts "Florida's Commitment to Equal Access and Equal Opportunity in
Public Higher Education: . . . . (Florida State Department of Education,
1978, pp. i–ii)

The most highly publicized example of recalcitrance on the part of a
state higher education system occurred in 1979, when the US Department of Health, Education and Welfare reported to the federal court that
North Carolina's desegregation plan, issued in accordance with the newly
released guidelines, "offered no realistic promise of desegregating the
University of North Carolina [System]"(*Adams v. Bell*, 1982, p. 2). Once
DHEW took the first steps in the complex administrative and judicial
process that must be followed in order to terminate federal funds, the
University of North Carolina filed suit to block enforcement of the guidelines. The suit was filed in the Eastern District Court of North Carolina,
outside the jurisdiction of Judge Pratt in the Washington, DC District who
had held sole jurisdiction in *Adams v. Richardson* (1973). Judge Dupree
in Raleigh denied DHEW's petition to return jurisdiction to Judge Pratt's
court in Washington and ordered an administrative hearing in Washington to settle the issue. In a recent description of the North Carolina litigation, the issues were summarized as follows:

As a result, the issues were framed between November 1979 and June 1980
as these: the history of OCR-UNC relations, 1965–1980; the nature of racial
segregation in higher education; evidence of segregative acts and outcomes;
states' rights; university governance and academic freedom; the Revised
Criteria for Desegregation; and so forth. (Dentler, Baltzell, & Sullivan, 1983,
p. 6)

Clearly, a long hearing was in the making. Judge Dupree in Raleigh, later in 1981, ratified a consent decree between the University of North Carolina and the newly formed US Department of Education (ED), negotiated by a private attorney, Douglas F. Bennett, on behalf of then-Secretary of Education Terrell Bell in Washington (*State of North Carolina v. Department of Education*, 1981). The decree remains in effect until December 30, 1988, allowing parties to the case to seek further proceedings in Judge Dupree's court until that date. The US Supreme Court refused in February, 1984 to review the North Carolina consent decree, despite plaintiff's arguments that the agreements do not conform to the desegregation guidelines nor require the University of North Carolina system to move far enough or fast enough to remedy the problem (*Chronicle of Higher Education*, Feb. 29, 1984, p. 11).

The University of North Carolina litigation constitutes one example of active resistance; other states like Mississippi, Louisiana, Ohio, and Alabama adopted similar postures, risking unfavorable rulings by the courts and withdrawal of federal funds. This strategy seems to have paid off in some ways, since in the cases of Louisiana and Mississippi no federally approved desegregation strategies were implemented until 1981, more than 10 years after DHEW issued its first set of findings.

Most states affected by Title VI appeared, on the other hand, to have reacted passively, adopting a strategy of seeming to comply, of submitting plans as required, of undertaking some commitments made in the plans, but of doing little on the whole to really accomplish desegregation objectives. To a large extent, the US Department of Education (ED) and earlier DHEW cooperated with the passive resistance strategy of the states inasmuch as the plans approved by the ED (or DHEW) officials have clearly not met the plaintiffs' and the district court's standards of remedy. On at least three separate occasions, plaintiffs petitioned with success for further relief from the court. In each case the court admonished the ED or DHEW for approving plans that clearly did not meet the guidelines and for failing to instigate compliance proceedings as required by statute (*Adams v. Weinberger*, 1975; *Adams v. Califano*, 1977; *Adams v. Bell*, 1983).

In an instance in 1982 when plaintiffs petitioned for further relief, Judge Pratt reviewed the progress of those states that have operated approved desegregation plans since the year 1978–79. Based upon its reading of approved plans and reports of progress, the court found that little has been accomplished. Judge Pratt's March, 1983 ruling concludes that where Arkansas, Georgia, Florida, Virginia, Oklahoma, and the community college system of North Carolina are concerned:

1. The Revised Criteria Specifying the Ingredients of Acceptable Plans to Desegregate State Systems of Public Higher Education (43 Fed. P 6658—Feb. 15, 1979) required each of the above states to desegregate its system of public higher education over a five-year period culminating in the 1982–83 academic year.
2. In 1978 and 1979 DHEW accepted plans to desegregate formerly *de jure* segregated public higher education systems from Arkansas, Florida, Georgia, Oklahoma, and Virginia, and from North Carolina's community college system. The plans expired at the end of the 1982–83 academic year.
3. Each of these states has defaulted in major respects on its plan commitments and on the desegregation requirements of the Criteria of Title VI. Each state has not achieved the principal objectives in its plan because of the state's failure to implement concrete and specific measures adequate to ensure that the promised desegregation goals would be achieved by the end of the five-year desegregation period. (*Adams v. Bell*, 1982, p. 2)

In view of his findings, Judge Pratt required the above states to submit another plan by June 30, 1983 that promised actions leading to the goals established in their earlier plans, to choose strategies that would meet with success by the fall of 1985, and to submit a progress report by February 1, 1984. The court ordered the ED's Office of Civil Rights (OCR) in the injunction to institute formal Title VI enforcement proceedings by September 5, 1983 if plans were not submitted, and/or to evaluate the progress reports by April 1, 1984 (*Adams v. Bell*, 1983, pp. 3–4).

The court also noted that Pennsylvania had refused to submit a desegregation plan as ordered by OCR in 1981 that included remedies affecting so-called "state-related" institutions—Pennsylvania State University, the University of Pittsburgh, Temple University, Lincoln University, and the 13 community colleges in addition to the "state-owned" four-year institutions. At issue since 1970 in Pennsylvania was the need to include state-related institutions. Judge Pratt in another injunction ordered OCR to begin enforcement proceedings against the State of Pennsylvania within 120 days of the hearing unless a plan was submitted. Pennsylvania has since then obtained approval for its desegregation plan including the specifications acknowledged (*Adams v. Bell*, 1983, pp. 4–5).

A legal stumbling block to Title VI regulation occurred in the Supreme Court's recent *Grove City College v. Bell* (1982) decision. The court ruled that under Title IX of the 1972 Higher Education Amendments, the federal government can regulate only those programs or units of a college or university that are guilty of sex discrimination, not the entire institution based upon an isolated finding as had been the case. The impact of this decision has been to curtail OCR regulatory activities in Title VI states. In a speech at the American Affirmative Action Association conference in Atlanta on March 13, 1986, Louis Bryson of the Atlanta regional OCR office reported that as a result of the *Grove City College* case OCR's efforts to achieve compliance with Title VI in higher education had been slowed. He also reported that OCR was involved in a review of progress in all state systems affected by Title VI toward the goal of determining future policy.

The details of the Reagan administration's Title VI policy in higher education are most clearly revealed in a speech Assistant Attorney General Bradford Reynolds presented at the Southern Education Foundation on February 10, 1983:

> The Civil Rights Division's enforcement activity is of a single purpose, and that is to achieve quality education in a desegregated environment. . . .
>
> At the primary and secondary levels, mandatory assignment programs requiring extensive dislocations of students have, in educational terms, seriously harmed school systems across this land, particularly in the larger metropolitan areas. Nor do you need me to tell you that the gradual erosion of public education that occurs at the preparatory grade levels has an equally distressing impact on our public institutions of higher education. . . .
>
> Our efforts in the Civil Rights Division have thus been to strive for a greater degree of sensitivity to the educational needs of particular communities that must respond to the constitutional and moral imperative of desegregation. . . .
>
> Not surprisingly, employing a similar philosophy to desegregate institutions of higher learning has met with considerably less resistance, principally because forced busing is not a viable option at this level. . . .
>
> The states of North Carolina, Louisiana, and most recently Virginia have entered into amiable settlements, and several other states are close to a final resolution of their higher education cases.
>
> A principal reason for these positive results is this Administration's attitude toward black colleges and universities in this country. . . .
>
> Unlike our predecessors we believe the effort should be made to preserve and enhance predominantly black institutions, while promoting desegregation, rather than looking to merge them with white colleges or discontinue them altogether. . . .
>
> As with elementary and secondary education, at the centerpiece of our higher education desegregation program is the guiding hand of educational quality. An effective dismantling of dual systems of higher education depends upon eliminating all barriers which deny equal access to any public college or university in the state. . . . With respect to predominantly white institutions, we have employed a variety of techniques to increase other-race enrollments. Considerable emphasis has been placed on programs designed

to inform students of available educational opportunities and to recruit other-race students. Developmental or remedial education programs have been utilized to reduce black attrition rates. Cooperative efforts between geographically proximate institutions have been required, including faculty and student exchanges and joint degree programs. These and other measures that we have adopted help to ensure equal access for all students, regardless of race, to a quality educational institution of their own choosing. (Reynolds, 1983, pp. 10–11)

In keeping with the administration's new policy of diminishing Title VI regulation, the Justice Department changed its role in several pending court proceedings affecting higher education. The 1985–86 Annual Report of the NAACP Legal Defense Fund (LDF) summarized its more current actions:

Recently the Justice Department challenged the standing of black parents and students to sue as plaintiffs, claiming that only the federal government has the right to bring suit under Title VI. The challenge came after LDF won two strong court orders in 1983 calling for definite time frames and immediate measurable progress. LDF has responded with a motion in the district court asserting that the black plaintiffs meet all of the judicial tests for standing, i.e. all are enrolled in schools covered by *Adams*, all suffer injury from racial discrimination in education, the injury is traceable to the Department of Education's inaction, and the relief sought is necessary to redress the plaintiff's injury.

A hearing on the standing and separation-of-powers issues was held in December 1985; a decision is pending. (NAACP LDF, 1986, p. 14)

Additionally, desegregation plans expired for several states in 1985 and 1986. The Department of Education must now decide whether to ask for new plans, or to declare the affected higher education systems in compliance with Title VI. The states awaiting the judgment of the Department are Arkansas, Delaware, Florida, Georgia, North Carolina (the community college system), Missouri, Oklahoma, South Carolina, Virginia, and West Virginia. The ruling of the Department and Judge Pratt's ruling on the standing of plaintiffs in the original *Adams* case are likely to be met with controversy.

THE IMPACT OF *DE JURE* DESEGREGATION REGULATION

The data that follow are drawn from Office of Civil Rights compliance reports (DBS Corporation, 1983). They illustrate the extent to which desegregation has taken place in the states affected by Title VI regulation.

For the most part, the data portray progress in the six states that operated Department of Education approved plans for desegregation over the period 1978 to 1983. These states are Arkansas, Florida, Georgia, Oklahoma, Pennsylvania, and Virginia. The data measure (1) changes in initial access to higher education for black high school graduates, (2) trends in systemwide enrollment by race, (3) status of black college enhancement, (4) trends in hiring black faculty and administrative staff, and (5) changes in racial composition of college and university system governing boards.

Data in Table 1.1 suggest the extent to which initial access to higher education for black high school graduates increased or reached parity with whites in five states over the period 1978 to 1983. Florida is the only state that shows a substantial change (greater than 1000 students) in the number of blacks graduating from high school. In the other four states the numbers remain relatively unchanged. The states' task then was to increase the proportion of blacks who graduate from high school and enter the college system from a stable pool of students. One hypothesis suggests that the students who graduate from high school are fewer, but since they remained in school, they are better motivated for college participation. Therefore, the percent who later enroll in college should be expected to increase. This hypothesis is consistent with new policies for increased high school graduation requirements (*Education Week*, 1983).

But the data in Table 1.1 suggest, on the contrary, both stable (or increased) high school graduation rates, and lowered access rates for black students. The percentages of high school graduates enrolling in college increased slightly during the first year of the desegregation plans, but later over a three-year period in five states, it declined (Arkansas Department of Education, 1983, pp. 4–5; State University System of Florida, 1983, p. 18; Oklahoma State Regents for Higher Education, 1983, p. 12; Dodds to Casteen, 1983, p. 2). Georgia, the sixth state for which data are presented, shows an increase from 17.2% to 18.8% systemwide between 1980 and 1982, but between the 1981–83 years declines also occurred (University System of Georgia, 1983, p. 5).

In Florida, Georgia, and Oklahoma increases in the percent of black high school graduates entering four-year traditionally white institutions occurred at the expense of two-year institutions, while the reverse trend seems to have occurred in Arkansas.

The percent of baccalaureate degrees awarded to black state residents follows a similar pattern in most of the states (see Table 1.2). The rates increased during the initial year of the desegregation plans, but subsequently decreased. Such decreases not only offer evidence of deteriorating participation by blacks, but perversely lower expectations for the

TABLE 1.1. Initial Access to Higher Education for Black High School Graduates: Statewide Summaries

	Number and Percentage per Academic Year							
	1978–79		1979–80		1981–82		1982–83	
	number of blacks	*% of black enrollment*	*number of blacks*	*% of black enrollment*	*number of blacks*	*% of black enrollment*	*number of blacks*	*% of black enrollment*
ARKANSAS								
Public H.S. Seniors in Preceding Year	6,430		6,583		6,745		6,138	
First-Time Within-State Entrants to:								
Two-year institutions	626	9.74	695	10.56	819	12.14	813	12.05
Four-year institutions	1,657	25.77	1,661	25.23	1,555	23.05	1,325	19.64
TOTAL	2,283	35.51	2,356	35.79	2,374	35.20	2,138	31.70
FLORIDA								
Public H.S. Graduates in Preceding Year	17,497		17,497[1]		15,777		16,470	
First-Time Entrants to:								
Two-year institutions	6,420	36.69	6,270	35.83	6,032	38.23	5,145	31.24
Traditionally white four-year	532	3.04	471	2.69	487	3.09	663	4.03
Traditionally black four-year	524	2.99	933	5.33	624	3.96	660	4.01
Total four-year	1,056	6.04	1,404	8.02	1,111	7.04	1,323	8.03
TOTAL	7,476	42.73	7,674	43.86	7,143	45.27	6,468	39.27
GEORGIA								
Public H.S. Graduates in Preceding Year	19,793		19,793[1]		19,179		20,741	
First-Time Within-State Entrants to:								
Two-year institutions	1,035	5.23	891	4.50	880	4.59	1,057	5.10
Four-year institutions	2,422	12.24	2,516	12.71	2,724	14.20	2,773	13.37
TOTAL	3,457	17.47	3,407	17.21	3,604	18.79	3,830	18.47

OKLAHOMA								
Twelfth-Grade Enrollment in Preceding Year	3,456		3,661		3,616		3,561	
First-Time Within-State Entrants to:								
Two-year institutions	1,105	31.97	1,129	30.84	1,077	29.78	1,186	33.31
Four-year institutions	819	23.70	873	23.85	863	23.87	905	25.41
TOTAL	1,924	55.67	2,002	54.68	1,940	53.65	2,091	58.72
PENNSYLVANIA								
Public H.S. Graduates in Preceding Year	11,420		11,420[1]		13,920		13,782[2]	
First-Time Within-State Entrants to:								
Traditionally white four-year	833	7.29	873	7.64	797	5.73	729	5.29
Traditionally black four-year	465	4.07	467	4.09	268	1.93	197	1.43
TOTAL	1,298	11.37	1,340	11.73	1,065	7.65	926	6.72
VIRGINIA								
Public H.S. Graduates in Preceding Year	13,665		13,885		13,740		14,598	
First-Time Within-State Undergrad Freshmen	4,292	31.41	6,481	46.68	4,384	31.91	4,453	30.50

[1] Figure for 1977–78, instead of 1978–79, was used in source.
[2] Includes graduates of private high schools.

increased enrollment of blacks in postbaccalaureate programs. This is the case because goals for postgraduate enrollment, according to the desegregation guidelines, must reflect the availability pool of black baccalaureate degree holders, measured by the percentage of black graduates each year in each state system.

But lowered enrollment goals cannot mask the trend illustrated in Table 1.2 toward little improvement in the number of blacks attending postbaccalaureate schools in the six states. These data show that the six states' colleges and university systems have failed to show great improvement. Decreases in the percentage of undergraduate degrees awarded to blacks have been accompanied by declines in the percentages of blacks enrolled in postgraduate programs. Despite increases since the 1981–82 year, data for the following year suggest that in Georgia and Florida, like the other four states, the percentages of blacks admitted to professional schools have also declined (University System of Georgia, 1983, pp. 9, 189; State University System of Florida, 1983, pp. 18, 48).

As one might predict from these data, black enrollment as a percentage of total student enrollment at traditionally white public colleges and universities in the six states has not increased substantially (see Table 1.3). Declines in both headcount and percentage enrollments were apparent in Florida by 1982, and in the other states a less than 1% increase took place per year. This trend continued into the 1982–83 year when: (1) decreases in total and percent enrollment of blacks occurred in Arkansas; (2) the percentage of blacks at traditionally white institutions in Georgia remained the same, although the total number of black enrollees increased slightly; (3) a less than 1% increase occurred in Oklahoma; and (4) in Virginia the total number of blacks enrolled increased, but the percentage remained unchanged (Arkansas Department of Higher Education, 1983, pp. 45, 79).

The only state to show a very small (less than 1%) decrease in white enrollment at traditionally black institutions over the period from 1978 to 1982 is Florida (see Table 1.4). The rest show increases, some of which are fairly substantial, but only up to the level of 15%. It is also important to note that most white students at traditionally black institutions are registered part-time. This may mean that most do not live on campus and are likely enrolled in "high-demand" degree programs recently inaugurated and unavailable at other institutions.

Data describing the extent to which state-proposed enhancement measures at traditionally black colleges and universities have actually been undertaken are not presented in the compliance data analysis. But the ED's Office of Civil Rights reported some assessments of black college enhancement activities.

In 1983, the Office of Civil Rights indicated that in Florida:

Plans to enhance the State's traditionally black institution, Florida A&M University (FAMU), have lagged behind schedule and actions proposed to access its resources and facilities have not been implemented fully. Further, although the State has committed itself to increase the total proportion of white students attending FAMU, its white enrollment has decreased since 1978–79 from 620 (10.9%) to 519 (10.6%). Other major deficiencies are summarized below.

Implementation of New Programs.   Florida has not met its timetables for implementation of new programs at FAMU. Only five of eleven new programs planned to enhance FAMU have been implemented. Six new programs have been delayed for at least one year beyond the revised implementation dates agreed to in April 1981.

Resources and Facilities.   Florida has not provided the results of an updated study of resource comparability among system schools. It also has delayed completion of a physical plant study. Both studies, which are cited in the *Plan*, were intended to identify deficiencies in FAMU's facilities and resources when compared with similar universities. The correction of any deficiencies is a fundamental component of Florida's *Plan*. (Thomas to Graham, 1983, p. 2)

In the State of Georgia, the Office of Civil Rights concluded:

Many of the measures aimed at desegregating the TBIs have been implemented: however, some activities have not occurred as committed in the *Plan*.

While some progress has been made, it is clear that additional actions need to be taken to further enhance and desegregate Albany State. While no similar commitments were made for the other two TBI's, they are also in need of additional actions. (Thomas to Harris, 1981, pp. 2–3)

Similarly in Virginia:

The 1978 *Plan* contained various measures designed to enhance the programs and facilities of Norfolk State University (NSU) and Virginia State University (VSU), Virginia's TBIs. In our November 1981 evaluation letter, we detailed serious shortcomings in the progress made toward enhancement, particularly in regard to Virginia State University.

Since this evaluation letter, the Commonwealth has taken action to promote the enhancement of NSU and VSU.

Even with these actions, additional resources and effort must be directed at the enhancement of the TBIs if they are to become comparable to their peer level TWIs and are to offer programs that will attract both white and black students. (Dodds to Casteen, 1983, pp. 3–4)

TABLE 1.2. Entrance of Blacks to Postbaccalaureate Study, 1978–82

	1978–79		1979–80		1981–82	
	Number	% of total enrollment	Number	% of total enrollment	Number	% of total enrollment
ARKANSAS						
Black Bacc. in Prec. Year[1]	499	10.19	663	12.80	747	12.77
First-Time Black Enrollment in:						
Graduate						
Full-time	67	7.09	79	8.32	40	5.75
Part-time	195	8.31	198	9.22	82	8.38
TOTAL	262	7.96	277	8.94	122	7.29
First-Professional						
Full-time	29	5.74	24	5.52	21	5.45
Part-time	10	13.51	8	8.51	1	1.82
TOTAL	39	6.74	32	6.05	22	5.00
Total						
Full-time	96	6.62	103	7.44	61	5.64
Part-time	205	8.47	206	9.19	83	8.03
TOTAL	301	7.78	309	8.52	144	6.81
FLORIDA						
Black Bacc. in Prec. Year[2]	1,515	7.94	1,651	8.77	1,631	8.48
First-Year Black Enrollment in:						
Graduate						
Full-time	69	7.97	74	7.52	43	4.96
Part-time	79	7.24	66	8.80	60	7.08
TOTAL	148	7.56	140	7.66	103	6.01
First-Professional						
Full-time	59	6.18	39	5.45	48	7.41
Part-time	0	0.00	0	0.00	0	0.00
TOTAL	59	6.17	39	5.43	48	7.40

Total					
Full-time	298	5.85	301	5.85	91	6.01
Part-time	588	13.33	396	9.01	60	7.07
TOTAL	886	9.32	697	7.31	151	6.39
GEORGIA					
Black Bacc. in Prec. Year[1]	1,091	10.19	1,285	10.35	1,064	9.78
First-Time Within-State Black Enrollment in:					
Graduate	531	15.21	348	10.72	333	10.79
First-professional	29	6.22	22	4.65	51	10.62
TOTAL	560	14.16	370	9.95	384	10.77
OKLAHOMA					
Black Bacc. in Prec. Year[1]	439	4.74	373	4.02	388	4.32
First-Year Black Enrollment in:					
Graduate					
Full-time	37	3.94	34	3.53	40	3.24
Part-time	58	4.74	56	4.98	80	4.89
TOTAL	95	4.39	90	4.31	120	4.18
First-Professional					
Full-time	12	2.04	11	1.89	9	1.53
Part-time	0	0.00	0	0.00	0	0.00
TOTAL	12	2.04	11	1.89	9	1.53
Total					
Full-time	49	3.21	45	2.91	49	2.69
Part-time	58	4.74	56	4.98	80	4.89
TOTAL	107	3.89	101	3.78	129	3.73

TABLE 1.2. (*continued*)

	1978–79		1979–80		1981–82	
	Number	% of total enrollment	Number	% of total enrollment	Number	% of total enrollment
VIRGINIA						
Black Bacc. in Prec. Year[1]	1,497	11.10	1,492	11.04	1,473	10.50
First-Year Black Enrollment in:						
Graduate						
Full-time	359	7.26	233	4.54	199	4.79
Part-time	679	8.87	594	7.54	341	9.25
TOTAL	1,038	8.24	827	6.36	540	6.89
First-Professional						
Full-time	45	4.72	47	4.03	44	4.08
Part-time	0	0.00	1	0.34	3	2.70
TOTAL	45	4.72	48	3.30	47	3.95
Total						
Full-time	404	6.85	280	4.45	243	4.65
Part-time	679	8.87	595	7.29	344	9.06
TOTAL	1,083	7.99	875	6.05	587	6.50

[1]Baccalaureates granted to black state residents in the preceding academic year.
[2]Baccalaureates granted to black students in the state university system in the preceding academic year.

The Office of Civil Rights noted a different situation in Oklahoma:

> Although the implementation of most *Plan* measures was several years be-
> hind schedule, the Regents' commitments to Langston as outlined in the New
> Mission document (September 1978) have now been fulfilled. The year
> 1982–83 is actually the first academic year that all measures are completed
> and in place. Despite these actions, there has been no progress in the de-
> segregation of student enrollment at the main campus. Moreover, fewer black
> students are enrolling or finishing their degrees at Langston. In the Fall of
> 1981, the main campus enrolled 930 students, 75% black, 2% white and 23%
> "all others." The New Mission document projects 38.5% or 500 white stu-
> dents to be enrolled on the main campus by 1983–84. The State committed
> itself to recommend to the 1983 Oklahoma legislature that Langston be
> transferred to Tulsa or Oklahoma City by the Fall of 1983, if by November
> 1982 it appeared that Langston was not meeting its desegregation goals as
> specified in Table III of the *Plan*. As indicated above, Langston did not
> achieve its interim desegregation goal for 1982–83 of 32.7% white enroll-
> ment on its main campus, and it appears to be virtually impossible for
> Langston to achieve its fifth-year goal of 38.5% white enrollment on its main
> campus by 1983–84. The Regents have initiated a study to evaluate Langs-
> ton's desegregation progress; the study is scheduled to be completed in
> March, 1983. (August to Nigh, 1983, p. 3)

Similar to Oklahoma, enhancement strategies in Arkansas are largely
completed. On the other hand, the Office of Civil Rights' assessment
found a dormitory desperately in need of repair, and discovered the possibility of eliminating some of the new degree programs due to "state fiscal" constraint. The Office of Civil Rights warned that:

> In view of the limited progress that has been made in desegregating UAPB,
> the State should expand UAPB's program offerings and take steps to reduce
> duplicative programs at TWI's that share UAPB's service area. (August to
> Clinton, 1983, p. 5)

The data in Tables 1.5 and 1.6 show little progress in the employment of black faculty and administrators at traditionally white institutions in the six college and university systems. Change patterns are
difficult to discern because few additional personnel were hired. Indeed,
some decline is apparent in all five states and among masters as well as
doctoral degree personnel. It is worth noting that blacks constituted 1.25%
of the total pool of faculty holding doctoral degrees in the lowest state,
Oklahoma, and only 2.39% in the highest state, Florida.

In view of such low percentages and little change over the years, the
data in Table 1.7 survey the extent to which the college systems have ac-

TABLE 1.3. Black Undergraduate Enrollment at Traditionally White Institutions, 1978–82

	1978–79		1979–80		1981–82	
	Number	% of total enrollment	Number	% of total enrollment	Number	% of total enrollment
ARKANSAS						
Full-time	4,535	12.26	4,977	12.82	5,189	13.07
Part-time	1,138	9.80	1,147	9.63	1,117	9.46
Full-time unclassified	33	7.07	48	9.07	46	6.97
Part-time unclassified	167	6.74	173	6.94	110	5.17
TOTAL	5,873	11.39	6,345	11.81	6,462	11.90
FLORIDA						
Full-time	14,967	23.88	14,034	22.43	12,669	19.67
Part-time	10,557	17.46	11,068	17.13	11,091	16.23
Full-time unclassified	595	27.74	532	25.10	444	21.72
Part-time unclassified	2,316	18.63	2,304	18.55	2,384	17.99
TOTAL	29,435	26.48	27,938	19.53	26,588	17.77
GEORGIA*						
Full-time	8,747	11.38	7,954	10.38	8,943	11.05
Part-time	4,274	11.38	4,455	11.60	4,575	11.81
Full-time unclassified	495	22.71	208	12.65	368	16.05
Part-time unclassified	257	10.20	231	9.25	348	11.03
TOTAL	13,773	11.57	12,848	10.78	14,234	11.38

OKLAHOMA

Full-time	2,793	5.06	2,965	5.32	3,033	5.42
Part-time	768	6.57	679	6.09	734	6.32
Full-time unclassified	22	6.96	24	7.45	13	6.37
Part-time unclassified	77	4.66	47	3.42	22	1.44
TOTAL	3,660	5.31	3,715	5.42	3,802	5.49

PENNSYLVANIA

Full-time	2,632	4.69	2,746	4.85	2,932	4.97
Part-time	159	3.03	205	3.35	182	2.86
Full-time unclassified	31	2.67	21	2.84	42	6.33
Part-time unclassified	38	1.62	63	2.78	73	3.11
TOTAL	2,860	4.41	3,035	4.62	3,229	4.72

VIRGINIA

Full-time	3,815	5.40	4,427	6.07	5,325	6.86
Part-time	552	6.37	608	6.83	655	7.05
Full-time unclassified	147	12.75	161	13.21	102	8.92
Part-time unclassified	779	10.40	946	9.83	849	10.61
TOTAL	5,293	6.02	6,142	6.62	6,931	7.22

*Includes undergraduate, graduate, and professional school enrollment.

TABLE 1.4. White Student Enrollment at Traditionally Black Institutions, 1978–82

	1978–79		1979–80		1981–82	
	Number	% of total enrollment	Number	% of total enrollment	Number	% of total enrollment
ARKANSAS						
Full-time	214	8.36	183	7.72	174	7.19
Part-time	112	30.52	102	28.98	84	37.84
Full-time unclassified	4	28.57	13	22.03	41	51.25
Part-time unclassified	24	42.11	69	55.65	136	72.73
Total	354	11.81	367	12.63	435	14.95
FLORIDA						
Full-time	270	6.19	228	5.20	145	3.65
Part-time	251	24.93	198	23.54	225	34.78
Full-time unclassified	29	30.21	19	67.86	7	53.85
Part-time unclassified	70	29.29	50	34.48	142	52.21
Total	620	10.87	495	9.17	519	10.57
GEORGIA						
Full-time	186	3.63	487	9.92	471	9.48
Part-time	242	40.13	128	23.93	232	31.69
Full-time unclassified	6	7.69	6	46.15	12	30.00
Part-time unclassified	15	36.59	6	40.00	19	31.67
Total	449	7.67	627	11.46	734	12.66

PENNSYLVANIA						
Full-time	55	2.61	150	7.12	161	8.12
Part-time	103	20.28	119	29.60	99	35.61
Full-time unclassified	2	11.11	0	0.00	0	0.00
Part-time unclassified	0	0.00	0	0.00	0	0.00
TOTAL	160	6.07	269	10.72	260	11.50
VIRGINIA						
Full-time	237	2.72	244	2.82	367	3.90
Part-time	306	12.62	221	12.91	276	17.65
Full-time unclassified	10	7.87	13	6.40	21	18.92
Part-time unclassified	141	27.81	314	33.16	349	34.32
TOTAL	694	5.90	792	6.88	1,013	8.38

TABLE 1.5. Black Faculty and Administrative Staff at Traditionally White Institutions, by Highest Degree Held

	1978–79		1979–80		1981–82	
	Number	% of total staff	Number	% of total staff	Number	% of total staff
ARKANSAS						
Executive/Administrative/Managerial						
Holding doctoral degree	5	2.40	5	2.45	6	3.33
Holding master's degree	12	8.82	9	7.26	10	7.58
Holding all others	8	4.02	7	3.20	8	3.49
Faculty						
Holding doctoral degree	20	1.38	25	1.50	24	1.42
Holding master's degree	29	3.74	27	3.94	34	4.57
Holding all others	5	4.35	4	4.60	7	4.70
FLORIDA						
Executive/Administrative/Managerial						
Holding doctoral degree	34	4.91	38	5.64	38	5.15
Holding master's degree	26	6.79	28	7.25	33	8.03
Holding all others	16	5.46	13	3.96	15	4.26
Faculty						
Holding doctoral degree	90	2.19	93	2.24	107	2.39
Holding master's degree	55	5.06	60	5.84	49	4.65
Holding all others	19	5.15	25	7.06	20	6.17
GEORGIA						
Executive/Administrative/Managerial						
Holding doctoral degree	10	1.79	8	1.45	9	1.44
Holding master's degree	18	4.41	19	4.36	25	5.46
Holding all others	14	2.64	11	1.92	18	3.27
Faculty						
Holding doctoral degree	35	1.00	51	1.43	57	1.58
Holding master's degree	63	3.94	61	3.99	68	4.49
Holding all others	11	2.98	14	3.67	7	3.18

OKLAHOMA						
Executive/Administrative/Managerial						
Holding doctoral degree	2	0.69	2	0.67	8	2.33
Holding master's degree	7	4.14	6	3.45	5	2.63
Holding all others	15	3.54	19	4.41	20	4.45
Faculty						
Holding doctoral degree	27	1.19	21	1.01	27	1.25
Holding master's degree	38	2.94	38	2.73	44	2.94
Holding all others	1	2.94	6	8.33	3	4.41
PENNSYLVANIA						
Executive/Administrative/Managerial	27	5.16	20	4.27	24	4.63
Faculty	89	1.97	105	2.30	94	2.18
VIRGINIA						
Executive/Administrative/Managerial						
Holding doctoral degree	15	4.32	15	5.26	20	5.33
Holding master's degree	32	5.52	26	4.91	36	5.74
Holding all others	25	4.82	29	4.13	29	5.29
Faculty						
Holding doctoral degree	48	1.05	35	0.96	78	1.57
Holding master's degree	49	2.87	42	3.02	42	2.67
Holding all others	20	2.63	38	1.89	22	2.76

tually hired new black personnel. The numbers of black personnel added to the staff and faculty and the percentage of total newly hired personnel are presented. Trends are also difficult to discern because of the way the data are aggregated and because of the small numbers involved. Nonetheless, no state demonstrated sustained, substantial success in hiring new black personnel.

Between 1978 and 1980 three states increased overall the number and percentages of new black employees hired, but three states did not. Increases occurred in the faculty category in Arkansas, Florida, Georgia, and Pennsylvania. But although Arkansas increased the number and percent of black faculty who were newly hired during this period, the number and percentage of black administrators hired decreased, resulting in an overall decline of new black hires. In this table, Pennsylvania was the only state shown consistently to hire more black administrators between 1978 and 1980, and the only state as well to show consistent increases in both the faculty and administrator categories.

Between 1980 and 1982 (data for 1980–81 are missing) total increases, taking into account both faculty and administrator categories, occurred only in Oklahoma and Virginia. The total increase in Virginia was largely due to increased black faculty appointments; appointment rates and numbers of new black administrators decreased. The overall decreases in Arkansas, Georgia, Florida, and Pennsylvania occurred largely due to reductions in the faculty category. Oklahoma was the only state where improvement in both categories occurred between 1980 and 1982. This observation should not be over-emphasized, however, because Oklahoma appointed no new black administrators in the 1979–80 year.

The data in Tables 1.5 and 1.7 together suggest two important facts: (1) positions at the college systems seem to be available, but the jobs simply have not been filled with new black personnel; and (2) as one would expect, hiring small numbers of blacks results in sustained low percentages of black faculty systemwide. Even where the number of new black hires is fairly substantial, the percentages systemwide of black personnel remain relatively small. For example, a total of 44 new black faculty and 11 new black administrators were hired in Virginia during the 1981–82 school year. This number amounted to only 4.4% of the total new college personnel in the state for that year. Furthermore, the percentage of blacks in faculty and administrative jobs at best remained stable. Negative trends are clear in Arkansas, Florida, Georgia, and Pennsylvania. The number of new personnel appointed has declined consistently at the same time that percentages of black administrators and faculty remained at low levels or declined.

The aggregate data describing membership of blacks on governing boards in the states' higher education systems show mixed results (see Table 1.8). Georgia, Virginia, and Oklahoma failed as of 1982 to appoint blacks in equal proportion to their numbers in the state population. In Georgia the number of black governing board officials remained unchanged, while the number of whites increased by one. In Virginia the number of blacks declined by two, while the number of whites increased by 24. And in Oklahoma the number of blacks increased by one, while the number of whites increased by four. The states of Arkansas, Pennsylvania, and Florida have achieved a percentage of black membership proportionate to their total black populations.

The data cited are neither definitive nor complete. They suggest little progress toward the desegregation goals enunciated in the federal guidelines, but offer scarcely any information on the question of why desegregation has proven to be difficult to achieve. More specifically, the data do not differentiate two categories of competing hypotheses about the causes of continued noncompliance: (1) choice of inappropriate remedial action, resulting in no policy impacts; and (2) poor implementation of promised remedies, their potential impact notwithstanding.

In its later ruling, the federal district court found evidence to support both kinds of hypotheses. It ruled that several states, including the ones for which data were reported earlier, have "not achieved the principal objectives in [their] plan[s] because of the state[s'] failure to implement concrete and specific measures adequate to ensure that the promised desegregation goals would be achieved. . ." (*Adams v. Bell*, 1982, p. 2).

This statement implies both failure to propose remedies that might work and failure to implement potentially promising remedies. These two related but separate problems are also reflected in findings of the Office of Civil Rights, which issues annual evaluation letters to the states acknowledging their accomplishments and highlighting their failures as reported in annual compliance reports. For example, the January, 1983 evaluation letter to the Governor of Florida indicated that:

> This is the third evaluation letter we have sent to you assessing progress in implementing Florida's *Plan* and seeking improvements in *Plan* performance. Although the *Plan* does not expire until the end of academic year 1982–83, it seems certain that important *Plan* goals and objectives will not be achieved by that time. As noted above, there has been virtually no improvement in reducing the gap between the enrollment of blacks and whites at the undergraduate level. On the graduate and professional level, the black/white enrollment gap is increasing. In contrast to the community colleges' success in achieving their employment goals for blacks, the State universities' lack of measurable progress is a serious problem and affects Florida's ability to achieve the goals of its *Plan*. The inability of the State to

TABLE 1.6. Black Administrators Employed at Central Coordinating Agencies, by Highest Degree Held

	1978–79		1979–80		1981–82	
	Number	*% of total staff*	*Number*	*% of total staff*	*Number*	*% of total staff*
ARKANSAS						
Employed by Department of Higher Education						
Holding doctoral degree	0	0.00	0	0.00	0	0.00
Holding master's degree	1	25.00	1	20.00	0	0.00
Holding all others	0	0.00	1	50.00	0	0.00
FLORIDA						
Employed by Board of Regents						
Holding doctoral degree	0	0.00	2	8.00	0	0.00
Holding master's degree	3	10.34	2	16.67	1	11.11
Holding all others	2	7.69	1	2.86	2	8.33
GEORGIA						
Employed by Board of Regents						
Holding doctoral degree	0	0.00	0	0.00	2	16.67
Holding master's degree	0	0.00	0	0.00	0	0.00
Holding all others	0	0.00	0	0.00	0	0.00
OKLAHOMA						
Employed by State Agencies						
Holding doctoral degree	0	0.00	0	0.00	1	14.29
Holding master's degree	0	0.00	0	0.00	0	0.00
Holding all others	0	0.00	0	0.00	1	100.00
PENNSYLVANIA						
Employed by State Department of Education	3	16.67	1	11.11	1	11.11
VIRGINIA						
Employed by State Higher Education Agencies						
Holding doctoral degree	0	0.00	0	0.00	2	13.33
Holding master's degree	0	0.00	1	11.11	0	0.00
Holding all others	2	8.70	2	8.00	1	7.69

TABLE 1.7. Number of New Black Employees Hired at Traditionally White Institutions between October and September of Preceding Year

	1978–79		1979–80		1981–82	
	Number	% of total staff	Number	% of total staff	Number	% of total staff
ARKANSAS*						
Executive/Administrative/Managerial	5	13.16	2	6.06	2	8.70
Faculty	16	4.11	21	4.67	10	1.92
TOTAL NEW EMPLOYEES	21	4.92	23	4.76	12	2.20
FLORIDA*						
Executive/Administrative/Managerial	17	11.64	12	7.84	14	11.29
Faculty	25	3.01	38	5.48	26	2.67
TOTAL NEW EMPLOYEES	42	4.30	50	5.91	40	3.65
GEORGIA*						
Executive/Administrative/Managerial	9	8.49	7	6.19	8	7.08
Faculty	38	3.44	38	4.00	20	2.68
TOTAL NEW EMPLOYEES	47	3.88	45	4.23	28	3.26
OKLAHOMA						
Executive/Administrative/Managerial	5	9.26	0	0.00	7	7.95
Faculty	10	2.01	6	1.41	15	2.87
TOTAL NEW EMPLOYEES	15	2.72	6	1.24	22	3.60
PENNSYLVANIA						
Executive/Administrative/Managerial	1	2.17	2	4.76	5	9.80
Faculty	13	2.83	20	4.50	7	1.80
TOTAL NEW EMPLOYEES	14	2.77	22	4.53	12	2.73
VIRGINIA						
Executive/Administrative/Managerial	11	6.59	13	5.28	11	6.92
Faculty	32	2.72	23	2.14	44	4.03
TOTAL NEW EMPLOYEES	43	3.20	36	2.73	55	4.40

*Indicated Employment at Four-year Institutions Only.

TABLE 1.8. Comparison of Higher Education Governing Boards

| | Racial Composition of State Population | | | | Racial Composition of Governing Board Memberships | | | | | |
| | 1976 | | 1980 | | 1978–79 | | 1979–80 | | 1981–82 | |
	Number	Percent	Number	Percent	Number	Percent	Number	Percent	Number	Percent
ARKANSAS										
Black	366,000	17.22	373,768	16.35	8	14.81	11	17.19	11	17.19
White	1,747,000	82.21	1,890,322	82.68	46	85.19	53	82.81	53	82.81
TOTAL	2,125,000	100.00	2,286,435	100.00	54	100.00	64	100.00	64	100.00
FLORIDA										
Black	1,319,000	15.52	1,342,688	13.78	58	14.50	30	14.85	30	14.42
White	7,122,000	83.82	8,184,513	83.98	338	84.50	171	84.65	176	84.62
TOTAL	8,497,000	100.00	9,746,324	100.00	400	100.00	201	100.00	208	100.00
GEORGIA										
Black	1,336,000	27.21	1,465,181	26.82	—	—	2	14.29	2	13.33
White	3,539,000	72.08	3,947,135	72.25	—	—	12	85.71	13	86.67
TOTAL	4,910,000	100.00	5,463,105	100.00	—	—	14	100.00	15	100.00
OKLAHOMA										
Black	179,000	6.68	204,674	6.77	6	5.04	7	5.88	8	6.35
White	2,406,000	89.82	2,597,791	85.87	110	92.44	109	91.60	113	89.68
TOTAL	2,681,000	100.00	3,025,290	100.00	119	100.00	119	100.00	126	100.00
PENNSYLVANIA										
Black	1,021,000	8.75	1,046,810	8.82	13	10.66	10	8.93	13	10.92
White	10,596,000	90.80	10,652,320	89.79	109	89.34	102	91.07	105	86.24
TOTAL	11,669,000	100.00	11,863,895	100.00	122	100.00	112	100.00	118	100.00
VIRGINIA										
Black	779,000	18.85	1,008,668	18.86	33	14.35	32	14.81	30	12.61
White	4,072,000	82.87	4,229,790	79.11	197	85.65	184	85.19	208	87.39
TOTAL	4,914,000	100.00	5,346,818	100.00	230	100.00	216	100.00	238	100.00

fulfill its commitments to FAMU, as shown in the lack of progress in implementing new programs, and declines in student enrollment (both black and white), have thwarted the enhancement process that was projected in the *Plan*. In some instances, it appears that failure to achieve these goals is due to lack of vigorous and complete *Plan* implementation. In others, it appears that the *Plan* did not contain sufficient measures to achieve the goals. (Thomas to Graham, 1983, p. 5)

The important aspect of the findings related in this letter is twofold: Florida took some steps that were not successful in remedying prior segregation, while other steps simply were not taken. Both problems constitute, in other states as well, a cause for the patterns of continued noncompliance illustrated in the data presented earlier.

AN ANALYSIS OF IMPORTANT ASSUMPTIONS UNDERLYING TITLE VI IMPLEMENTATION

An obvious question emerges from the data just reported: What factors prevent full implementation and choice of appropriate Title VI remedies? Available compliance data aim at directly discerning outcomes and are typically unsuited for an exploration of failure or success. Also missing, however, is a set of hypothetical propositions useful for undertaking an exploration of the causes of nonimplementation determined to exist by the district court.

Deriving explorable explanations for nonimplementation involves examining the assumptions underlying *de jure* desegregation regulation policies. In general, where nonimplementation seems to occur one might reasonably reconsider whether the assumptions that constitute the basis for establishing a set of regulatory actions remain adequate. In the following discussion four broad assumptions underlying existing *de jure* desegregation regulation policy are explored. This approach is taken as a means of taking a closer look at implementation problems clearly associated with Title VI regulation.

State higher education systems, colleges, and universities ordered to desegregate will choose potentially successful strategies for remedy and implement them fully if the following assumptions are correct: (1) clearly articulated statutes and regulations provide the basis for *de jure* desegregation, (2) political environments supportive of *de jure* desegregation exist within higher education, and (3) sufficient knowledge exists about how to achieve the desired results, and (4) governance authorities hold the necessary organizational capacity to propose and implement successful remedies (Hargrove, 1981).

The first assumption seems inadequate, since Title VI of the 1964 Civil Rights Act is vague. Its goals are unclear and it is demonstrably difficult in other institutional settings to implement (Orfield, 1969). One would expect it to be so. Any law aimed at providing appropriate authority for the federal government to remedy so widely practiced, multifaceted, and insidious a problem as public school desegregation will be loosely drawn. A more clearly structured statute that tightly limits the basis upon which the federal government can intervene in public school desegregation and circumscribes pursuable outcomes would have done little to lift persistent deadlocks encountered between 1954 and 1964 in implementing the famous *Brown v. Board of Education* (1954) decision. A more tightly constructed statute would have been easy to circumvent. Not unexpectedly, Title VI in 1964 did not clearly prescribe needed evidence of desegregation in education, nor did it prescribe the remedies required for full compliance. Much was left to the discretionary authority of the administrative branch of government.

In earlier years standards for making such determinations evolved through a tedious process including judicial review of almost every detail of federal administrative action toward public school desegregation (Orfield, 1969). But guidelines for remedy in higher education were not provided until 1978, approximately 10 years after the original 10 college and university systems were notified of noncompliance, and as illustrated earlier the guidelines have not been treated as sacrosanct by either the Department of Education or the state higher education systems.

Where Title VI interventions are undertaken, a trade-off of the federal administrative branch's broad powers to intervene in public education may be the lack of specificity required to assure smooth implementation of remedies. Improved specificity of Title VI requirements, provided in judicial rulings and elsewhere, have not necessarily had the effect of clarifying the nature and scope of Title VI's application in higher education because college attendance is neither free nor compulsory.

In theory, tension exists between government setting out in vague ways to reach several difficult, equally valued, and sometimes contradictory goals; and the alternate approach involving fewer, more specific, and less comprehensive goals and comparatively limited means. Full implementation seems most closely associated with fewer goals and limited means, while in the long run having a strong impact seems more clearly associated with sustained and complete government authority (Berman & McLaughlin, 1975; Ciarlo, 1977; Elmore, 1980; Hill, 1979; Roos et al., 1978). (This finding may constitute an artifact, however, since clear goals and means make evaluations of implementation and impact easier to conduct.)

The fact that clarity may constitute a short-run barrier to implementation does not necessarily argue for narrowing interpretations of Title VI even though this course of action by the federal government seems to be underway. Such a strategy may not be desirable since it may compromise achievement of more comprehensive, and in some instances unanticipated, desegregation benefits over time. A strategy of clarifying desegregation goals through the courts or the federal legislature, or by issuing more simply defined administrative guidelines may constitute a desirable short-range strategy only if the comprehensive character and more long-range potential for change underlying current Title VI legislation can be preserved.

Clearly, political support for Title VI regulation is waning at the federal level. Evidence of the true meaning of Assistant Attorney General Reynolds' 1983 speech emerged, among other places, in the Tennessee case. According to the 1986 NAACP Legal Defense Fund Annual Report:

> As reported last year, we had achieved a comprehensive settlement in *Geier v. Tennessee* in a case to desegregate the state's public higher education systems. . . . Although the State of Tennessee agreed to the settlement, the Justice Department—an intervenor in the case since 1968—opposed it on the ground that it established too many numerical goals and was not based upon proof that any specific black student is being discriminated against today.
>
> The district court rejected the Justice Department's objections. The Department of Justice appealed; LDF is requesting that the Sixth Circuit affirm the district Court order. A decision is pending. (NAACP LDF, 1986, p. 14)

Despite the federal government's current posture, some evidence of local support does exist. Local litigative initiative is interesting because it suggests increasing political support for desegregation as a policy. Individually initiated requests for judicial review of persistent problems of desegregation at individual institutions and at state systems have emerged in recent months in Alabama, Mississippi, and Arkansas (*Chronicle of Higher Education*, Jan. 4, 1984, p. 17; August 10, 1983, p. 9). The NAACP Legal Defense Fund has in the past pressed for federal administrative action for higher education desegregation through the District Court in Washington, D.C. on the basis of Title VI's commonly understood purposes. A necessary change may be underway.

But regardless of the weight of emerging evidence, enthusiastic political support for *de jure* desegregation remedies in higher education is difficult to generate. The self-interests of groups and individuals involved are constrained by naturally occurring broader circumstances. Comparatively few youths—only about 30% of 18- to 25-year-olds—ever attend college; the relative size of the 18- to 25-year-old traditional college-eligible cohort is declining in comparison to earlier generations even though the proportion of blacks in this cohort in relation to whites is increasing; belief in the future value of a college degree and thus demand for access dwindles; families are concerned about higher education only for the period of time when family members aged 18 to 25 actively consider attending; and confidence in desegregation as a federal remedy for social inequality diminishes as a result of the elementary and secondary battles (McCorkle & Archibald, 1982, pp. 3–4). For these and other reasons the constituency for a desegregation policy in higher education is obscure.

Searching for groups that stand to gain from full implementation of *de jure* desegregation remedies, black citizens in communities in Title VI states seem likely candidates, especially since black colleges and universities stand to gain or lose a great deal through successful implementation of Title VI. But unqualified support for traditionally black colleges and universities does not exist even within the communities in which they are located. Many black, college-eligible students and their families view attendance at predominantly white institutions as the most desirable avenue for reaping the benefits of American society. This view seems to grow despite the visibility of increasingly sizable numbers of blacks withdrawing before graduating from predominantly white institutions recently opened to blacks. Decreases in black enrollment at traditionally black institutions and the persistent low retention rates of blacks at white institutions provide evidence of a variety of dynamics at work in black communities. Mirroring the opinion of many whites, black youth and their families may also increasingly suspect the prospect of achieving personal advancement through participation in formal higher education.

Groups of white citizens in Title VI states who stand to benefit from desegregation are hard to identify because of cohesive customs of racial exclusivity that persist in many communities. Those whites who might favor desegregation for political, social justice, or economic reasons must think carefully about the trade-offs. Thus most white political and education leaders end up advocating desegregation in principle, but disagreeing with required remedies and with the federal involvement with the problem.

In a personal way, desegregation may not be perceived to coincide with the best interests of white citizens because of potential losses they imagine. Tangible losses would seem negligible since the number of vacant places at white colleges increases as the overall cohort of 18- to 25-year-olds diminishes. More serious perhaps are intangible aspects of a racially exclusive higher education environment that, though unmentioned and perhaps unrecognized, constitute an arena for personal loss for some whites.

Apparently many whites are also convinced that admitting blacks will decrease the quality of the instruction offered at traditionally white institutions. The American Council on Education recently reported that 88 percent of four-year colleges and universities in the nation offer some form of remedial instruction (American Council on Education, 1986). Since minority enrollment is so small and since it is increasingly concentrated in certain kinds of institutions located in certain regions of the country, it is unlikely that the majority of students enrolled at all of the approximately 2600 institutions offering remedial programs are minority. Therefore, the problem of preserving quality probably already exists, regardless of the presence of minority students. Nonetheless, for these reasons it is difficult to identify white constituencies that might profit from desegregation in a manner they could actively agree upon, except perhaps the small number of faculty and college administrators who may lose their jobs if black students do not begin to fill potentially empty college classrooms.

The third assumption—that "technology" needed to implement the unclear Title VI statute in an increasingly unsupportive political environment is on hand—is also questionable. As indicated earlier, most resistance to Title VI centers upon the guidelines that in one sense suggest the "technology" or steps required at the state and campus levels to achieve compliance. Any federally mandated strategy, regardless of how much discretion remains with the complying agency, would seem to contradict a widely held and hard-won tradition of academic freedom in American higher education. But beyond this very general objection, another problem for desegregation exists. Where changing higher education in a prescribed manner toward any new set of goals is concerned, little is known about how to do so properly.

Consider the issue of influencing student decisions to attend college. Since students cannot be compelled to attend, or to attend a specific institution, achieving changes in the racial distribution of student enrollment within state systems is dependent upon successfully influencing the choices students themselves make. Student enrollment decisions since 1970 have constituted an increasingly important issue for higher education managers and decision-makers, their motivation extending far beyond the more parochial concern of achieving positive racial distributions of students. Many colleges and universities are today dependent for their survival upon successfully enrolling a mix of students who can pay their own way and those eligible to receive some form of federal student financial aid. Consequently, determining salient elements of student choice decisions spawned a literature potentially useful, despite its original intent, for fashioning strategies that may result in favorable black student enrollment rates.

This research confirms the fact that policy-relevant conditions—like the existence of adequate student financial aid and the establishment of campus-level support programs—are reliable albeit insufficient determinants of black student enrollment (Astin, 1982). Knowledge of this kind clearly is useful for establishing the potential impact of selected desegregation strategies, since colleges that fail to provide sufficient aid and support programs are not likely to enroll large numbers of black students.

On the other hand student choice is most convincingly portrayed in research literature as a consistent function of the student's family background (Terkla & Jackson, 1984). For a variety of social, political, and economic reasons, family background is in more complicated, less successful, and less immediate ways influenced by public policy than factors like the existence of student support programs at the campus level. The student-choice research leads to the conclusion that desegregation achieved only by adding more black students may be subject to comparatively feeble influence through federal policy intervention. If other more substantial, reliably substantiated and manipulable determinants of choice exist, it would be useful to know about them. But the research has not proceeded sufficiently in this direction. Particularly absent is research that attempts to differentiate policy-relevant determinants of student choice by race.

To illustrate the absence of documented knowledge about how to recruit, enroll, and graduate special categories of underserved students, consider the literature describing ways in which the "college experience" exerts an impact upon any student once he or she enrolls. Despite a voluminous literature addressing this basic question and despite a fairly broad consensus based upon history and experience that college certainly does exert an influence, the literature does not provide definite policy-relevant variables to serve as clues for understanding the complex processes involved in producing desirable changes in students (Feldman & Newcomb, 1973; Bowen, 1977; Salmon & Taubman, 1973). More certain findings about college impacts would be useful for fashioning desegregation remedies, since, arguably, black and white students who participate in desegregated colleges are changed in more desired and highly valued ways than students in other environments. Knowing whether and how such changes take place could lead to the establishment of a clearer focus for desegregation remedies.

Sadly, too, little research has been devoted to an understanding of the differential impact of desegregated versus segregated college experiences, and most studies that do investigate the matter are solely concerned with comparative impacts upon blacks. Most recently, for example, Baratz and Finklen (1983) compared patterns of graduate school enrollment and employment for blacks graduating from traditionally black and predominantly white colleges and universities. They found that in most areas black graduates of traditionally black and predominantly white institutions behave the same: (1) they report satisfaction with their undergraduate degree programs in similar patterns; (2) they enter predominantly white graduate programs at similar rates and in similar distribution by field; and (3) both groups tend to obtain employment at similar rates and in similar types of jobs, although traditionally graduates of black colleges tend to earn less money. Studies that compare the behavior of whites graduating from desegregated and exclusively white colleges are virtually nonexistent.

Another important "technology void" exists where black college enhancement is concerned. A Research Triangle Institute study of the impact of the federal Aid to Developing Institutions Program (ADIP), which over the years has awarded categorical grants to "underdeveloped" colleges to accelerate their increased visibility, began by stating a dilemma: "Is it plausible to expect that institutions with limited means and resources and which focus on students of limited financial resources, can indeed generate, through Title III or other activities, increased fiscal support that may guarantee both survival and a program of reasonable quality?" (Davis & Ironside, 1981, p. *xi.*) Concerning prior studies of Title III, the study concluded that "in short, not much of utility in evaluating how Title III activities contribute to institutional development has emerged" (Davis & Ironside, 1981, p. I.3). Based upon their own further research, the RTI investigators concluded that:

> In terms of the usual requirements of evaluation design—that standard and accepted measures of input, process, context and outcomes exist and are or may be routinely applied; that interactions among program and other institutional variables may be recognized and appropriately controlled—it must be concluded that the program (Title III) is not evaluable as currently operated. (Davis & Ironside, pp. *xvii–xviii*)

Little is documented with great certainty from evaluation studies of such programs and related research about the best strategies for government to use to help black colleges become more viable. Research offers few definitive suggestions for speeding the development of any kind of college or university. One would even encounter difficulty reaching agreement within higher education communities on the meaning of the term "development" when it is applied to colleges and universities. For all these reasons, it is not known whether adding new instructional programs, enhancing campus facilities, and equalizing public funding at black colleges will result in their ability to compete for students with other institutions in the same system.

On this subject the desegregation guidelines assume a comprehensive, politically desirable approach. In a manner that begins to add credibility to the process, monitoring by OCR in recent times seems to reflect an acceptance of long-term trial and error with sustained persistence needed to make sure the black colleges are enhanced. Nonetheless, the Title III ADIP program constitutes the only precedent for achieving renewed institutional viability in recent times through federal policies of intervention, and its track record is at best unknown.

Evidence of lack of consensus upon the "technology" for higher education desegregation therefore exists in two forms: (1) disputes involving the courts, the Department of Education, and the states over the guidelines and subsequent strategies included in state desegregation plans; and (2) lack of documentation in research and development literature about most successful strategies for "desegregating" a college or university.

The fourth assumption of the necessary organizational capacity by federal and state government and by the colleges and universities to carry out remedies for desegregation also deserves close attention. The limited capacity of the Office for Civil Rights at the Department of Education to undertake its numerous regulatory responsibilities is noted elsewhere. In most recent years funds for civil rights regulation in education have allegedly been reduced with priority within OCR assigned to the elementary and secondary arena (*Chronicle of Higher Education,* Dec. 15, 1982, p. 22; May 4, 1983, p. 17). Other evidence of diminished political and staff capacity include the following: (1) guidelines for Title VI regulation of higher education were not written until 1977, but similar ones for elementary and secondary school were first prepared in 1968; (2) OCR did not begin until 1980 to issue written responses to the evidence of compliance supplied on a yearly basis by state college and university systems as required by the guidelines; (3) despite threats few compliance proceedings occurred and usually only under pressure from the courts and in response to long delays at the state level; (4) compliance data for only three years have been computer processed and analyzed even though several states have been submitting required surveys and narrative reports since 1976.

Another indicator of the limited capacity of the federal government to regulate college and university systems for civil rights purposes is dogged interference from federal legislators and other political actors. Apparently a great deal of interference took place where Title VI regulation was concerned preventing action by OCR and the Justice Department. Limits upon such interference are not included in implementation regulations, as is the case where other federal policies are concerned.

It was only during the 1970s that in most state governments higher education emerged as a concern worthy of full representation by a strong, separate administrative agency (Kerr, 1980). During the 1970s most states culminated plans to establish or strengthen the role of higher education authorities. The federal requirement for so-called "1202" commissions influenced choices in this direction, but this means that most higher education authorities are relatively new units of government, or that they have only recently assumed substantial statewide policy-making authority after a longer period of limited visibility. Their relative newness suggests evidence of their perhaps growing, but at the present time limited, capacity to regulate the colleges and universities comprising the state systems.

According to a 1983 study by the Education Commission of the States, most state higher education agencies are concerned with a range of responsibilities that typically include systemwide planning, budget development, and (instructional) program renewal or approval (Burnes et al., 1983, pp. 27–28).

Two states in our sample of six—Georgia and Florida—have consolidated higher education governing boards that hold more control in terms of program review and budgeting authority than the higher education coordinating boards in Arkansas, Oklahoma, Pennsylvania, and Virginia. In Florida, however, a major change in law took place in 1981, creating a situation where the board of regents' authority is more similar to that of a coordinating board. The public universities gained greater independence from the board of regents, and authority was granted to the State Postsecondary Education Planning Commission, an advisory group to the State Board of Education, for higher education master plan development (Burnes et al., 1983, p. 30).

These governance structures suggest that five of the six states involved in desegregation over the longest period govern their state colleges and universities through means more limited than about half the states in the country. Georgia is the only state in our sample that falls in the category of strong board control over higher education. Evidence of low state capacity to regulate the institutions is reflected in these findings, and desegregation compliance may be harder to achieve at the campus level as a result.

It is also worth noting that the authority nationwide for running higher education systems, though increasingly located in state agencies created or strengthened for this purpose, is shared between the legislative and executive branches of state government. Moreover, the legislature plays a dominant role historically in government in many of the states we investigated, and this balance of power has demonstrably reduced the pace of Title VI compliance despite the expressed intentions of the governor and chancellor in some states. This is sometimes notably an outcome where attempts have been made to have the legislature appropriate supplementary funds for the enhancement of traditionally black colleges. The narrative compliance reports submitted by state systems each year to the Department of Education contain a great deal of evidence on this problem. In many instances a state confirms that the chief state higher education official, with the governor's approval, submitted a request for additional funds for the enhancement of traditionally black colleges and universities. A year later the same state often reports that the request was turned down, partially funded, or tabled for further consideration.

For example, the 1980 Virginia compliance report notes that: "Virginia State University requested through the 1980–82 capital outlay process 17 major projects amounting to $25,379,442. Of this amount, $20,327,671 was from State General Funds, $4,525,805 was from revenue bonds, and $525,966 was from total higher education operating funds. Of the total requested funds, 19.3 percent was appropriated. This is 24.2 percent of the State General Funds requested for the 1980–82 biennium. No appropriations were made in the other two categories for the 1980–82 biennium" (State Council of Higher Education for Virginia, 1980, p. 5). The heavy influence of the legislative branch in relation to the administrative branch of state government may further suggest limited organizational capacity at the state level in implementing desegregation.

Where the organizational capacity of the predominantly white colleges and universities constituting the six state systems is concerned, the Department of Education compliance reports do not request evidence of exceptionally limited capacity for implementation. On the other hand, since the colleges have been segregated for a long time, few personnel at the campus level would seem to have had experience conducting the kinds of programs needed to recruit and retain black students. Moreover, few new staff experienced at other institutions seem to have been hired for this purpose. The very low number of black faculty and administrators—new hired in particular—supports this impression. Indeed, most colleges nationwide have not had experience recruiting students. Furthermore, competition for increasingly diminished resources also seems to dampen enthusiasm for any attempt to develop the capacity to implement such desegregation strategies. More seriously, active leadership to undertake and design such programs would seem to be particularly absent at institutions ordered to assume desegregation tasks despite evidence that most colleges and universities that voluntarily desegregated in earlier decades encountered difficulty meeting the needs of minority students. Among the deficiencies reported were lack of student support programs, limited curricular offerings, and lack of appropriately trained and experienced faculty and administrative personnel (Willie & McCord, 1972; Peterson, 1978).

SUMMARY

Implementation in public higher education of Title VI of the 1964 Civil Rights Act promises far-reaching outcomes, and a broad range of state systems, colleges, universities, and individuals are potentially affected. The 15-year history of implementation of the statute is not distinguished, however, by circumstances of tremendous success.

This is the case in the judgment of the federal courts because the US Department of Education and responsible elements of state governments have not exerted great effort in choosing potentially successful desegregation remedies; nor have chosen remedies, their potential notwithstanding, been fully implemented. In particular, little sustained increase has occurred in black student enrollment at predominantly white institutions in Title VI states; enhancement activities at traditionally black colleges and universities have not unfolded rapidly with sufficient resources; and increased hiring of black faculty and administrators has generally not materialized. In too many instances, declines in black participation in most areas of higher education occurred over the period 1981 to 1983.

Directions for improvement that emerge from an analysis of broad assumptions underlying Title VI implementation include: (1) revising the desegregation guidelines or refining Title VI itself in ways that enhance implementation but also preserve the far-reaching potential for increasing black participation in higher education; (2) mustering local political support for desegregation enforcement; (3) systematically identifying and exploring successful campus and state-level desegregation remedies, simultaneously conducting inquiries aimed at producing good evidence useful for constructing and implementing new remedies and influencing the establishment of a consensus about the best avenue for reaching compliance; and (4) increasing the organizational capacity at the federal, state, and campus levels to address Title VI regulation of public higher education.

A SUMMARY OF POLICY-MAKING EVENTS
ACCOMPANYING TITLE VI REGULATION, 1964–1984

1964

The Civil Rights Act enacted by Congress. Title VI and related decisions prohibit discrimination on the basis of race, and provide for the withholding of federal funds where such discrimination is found.

1969

DHEW charged 10 states with operating dual systems of higher education in violation of Title VI, and requested that each state develop and submit a desegregation plan. Five states (Florida, Louisiana, Mississippi, North Carolina, and Oklahoma) did not submit a plan, and five (Arkansas, Georgia, Maryland, Pennsylvania, and Virginia) submitted plans considered unacceptable. Yet the Office of Civil Rights took no enforcement action.

1970

OCTOBER   The NAACP Legal Defense Fund (LDF) filed a class action suit, *Adams v. Richardson* (1973) in the US District Court for the District of Columbia. LDF charged that DHEW and the Office of Civil Rights (OCR) had failed to enforce Title VI, as federal funds had not been withheld from those 10 state systems found to discriminate on the basis of race.

At this time the National Association for Equal Opportunity in Higher Education (NAFEO), an organization representing black colleges, filed an *amicus curiae* brief requesting that the suit be dropped.

1971

FEBRUARY   The US District Court ruled that DHEW was obligated to commence enforcement proceedings against the 10 state systems. DHEW was ordered to initiate those proceedings within 60 days.

The circuit court affirmed the district court order, but granted DHEW 10 months of additional time, noting that "HEW must carefully assess the significance of a variety of new factors as it moves into an unaccustomed area" (*Adams v. Richardson*, 1973).

1974

JANUARY   US suit against Louisiana filed in US District Court for Eastern Louisiana to enforce the Fourteenth Amendment and Title VI.

JUNE   By this time, OCR had accepted plans from eight of the 10 states. Louisiana had refused to submit a plan; Mississippi did not include junior colleges in its plan.

1975

MARCH   The US Department of Justice filed suit against Mississippi.

AUGUST   The *Adams v. Richardson* (1973) plaintiffs petitioned the court for further relief, arguing that the plans DHEW had accepted were inadequate, and that DHEW had failed to obtain implementation.

1976

NAFEO filed a second *amicus curiae* brief in opposition to the LDF's position on the grounds that it required the merger of traditionally black institutions into predominantly white institutions.

1977

JANUARY   The district court granted the *Adams v. Richardson* (1973) plaintiffs relief with regard to six state systems.

APRIL   The district court issued a written order that included instructions to OCR to develop final guidelines or criteria for compliance with Title VI, to seek revised desegregation plans from the six states, and to follow a specified time frame in dealing with the states.

JULY   OCR filed with the court and sent to the affected states a document entitled "Criteria Specifying the Ingredients of Acceptable Plans to Desegregate State Systems of Public Higher Education" (*Federal Register*, 1978).

SEPTEMBER   The six states submitted revised plans.

1978

OCR's guidelines published in the *Federal Register* signaling their formal approval. Plans for all but three states found adequate. Georgia, Virginia, and the University System of North Carolina (UNC) required to submit adequate plans within 45 days or face enforcement proceedings.

MARCH   Georgia and Virginia submitted amended plans.

APRIL   Enforcement proceedings initiated against UNC.

1979

APRIL   North Carolina filed suit in US District Court for the Eastern District of North Carolina, seeking to enjoin the administrative hearing.

JUNE   The district court enjoined the Department of Education from deferring financial assistance prior to holding an administrative hearing on evidence concerning Title VI.

1981

Consent decree entered in the *State of North Carolina v. US Department of Education* (1981).

SEPTEMBER   Consent decree entered in *The United States of America v. State of Louisiana* (1981).

1982

JANUARY   OCR provisionally accepted the Kentucky Plan, but asked the Justice Department to begin enforcement proceedings against Alabama for failure to submit an acceptable plan.

FEBRUARY   OCR asked the Justice Department to begin enforcement proceedings against Ohio.

MAY   The NAACP Legal Defense Fund returned to district court charging that several states had not met their plan commitments; LDF blamed the federal administration for failing to enforce these plans, and asked the court for further relief.

JULY   At OCR's request, Virginia agreed to modify its state plan.

1983

MARCH   US District Court for the District of Columbia granted NAACP Legal Defense Fund's petition and ordered Arkansas, Florida, Georgia, Oklahoma, North Carolina community college system, and Virginia to submit new plans. The court also ordered Pennsylvania to submit a new plan that included "state related" institutions. OCR was ordered to undertake compliance proceedings within 10 days as required by law against all of these states plus Kentucky and Texas. The latter two had failed to make revisions in their desegregation plans as ordered by OCR. West Virginia, Missouri, and Delaware were excluded from further relief.

1984

FEBRUARY   The US Supreme Court refused to consider NAACP's appeal of Eastern District Court of North Carolina ratification of 1981 consent decree between the University (System) of North Carolina and the US Department of Education.

Source: Adapted from Clark, Phipps, Clark, and Harris. *Technical Assistance on Higher Education: A Report to the Office for Civil Rights, US Department of Education,* mimeo, Oct. 2, 1982, Appendix B.

REFERENCES

Adams v. Bell, D.C. Civil Action No. 70-3095, March 24, 1982.
Adams v. Califano, 430 F. Supp. 118, 121 (D.D.C. 1977).
Adams v. Richardson, 356 F. Supp. 92 (D.D.C. 1973).
Adams v. Weinberger, 391 F. Supp. 269 (D.D.C. 1975).
American Council on Education. *Summary Statistics: Annual Survey of Colleges, 1986–87.* Washington, D.C.: ACE, 1986.
Arkansas Department of Higher Education. *Annual Report of the Arkansas College and University Plan for Compliance with Title VI of the Civil Rights Act of 1964.* Mimeo, Fall 1983.
Astin, Alexander W. *Minorities in American Higher Education.* San Francisco: Jossey-Bass, 1982.
August, Taylor D., Office for Civil Rights Regional Director, letter attachment to Bill Clinton, Governor of Arkansas, Jan. 28, 1983.
August, Taylor D., Office for Civil Rights Regional Director, letter to George Nigh, Governor of Oklahoma, Jan. 28, 1983.
Baratz, Joan C., and Myra Finklen. *Participation of Recent Black College Graduates in the Labor Market and in Graduate Education.* Princeton: Educational Testing Service, 1983.
Berman, Paul, and Milbrey McLaughlin. *Federal Programs Supporting Educational Change: The Findings in Review.* Santa Monica: Rand, 1975.
Bowen, Howard R. *Investment in Learning.* San Francisco: Jossey-Bass, 1977.
Brown v. Board of Education, 347 US 483 (1954).
Brown, Cynthia G., Assistant Secretary for Civil Rights, Department of Education, letter to Mark White, Attorney General of Texas, Jan. 15, 1971.
Burnes, Donald W., Robert M. Palaich, Aims McGuiness, and Patricia Flakus-Mosqueda. *State Governance of Education: 1983.* Denver: Education Commission of the States, 1983, pp. 26–33.
Carnegie Council on Policy Studies in Higher Education. *Making Affirmative Action Work in Higher Education.* San Francisco: Jossey-Bass, 1975.
Chronicle of Higher Education, Vol. 26, No. 22, July 27, 1983, p. 8; Vol. 28, No. 1, Feb. 29, 1984, p. 11; Vol. 27, No. 17, Jan. 4, 1984, p. 17; Vol. 26, No. 24, Aug. 10, 1983, p. 9; Vol. 27, No. 20, Jan. 25, 1984, pp. 17–18; Vol. 25, No. 16, Dec. 15, 1982, p. 22; Vol. 26, No. 10, May 4, 1983, p. 17.
Ciarlo, J.A. "Monitoring and Analysis of Mental Health Program Outcomes Data," in Marcia Guttentag and S. Sarr (eds.), *Evaluation Studies Review Annual*, Vol. 2. Beverly Hills: Sage, 1977, pp. 647–656.
Davis, Junius A., and Roderick A. Ironside. *An Evaluability Assessment of the Strengthening Developing Institutions Program.* Research Triangle Park, North Carolina: Research Triangle Institute, 1981.
Davis v. East Baton Rouge Parrish School Board 398 F. Supp. 1013, vac. 570 F. 2d 1260, *cert. denied, East Baton Rouge Parrish School Board v. Davis* 439 U.S. 1114 (1979).
Dayton v. Brinkman 433 U.S. 406 (1977).

DBS Corporation. *Data Processing and Analysis of the Seventh Annual Report on Progress in Implementing Statewide Higher Education Desegregation Plans*, Mimeo, Sept. 1983.

Dentler, Robert A., D. Catherine Baltzell, and Daniel J. Sullivan. *University on Trial*. Cambridge, MA: Abt Associates, 1983, p. 6.

Dodds, Dewey E., Regional Civil Rights Director, Region III, Department of Education, letters to John D. Rockefeller IV, Governor of West Virginia; to Pierre S. Dupont IV, Governor of Delaware, Jan. 7, 1981; to John T. Casteen, Secretary of Education, Commonwealth of Virginia, Jan. 31, 1983.

Education Week, Vol. 3, No. 13, Dec. 1983, pp. 5–17.

Elmore, Richard. "Mapping Backward: Using Implementation Analysis to Structure Policy Decision," in *Political Science Quarterly*, Vol. 94, Winter 1980.

Federal Register 1977, Vol. 42, No. 155, pp. 40780–40785; 1978, Vol. 43, No. 32, pp. 6658–6664.

Feldman, Kenneth A., and Theodore M. Newcomb. *The Impact of College on Students*. San Francisco: Jossey-Bass, 1973.

Florida State Department of Education. *Florida's Commitment to Equal Access and Equal Opportunity in Public Higher Education*. Tallahassee: Florida State Department of Education, Feb. 1978.

Georgia State Board of Regents. *A Plan for the Further Desegregation of the University System of Georgia*. Atlanta: Georgia State Board of Regents, Sept. 1977.

Grove City College v. Bell 687 F. 2nd 684 (C.A. 3 1982).

Hargrove, Erwin C. "The Search for Implementation Theory." Mimeo, Institute for Public Policy Studies, Vanderbilt University, Nashville, May, 1981.

High, Jesse, Office for Civil Rights, Region VII Director, letter to Christopher Bond, Governor of Missouri, Jan. 15, 1981.

Hill, Paul. *Enforcement and Informal Pressure in the Management of Federal Categorical Programs in Education*. Santa Monica: Rand, 1979.

Kelly v. Metropolitan County School Board of Nashville and Davidson County 20 F. 2d. 209 (6th Cir. 1959).

Kerr, Clark. "Coordination in a Changing Environment," in *Change*, Vol. 12, No. 2, Oct. 1980, pp. 19–23.

McCorkle, Chester O., Jr., and Sandra Orr Archibald. *Management and Leadership in Higher Education*. San Francisco: Jossey-Bass, 1982.

Mingle, James R. "The Opening of White Colleges and Universities to Black Students," in Gail E. Thomas (ed.), *Black Students in Higher Education*. Westport, CT: Greenwood, 1981, pp. 18–29.

NAACP Legal Defense and Educational Fund. *Annual Report, 1985–86*. New York: LDF, 1986.

National Center for Education Statistics. *Higher Education General Information Survey, 1983*. Washington, D.C.: Government Printing Office, 1984.

National Center for Education Statistics. *Higher Education General Information Survey, 1976*. Washington, D.C.: Government Printing Office, 1976.

Oklahoma State Regents for Higher Education. *Annual Report: Compliance with Title VI of the Civil Rights Act*. Mimeo, August, 1983.

Orfield, Gary. *The Reconstruction of Southern Education*. New York: Wiley, 1969.

Panetta, Leon, Director of the Office for Civil Rights, US Department of Health, Education, and Welfare, letter to Mills E. Godwin, Governor of the Commonwealth of Virginia, Dec. 2, 1969.

Peterson, Marvin W., Robert T. Blackburn, Zelda F. Gamson, Carlos H. Arce, Roselle W. Davenport, and James R. Mingle. *Black Students on White Campuses: The Impacts of Increased Black Enrollments*. Ann Arbor: University of Michigan Press, 1978.

Read, Frank T. "Judicial Evolution of the Law of School Integration Since *Brown v. Board of Education*," in *Law and Contemporary Problems*, Vol. 39, No. 1, Winter 1975, pp. 7–49.

Reynolds, William B. "The Administration's Approach to Desegregation of Public Higher Education," in *American Education*, 1983, Vol. 19, No. 4, pp. 9–11.

Roos, L., N.P. Roos, P. Micol, and C. Johnson. "Using Administrative Data Banks for Research and Evaluation: A Case Study," in Thomas D. Cook (ed.), *Evaluation Studies Review Annual*, Vol. 3, Beverly Hills: Sage, 1978, pp. 263–270.

Salmon, Lewis C., and Paul J. Taubman (eds.). *Does College Matter?* New York: Academic Press, 1973.

State Council of Higher Education for Virginia. *Annual Report*. Mimeo, August 31, 1980.

State of North Carolina v. US Department of Education, Eastern North Carolina Civil Action No. 79-217-CIV-5, *Consent Decree*, July 17, 1981.

State University System of Florida. *Annual Report of Progress, 1982–83*. Mimeo, Dec. 1, 1983.

Terkla, Dawn G., and Gregory A. Jackson. "State of the Art in Student Choice Research." Mimeo, Harvard Graduate School of Education, Jan. 1984.

Thomas, William H., Office for Civil Rights, Region IV Director, letters to Fob James, Governor of Alabama, Jan. 7, 1981; to Richard W. Riley, Governor of South Carolina, Jan. 7, 1981; to John Y. Brown, Jr., Governor of Kentucky, Jan. 15, 1981; to Bob Graham, Governor of Florida, Jan. 28, 1983; to Joe Frank Harris, Governor of Georgia, Jan. 31, 1983.

University System of Georgia. *Annual Progress Report: Implementation of a Plan for the Further Desegregation of Georgia*. Mimeo, Oct. 14, 1983.

United States v. Jefferson County Board of Education, 372 F. 2d 836, 847 N.S. (5th Circ. 1966).

United States v. Louisiana, Civ. No. 74-68 (M.D. La.), *Consent Decree*, Sept. 7, 1981.

Willie, Charles V., and Arline S. McCord. *Black Students at White Colleges*. New York: Praeger, 1972.

2

The Production of Black Doctoral Recipients: A Description of Five States' Progress

WILLIAM T. TRENT
ELAINE J. COPELAND
University of Illinois at Urbana-Champaign

Central to an assessment of black Americans' access to and completion of doctoral programs is financial support to pay the costs of enrolling in graduate school. Yet little information is available to indicate the level and quality of support black doctoral students receive, particularly from state government. The federal government has made a limited commitment to increasing access by supporting minority graduate students under programs like the Graduate and Professional Opportunity Program (GPOP). Astin (1982) maintains that individual states are viewed as primarily responsible for increasing student access, yet funding from states has basically been used to support minority, low-income undergraduate students. Enforcement of Title VI of the Civil Rights Law of 1964 has substantially influenced several states to provide financial aid to black students. Those states affected have supported dual systems of higher education and are legally required to provide special equal educational opportunity for black residents.

The research reported in this chapter examines the efforts of five states—Arkansas, Florida, Georgia, Oklahoma, and Virginia—to increase the production of black recipients of the doctoral degree. In the past these states operated racially dual systems of postsecondary education and, as a result of the *Adams v. Richardson* (356 F. Supp. 92 [1973]) court case, have been required to comply with Title VI by increasing black partici-

The research reported here is taken from a larger study funded by the Southern Education Foundation, entitled "The Effectiveness of State Financial Aid in Enhancing the Production of Black Ph.D. Recipients." We wish to thank the Foundation for their support and for permission to publish data from that report.

pation in public higher education in several ways (Haynes, 1978). This chapter is concerned with one of the areas of increased opportunity: graduate level enrollment and degree attainment.

Exploring this state responsibility, we report results from secondary analysis of national and state data, as well as from interviews with key informants in each of the five states and their respective doctoral degree-granting universities. Our assessment of the relationship between, on the one hand, availability and quality of states' financial support for black graduate students and, on the other, the extent of Ph.D. production is facilitated by an examination of statewide desegregation plans. Since these states were first instructed to submit desegregation plans as early as 1969, and because the plans include procedures to increase access of black students to doctoral programs, they provide an important source of data on the efforts and accomplishments in increasing the number of black Ph.D.s.

BACKGROUND RESEARCH

A number of researchers have examined the status of black Americans in higher education (Astin, 1982; Blackwell, 1975, 1981; Brown & Stent, 1977; Morris, 1979; Preer, 1982; Thomas, 1981). Each of these authors examines the status of black Americans in higher education and discusses those factors that impede or promote access, persistence, and success.

Several factors have been cited as major barriers to equal educational opportunity at both the undergraduate and graduate levels. Thomas (1981) reported that while the quality of financial aid constitutes a factor in increasing access of black Americans to all levels of higher education, family background, income, and the lack of any form of financial aid are major impediments for black students seeking advanced graduate and professional degrees. Lack of aid is due in part to the fact that both federal and state governments have historically provided less support for graduate than undergraduate low-income students. Not surprisingly, then, studies by Howard University researchers indicate that negative effects of family income were much greater at the postbaccalaureate level (Institute for the Study of Educational Policy, 1981).

Not only is the absence of state and federal financial aid an issue, but a report from the National Advisory Committee on Black Higher Education (1982) reveals that blacks are less likely than whites to have been supported with teaching and research assistantships in graduate school, despite the fact that the financial needs are greater for black graduate students than for their white counterparts. Black students have tended to rely on different sources of aid to support their graduate education (Morris, 1979).

If aid is very important and a shortage exists, then how is the status of blacks in graduate school negatively affected? In a recent study, Blackwell (1981) examined the status of black Americans in selected graduate and professional fields. His study consisted of two phases: an analysis of survey data from selected institutions offering advanced training for eight professional fields, and a trend analysis of first-year enrollment and graduation rates of black students for these same professional schools during the 1970s. The Blackwell study assessed the relative extent to which such factors as recruiting, presence and quality of retention programs, presence and quality of financial support, and the presence of special admission programs influenced the enrollment and retention of black students in eight graduate and professional programs. Blackwell's research results underscore the crucial role and importance of financial support among the various factors that he studied.

The American Council on Education, citing the concentration of doctoral degrees earned by blacks, reported 60% of the 1980–81 doctorates being awarded by 10% of doctoral-granting institutions, including Howard University, a traditionally black institution. In accounting for the institutional disparity, the ACE report cites a lack of recruitment, limited financial assistance, and restrictive admissions policies. Along this same line, Blackwell (1981) and Peterson and associates (1978) released studies demonstrating that commitment on the part of colleges and universities in the form of special support efforts, vigorous recruitment, and ample financial assistance can yield important improvements in enrollment, retention, and graduation for blacks at both the undergraduate and graduate levels.

The severity of the underrepresentation of blacks resulting from these factors identified at the Ph.D. level has also been addressed in recent research. Using data from the Higher Education General Information Survey, Trent (1984) reports a small gain in earned doctorates by blacks nationally from the 1975–76 to 1980–81 school years (from 1169 or 3.4% to 1265 or 3.7%), while overall a net decline for total earned doctorates occurred for the same period. Even with this modest gain, blacks lost ground with respect to parity. In 1970 blacks were 5.2% of the availability pool—persons 20 to 34 years old with at least four years of college— and by 1976 they were 5.7% of that pool. The 0.3% gain in their share of all earned doctorates was outdistanced by their 0.5% gain as a portion of the availability pool. Trent's research further showed the continuing concentration of Ph.D. degrees by major field for blacks: About half of all black Ph.D.s are earned in education.

The American Council on Education (1984) offers further evidence of the severity of the underrepresentation problem. In its survey of minority Ph.D. holders employed in academic settings, council researchers found that in 1979 about 3% of academic positions were held by native-born minorities, or about 5500 out of approximately 170,000 jobs. Native-born blacks held about 2150 of these positions.

States affected by Title VI hold a rather specific responsibility to increase access and to remedy underrepresentation problems. For these states, the production of black doctorates continues to be a challenge of major proportions. Since virtually all previous studies of the graduate enrollment issue report financial aid as a major factor in increasing or impeding access, an examination of these states' financial aid efforts at the doctoral level is not unreasonably a measure of their will to address the overall problem of remedying past segregation practices. Moreover their successes and failures may exemplify what others may expect in grappling with this same problem.

The principal concerns of this research are: (1) to describe and document the level, quality, and variety of expenditures directed toward the production of doctoral degrees for blacks within five states affected by Title VI enforcement; (2) to provide a detailed count of degree production by doctoral-degree-granting institutions for the five sample states for the period from 1975 to 1981; and (3) to provide a detailed count of enrollment by full- and part-time status and postbaccalaureate-degree level for each state for the period 1976 to 1982.

First, publicly available enrollment data for conferred degrees provide counts by race and gender for each higher education institution, and constitute an invaluable and immediately available means of describing production trends for each of the five states. The Higher Education General Information Survey (HEGIS) contains data for each state. Two additional types of precollected data also exist in the public domain. Of the original 10 states affected by Title VI, the five selected for this study have annually, over a five-year period, submitted survey reports to the US Office for Civil Rights indicating progress toward compliance with the objectives detailed in their respective statewide desegregation plans. These reports and supporting data, obtained from the US Office for Civil Rights, provide student counts and other program implementation measures that address the desegregation-related activities of each state. Finally, each of the five states involved in the study provides an annual narrative report, making available still another source of financial and student data that specifically addresses the concerns of this research.

A second type of data employed in this assessment identifies the quality, range, and function of state efforts to recruit, admit, support, and graduate black doctoral degree candidates. These were obtained through interviews with state- and campus-level respondents.

RESULTS

Tables 2.1 through 2.5 provide a summary of our findings for the five states. The summary findings are a compilation and synthesis of data derived from each of the sources described above. We begin with an overall description of enrollment and degree attainment and then turn to our core concern, the effectiveness of state financial aid in the production of black Ph.D.s.

For the purpose of this research we use three indicators of the effectiveness of financial aid:

1. Whether the aid produced an increase in the number of doctorates awarded to blacks.
2. Whether the increase in aid availability resulted in increasing rates of first-time black graduate enrollees.
3. Whether the quality of the aid as indicated by amount, length of award, and packaging suggests that it is sufficient.

We explore each of these indicators using both the empirical and the interview data.

Title VI regulations require states to achieve parity at the graduate level by equalizing proportions of black and white in-state bachelor degree recipients from public institutions who immediately enroll in graduate school. In general, the five states examined approached but did not consistently attain parity on this measure. The January 1983 letters of evaluation to the respective state governors reveal that with the exception of Virginia, no state achieved parity on this measure for the period 1979 through 1982. Thus, with respect to this standard measure of equity, continued effort is needed. Similarly, the elimination of black–white disparity with respect to degree attainment at the doctoral level has not been achieved. Tables 2.1 and 2.2 report overall first-time graduate enrollments and earned doctorates for each of the five states. Although these tables lack a specific base from which to assess parity, they do show broad disparities.

Tables 2.3 and 2.4 provide data on black degree attainment at the doctoral level and first-time graduate enrollment for institutions offering the doctoral degree for each of the five states beginning in 1976.

If a reasonable indication of "effectiveness" is an increase in the absolute number of black Ph.D.s produced, then, as indicated by the fig-

TABLE 2.1. Percentage of Full-Time Graduate Enrollment of Ethnic Groups in Public Colleges in Five States, 1976–1982

State/Ethnic Group	1976	1978	1980	1982
ARKANSAS (N=)	(2,102)	(2,114)	(2,388)	(1,678)
Nonresident Alien	6.52	8.47	8.33	10.97
Black	6.42	6.72	5.57	5.19
American Indian	.43	.99	1.09	.66
Asian Pacific Isl.	1.24	.80	1.26	1.25
Hispanic	.33	.71	3.22	.98
White	85.06	82.31	83.12	81.47
FLORIDA (N=)	(7,913)	(7,891)	(8,188)	(7,492)
Nonresident Alien	8.01	8.34	9.87	14.34
Black	4.49	4.70	4.70	4.71
American Indian	.11	.17	.20	.13
Asian Pacific Isl.	.57	.89	1.25	.92
Hispanic	2.58	3.16	3.57	2.75
White	84.24	82.85	80.42	77.15
GEORGIA (N=)	(7,862)	(7,403)	(6,787)	(7,353)
Nonresident Alien	5.51	6.93	10.79	12.05
Black	8.85	10.16	6.35	5.66
American Indian	.28	.10	.01	.20
Asian Pacific Isl.	.43	.69	.83	1.99
Hispanic	.32	.45	.65	1.29
White	84.61	81.67	81.32	78.81
OKLAHOMA (N=)	(4,457)	(4,092)	(4,149)	(4,128)
Nonresident Alien	19.3	25.4	25.4	27.3
Black	3.9	3.3	3.6	3.1
American Indian	2.3	2.5	2.9	2.7
Asian Pacific Isl.	1.1	.8	1.8	1.5
Hispanic	.5	.7	1.5	.8
White	72.8	67.3	64.8	64.6
VIRGINIA (N=)	(7,406)	(7,662)	(8,453)	(8,615)
Nonresident Alien	4.1	5.6	7.9	11.6
Black	5.7	6.5	5.7	4.1
American Indian	.08	.09	.31	.10
Asian Pacific Isl.	.98	1.14	1.8	1.0
Hispanic	.24	.33	.69	.46
White	88.8	86.1	83.4	82.5

ures in Table 2.3, the efforts of the five states individually and collectively have not achieved the hoped-for success. In Table 2.3, only two states (Arkansas and Virginia) awarded more Ph.D.s to blacks in the 1983–84 year than they awarded eight years earlier. Differences for Arkansas and Virginia were minimal—1 and 2, respectively—while the decreases for

TABLE 2.2. Percentage Distribution of Earned Doctorates by Race/Ethnicity in Public Colleges in Five States, 1975–76 to 1980–81

State/Ethnicity	1975–76	1976–77	1978–79	1980–81
ARKANSAS (N=)	(120)	(106)	(93)	(105)
Nonresident Alien	.8	3.8	5.4	15.0
Black	4.2	2.8	4.3	3.0
American Indian	.8	—	—	—
Asian Pacific Isl.	4.2	1.9	5.4	—
Hispanic	—	2.8	1.1	—
White	90.0	88.7	83.9	82.0
FLORIDA (N=)	(693)	(695)	(713)	(697)
Nonresident Alien	5.9	13.0	12.0	10.0
Black	4.9	6.0	4.0	5.0
American Indian	.3	.3	.3	.3
Asian Pacific Isl.	3.0	.4	2.0	.3
Hispanic	2.0	1.0	.1	2.0
White	84.0	79.0	80.0	82.1
GEORGIA (N=)	(445)	(440)	(413)	(436)
Nonresident Alien	.4	—	13.0	13.0
Black	4.0	2.3	5.0	5.0
American Indian	.4	.2	.5	—
Asian Pacific Isl.	.9	1.3	1.2	.7
Hispanic	.9	.2	.2	.2
White	93.3	96.0	80.0	81.0
OKLAHOMA (N=)	(395)	(373)	(395)	(353)
Nonresident Alien	11.0	13.0	15.7	22.9
Black	2.0	2.0	6.0	3.1
American Indian	.8	1.0	.7	1.1
Asian Pacific Isl.	.3	.5	1.0	2.3
Hispanic	.8	1.0	.5	.6
White	85.0	82.3	76.0	70.0
VIRGINIA (N=)	(475)	(467)	(499)	(529)
Nonresident Alien	3.4	6.2	8.0	11.0
Black	4.0	3.9	5.4	3.6
American Indian	—	—	—	.2
Asian Pacific Isl.	1.5	1.1	2.0	.2
Hispanic	.2	.2	—	—
White	90.9	88.7	84.6	85.1

Georgia and Oklahoma were much greater—4 and 5, respectively—with the latter being 50% less than eight years earlier. Similarly, the totals for the five states show that for the 1983–84 year, 78 black Ph.D.s were awarded, constituting six fewer than eight years earlier.

Perhaps a more accurate and more revealing description of the patterns in Table 2.3 are the year-to-year fluctuations that occur for each state. There are no clear trends in the data for any one state or across the five. At best, the period 1980 to 1983 appears relatively stable for each state except Georgia. The degree attainment figures suggest that the post-plan implementation period has offered no substantial improvements over the pre-plan period. In essence, the availability of a statewide program has not discernibly altered the number of black recipients of doctorates at public institutions in these states. It appears that rather than increasing the number of students aided, the new sources of aid are being used by the same-sized cadre of students.

A second criterion of effectiveness of state financial aid involves the access issue. If increased financial support is available, then we might expect increases in the number of first-time black graduate enrollees. This hypothesis is consistent with research findings reported earlier: that the absence of financial support constitutes a major barrier to continued schooling, especially for blacks. Table 2.4 presents the first-time graduate enrollment figures for 1976 through 1984.

The numbers in Table 2.4 show a pattern of unevenness similar to numbers for degree attainment. Unfortunately, the reported figures for 1983 and 1984 are compiled in a different manner from the prior years. In Arkansas, Oklahoma, and Virginia, we note evidence of considerable improvement for 1983 and 1984. Nonetheless, using the period 1976 to 1982 (based on HEGIS public-use data tapes), apparently the overall movement in black first-time graduate enrollment was downward. The 1978–79 year involved the highest first-time black graduate enrollment overall. By 1982 the enrollment figure ran about 30% lower. Note too that the 1978–79 year also marks the greatest number of doctorates awarded to blacks. It is likely that increased sources or amounts of financial aid could have influenced both degree attainment and enrollment in that first year of full implementation, especially in the limited case where near-Ph.D.s were assisted to completion in one year.

Despite progress in Oklahoma and Virginia, these two states showed the largest increases in Ph.D.s awarded to blacks between the 1976–77 and 1978–79 school years. It is still the case that enrollment figures do not reflect a general pattern of change suggesting that financial aid has been effective in increasing the pool of black candidates. We caution the reader that first-time graduate enrollment includes students who will terminate with a master's degree, and that in some fields strong financial incentives exist for doing so. On the other hand, the quality of direct aid available could increase the number of black students who will persist in their studies until the doctorate. Thus, first-time black graduate enrollment numbers, although not increasing, could contain a greater propor-

TABLE 2.3. Black Ph.D. Degree Attainment for Five Southern States

	1975–76[1]	1976–77[1]	1978–79[1]	1979–80[2]	1980–81[1]	1981–82[2]	1982–83[2]	1983–84[2]
Arkansas	5	3	4	5	3	6	6	6
Florida	36	39	27	26	34	28	30	36
Georgia	18	10	20	14	20	18	12	14
Oklahoma	10	6	22	7	11	11	13	5
Virginia	15	18	27	16	19	24	23	17
TOTALS	84	76	100	68	87	87	84	78

[1]Earned degree data for 1975–76, 1976–77, 1978–79, and 1980–81 are based on data from the Higher Education General Information Survey of degrees and other formal awards conferred between July 1 and June 30 of the respective years (HEGIS XI, XII, XIV, and XVI).

[2]Earned degree data reported for 1979–80, 1981–82, 1982–83, and 1983–84 are based on annual reports supplied by the state system-wide offices.

TABLE 2.4.   First-Time Graduate Enrollment for Black Students in Five Southern States[1]

	1976[2]	1978[2]	1980[2]	1982[2]	1983[3]	1984[3]
Arkansas	86	102	79	40	106	131
Florida	204	238	278	226	—	115
Georgia	488	554	334	309	144	136
Oklahoma	116	109	97	72	137	145
Virginia	263	215	277	215	164	230
TOTALS	1,157	1,218	1,065	862		757

[1]The enrollment data reported in this table are given only for those four-year institutions in each state that award the doctorate degree.
[2]First-time black graduate enrollments for 1976, 1978, 1980, and 1982 are based on data from the Higher Education General Information Surveys of Fall Enrollment, public use data tapes for the respective years (HEGIS XI, XIII, XV, and XVII).
[3]First-time black graduate enrollments for 1983 and 1984 are based on reports from the state system-wide offices for each of the five states.

tion of aspirants for the doctorate. We turn next to a discussion of aid quality.

Table 2.5 summarizes the states' current efforts in providing financial assistance to black doctoral students. In addition, it provides an indication of the availability of state funding for recruitment and financial aid. It is important to emphasize that the funds reported here are centrally administered state funds clearly designated for the support of black graduate doctoral candidates. The figures in the table do not include additional support made available by individual institutions, some of which may be private and public aid also awarded to blacks. The reported funds are made available through legislative action in response to Title VI requirements. Notably for Arkansas, the year 1985–86 saw the first availability of such support even though the Title VI regulatory intervention in Arkansas began in 1969. There are two grant programs in Florida: (1) Grant-in-Aid for Graduate Students Program, and (2) Employee Grant-in-Aid Program.

We begin first with a discussion of the amount of aid provided. For the average size of awards (column 1 of Table 2.5), the number of students supported (column 2, FTE), and total cost (column 3), there are considerable differences from one state to the next. For the average dollar amounts, Florida (Graduate Students Program), Georgia, and Oklahoma are quite comparable, offering grants of $5000 to $6000 annually. By contrast, Virginia offers an average award of $10,000 to $12,000 to qualified employees. The Virginia awards are comparable to Florida's

TABLE 2.5. Characteristics of State System-Wide Financial Aid for Black Doctoral and Graduate Students

| | Funding | | | | | Recruitment | | Student Support Services |
	Avg.	Students	Total $	Length	Additive	Funded	Centralized	Funded
Arkansas	—	—	$175,000	N/A	Yes	—	—	—
Florida[1,2]	$ 5,000	63	315,000	Renewable	Yes	No	No	Yes
	17,000	10	170,000	Renewable	Yes	No	No	No
Georgia	5,000	120	600,000	Renewable	Yes	No	Yes	No
Oklahoma	6,000	20	120,000	4 year	Yes	No	No	No
Virginia	10,000	10	100,000	Renewable	Yes	Yes	Yes	Yes

[1]Grant-in-Aid for Graduate Students Program.
[2]Employee Grant-in-Aid Program.

Employee Grant-in-Aid Program. As suggested earlier, some states have made explicit their support of doctoral candidates as an aid to their affirmative action promotion and hiring policies. In Virginia, Florida, and Oklahoma, these connections are clear. The newly implemented Arkansas program is constructed in the same fashion.

Georgia and Florida are clearly supporting larger numbers of students, perhaps reflecting the size of their black population. But Virginia also has a substantial black population, and currently shows the smallest total dollar amount and lowest number of students supported. The individual stipends for Virginia and Florida are large and do not preclude receiving other aid. The Florida and Virginia employee grant programs are also renewable for at least one additional year, and each carries a reciprocity work agreement based on leave time used. Each of these awards also includes a tuition payment, further enhancing the sufficiency of the award.

For the Florida, Georgia, and Oklahoma grant programs, the stipend quality is enhanced because the grants are used in conjunction with other forms of aid. For Oklahoma, the "packaging" of aid has been made an explicit requirement, with the resultant aid awards totalling up to $16,000 per year. For Florida, the grant program is renewable, but emphasis is placed upon new students with other institutional support coming into play in subsequent years. By contrast, Oklahoma followed a consistent plan of increasing the length of time a student may hold the award, from two years at its inception to the current four years. In each of the other states, the candidates who currently hold the awards are eligible to reapply, but the aid is not guaranteed. In this sense, only in Oklahoma can the grants be considered automatically retainable, but a similar provision has been proposed in Florida.

Note that the total amounts reported in Table 2.5 are annual appropriations, not cumulative totals. This means that new and continuing grantees annually compete for a fixed amount of dollars, even in Oklahoma where such funds in practice are retained automatically. Two potential outcomes emerge: The grant program could have a "revolving door" character if other aid sources are not forthcoming or are insufficient; or second, such an arrangement could encourage increased emphasis on "picking the best horse." In the first instance one future possibility is that students may come to view the aid as more a risk than an opportunity, or it could increase the pressure resulting from competition based on performance. Similarly, an emphasis on selection might tend to perpetuate rigid adherence to traditional admissions criteria, especially to test scores. This could have the effect of limiting the candidate pool and hence limiting the number of blacks earning the doctorate.

In general, we find the aid programs of good quality on each measure except length of eligibility for receiving aid. It may be important that states follow the lead taken by Oklahoma and increasingly structure their grants as retainable without restriction. Beyond that, enrollments (FTEs) are low in Virginia and Oklahoma, and also in Arkansas. In both Oklahoma and Virginia this concern is being addressed. The Oklahoma Regents have made repeated requests for increased funding, but additional appropriations have not been forthcoming. Virginia has made similar repeated requests, finally with somewhat greater success than Oklahoma. In 1985, the Virginia Council for Higher Education administered a pilot program, the Graduate Fellowship Program, offering a one-time, one-year graduate fellowship totalling $4400 each to 22 students.

RECRUITMENT AND SUPPORT SERVICES

In addition to direct aid to black graduate students, an effective state response to low black enrollment might consist of funded recruitment and student support services alone. In general, as Table 2.5 shows, only one state appears to have adopted both such measures, while one other state funds support services. We briefly describe the nature and funding of these services.

Only Virginia directly funds its recruitment effort. The current annual funding is $100,000 for two projects. The first is an annual workshop for potential graduate students currently enrolled as juniors in the state's public colleges. These workshops are also attended by the deans and other academic officials representing the doctorate-granting institutions. A second project, the Summer Undergraduate and Doctoral Program for Minority Virginians, provides undergraduates the opportunity to take one graduate course and receive orientation to graduate study during the summer.

Florida currently provides $342,000 to fund a special summer program for new, entering graduate and professional students. Each student receives a grant ranging from $1300 to $1500 to help defray the cost of tuition and living expenses.

While differently focused, each of these efforts seems quite appropriate based on the studies by Peterson and associates (1978) and Blackwell (1981) cited earlier. They serve the purpose of stimulating student interest in graduate study, increasing student familiarity, and communicating the interest of the state and university in the students.

SUMMARY AND DISCUSSION

In summary, the pattern of earned doctorates for blacks in these states is uneven with no clearly discernible trends for any one state or for all five together. The degree count for the 1983–84 year is slightly lower than the 1975–76 count. Using an average of four to five years for degree completion, it would be reasonable to expect to see positive changes as early as 1981–82 and certainly by the 1983–84 year in each of these states except Arkansas. That no increase in production occurred suggests at least two interpretations.

First, the 1975–76 degree count level may already reflect significant increases in each of these states, thereby making a search for further increments unreasonable. This may be the case, but the funding levels reported here were initiated after 1975 and should show some impact. A second interpretation raised earlier is that the funds are being used for replacement. Still, however, it is difficult to account for low degree levels given the numbers being supported in Florida and Georgia. An alternate suggestion—that the grants are being used disproportionately for professional students—is not borne out either. In Florida, for example, of 66 students supported as of fall 1983, 19 were reported enrolled in professional programs compared to 47 in traditional graduate fields leading to the doctorate.

The first-time black graduate enrollment rates underscore the lack of improvement in degree production. The decline over the six-year period from 1976 to 1982 in each state is notable. Table 2.6 underscores the 12-year pattern of national black graduate enrollment from 1972 to 1984. As shown, both in real numbers and as a percentage of all graduate students, blacks have experienced a precipitous decrease. Indeed, since 1980 there has been a 4000-student decline. The patterns reported in the Title VI states appear to correspond to national trends and force us to reconsider ways of increasing the candidate pool.

The direct aid being supplied by the states appears adequate on all but one of our criteria—its retentiveness. It may be important that students experience a sense of certainty about their financial support in order to maximize their planning and pursuit of graduate training. As repeatedly expressed by our respondents, the emphasis on new students is probably attributable to a concern for improving black–white parity in enrollment. Obviously both goals (entry parity and retention) are important, but the consequences of their current tensions could render the scholarship programs less effective.

The findings presented above offer a mixture of optimistic and cautious expectations. Optimistically, we can view the existing efforts of Title VI states to increase black doctoral candidates and degree recipients as tangible evidence of structured responses to this problem that can produce meaningful results: States can make financial aid available; states can fund and implement effective recruitment and support services; and col-

TABLE 2.6.   Black Full-Time Graduate Enrollment, 1972–1984

	Full-Time Graduate Students*	
	Black Students (in thousands)	Blacks as a Percent of All Students
1972	21	5.3
1974	22	5.5
1976	22	5.1
1978	21	4.9
1980	22	5.0
1982	19	4.2
1984	18	3.9

*Excludes (1) unclassified students (i.e., not candidates for a degree) and (2) students in US Service Schools.

Source: US Department of Commerce, Bureau of the Census, Current Population Reports, *School Enrollment—Social Economic Characteristics of Students*, Series P-20, Nos. 222, 303, 362, and 404.

leges and universities, given adequate direction and financial resources, can design and undertake programs that recruit, select, sustain, and move toward completion increased numbers of black doctoral candidates. Viewed in the narrow time frame, 1978 to 1984, six years after the acceptance of the plans submitted by the states reported on here, these are important accomplishments.

On the other hand, optimism has to be guarded, given the persistence of declining graduate-level enrollments and doctoral degree attainment. Moreover, programmatic efforts instituted in these states are not created voluntarily, and any further development will likely depend on increased funding through active enforcement. The current federal administration has been unequivocally lacking in its support for affirmative action and desegregation, the premises upon which Title VI decision-making rests. It is unlikely that incentives for greater compliance will be forthcoming at that level. This scenario places a premium on state-level leadership exemplified in Oklahoma, Virginia, and Florida, where state legislators continue to pursue funding increases.

Despite efforts to improve funding levels and to increase the range of support services funded, money has been difficult to obtain. At present, graduate-level state funding is rarely automatically retainable or cumulative, despite the fact that these represent key features of financial assistance for sustaining students and increasing the numbers of students supported.

In conclusion, the efforts of the five states reported here to increase the production of black doctorate recipients have improved in a variety of respects since their inception. Nevertheless, the net result of their programs after a number of years of operation has to be judged minimal if strict criteria are applied: an increase in the number of black Ph.D.s produced or an increase in first-time black graduate enrollment. The total 1983–84 counts are lower than both the 1978–79 and the 1975–76 counts. Also from national data, a precipitous decline in black participation in graduate education has occurred since the latter half of the 1970s. Even in those instances where legal decisions have required improvements, the evidence indicates that successes have not been forthcoming.

REFERENCES

American Council on Education. *Minorities in Higher Education: Third Annual Status Report.* Washington, D.C.: ACE, 1984.

Astin, Alexander W. *Minorities in American Higher Education.* San Francisco: Jossey-Bass, 1982.

Blackwell, James E. *Access of Black Students to Graduate and Professional Schools.* Atlanta: Southern Education Foundation, 1975.

Blackwell, James E. *Mainstreaming Outsiders: The Production of Black Professionals.* New York: General Hall Publishing Co., 1981.

Brown, Frank, and Madelon D. Stent. *Minorities in U.S. Institutions of Higher Education.* New York: Praeger, 1977.

Haynes, L.L. *A Critical Examination of the Adams Case: A Source Book.* Washington, D.C.: Institute for Services to Education, 1978.

Institute for the Study of Educational Policy. *Equal Education Opportunity Scoreboard: The Status of Black Americans in Higher Education, 1970–79.* Washington, D.C.: Howard University Press, 1981.

Morris, Lorenzo. *Elusive Equality.* Washington, D.C.: Howard University Press, 1979.

National Center for Education Statistics (NCES). *Higher Education General Information Survey of Earned Degrees, 1975.* Washington, D.C.: U.S. Department of Health, Education and Welfare, 1976.

National Center for Education Statistics (NCES). *Higher Education General Information Survey of Earned Degrees, 1976.* Washington, D.C.: U.S. Department of Health, Education and Welfare, 1977.

National Center for Education Statistics (NCES). *Fall Enrollment in Colleges and Universities, 1976.* Washington, D.C.: U.S. Department of Health, Education and Welfare, 1977.

National Center for Education Statistics (NCES). *Fall Enrollment in Colleges and Universities, 1980.* Washington, D.C.: Department of Education, 1981.

Peterson, Marvin W., Robert T. Blackburn, Zelda F. Gamson, Carlos H. Arce, Roselle W. Davenport, and James R. Mingle. *Black Students on White Campuses: The Impacts of Increased Black Enrollments.* Ann Arbor: Institute for Social Research, University of Michigan, 1978.

Preer, Jean. *Lawyers Versus Educators.* Westport, CT: Greenwood Press, 1982.

Thomas, Gail E. (ed.). *Black Students in Higher Education.* Westport, CT: Greenwood Press, 1981.

Trent, William T. "Comparisons of Race and Gender Degree Attainment in 1975–76 and 1980–81: A Focus on Equity." Paper presented to the Annual Meeting of the Southern Sociological Society, April 1984.

3
Title VI Issues
as Viewed from a Chancellor's Office

BARBARA W. NEWELL
Harvard University

The thrust of the activity initiated by litigation in the states affected by
Title VI enforcement has focused on how to increase the presence of
blacks in the predominantly white institutions, and upon determining the
appropriate role for historically black institutions. Although I could go on
at much length in both of these areas, I am not sure that—beyond the
McKnight Foundation grants and the activities of the Institute of Education—the Florida experience contributes uniquely to the body of
knowledge on Title VI regulation. It is rather in a third area I will con-
centrate: those activities that can be described as falling within the efforts
of the states to "push for excellence."

If the basic concern of Title VI is to expand opportunities for black
citizens, then the recent actions of boards and legislators to improve
standards must be analyzed to evaluate the impact of these changes on the
opportunities of black students and faculty. I fear that without care, we
may through sophisticated measures resegregate the schools. With care
we can provide more truly equal education.

Let me start by putting into context the movement for improved
standards. The profile of American industry is changing. Knowledge is
the basic ingredient for the development of new industries, the strategic
advantage of existing industries, and the ability to find a job. Therefore,
the economic well-being of our country is dependent on the quality of its
educational system and the sophistication of its work force and research.
Citizens, legislators, and boards see the country having a stake in quality.
The rapid rise in recent years of the Japanese high-tech industries has
shaken our complacency and put the fear of the market behind the quality movement.

At the same time as quality has been underscored, we find a majority of our youth going on to some postsecondary education. This move

71

toward education should provide the labor force future industry needs, but it also means a marked increase in the dollars required for the support of education. Today education consumes the largest part of state budgets. America is, at this moment, going through a major tax revolt, both at the federal and the state level. All state expenditures are under close scrutiny. The education industry is labor-intensive, and it is not easy to decrease costs and increase productivity. Legislators are asking "Are we getting our money's worth for the dollars spent on education?"

This cry is not only the product of increased tax sensitivity, but also because the public has lost faith in educational standards. They see lawyers who cannot write, teachers who cannot compute.

One way to increase educational standards and increase the resources available per student is to reduce the number of students one tries to educate. The decade of the 1980s is an appropriate time for such a realignment because of the drop in the number of traditional-age high school graduates. The 1980s might be a period during which the universities could make up for the inroads of the inflation of the late 1970s and the lack of appropriations to correspond to the increased enrollments of the baby boom. For legislators to require an increase in standards and provide an increase in the resources per student presents a good public image. It shows public money producing the quality of education needed for the new knowledge-based industries and used to educate well those who can "take advantage" of an education.

Any academic will tell you that the easiest way to increase the "standards of output" of an educational institution is to improve the level of accomplishment of incoming students. As the director of Georgia prisons said when asked to raise the standards of his institution, what he really needed to raise standards was "a better grade of prisoners."

Much activity has been initiated to improve the performance of students entering universities. In Florida the move toward excellence has given us testing of levels of academic accomplishment at the third, fifth, eighth, and tenth grades, as well as a high school graduation exam. Standards must be met before moving to the next level, thus assuring that students have the academic base for the work that follows. Although we have increased the hurdles through primary and secondary school, we have yet to put in place an adequate measure of those who drop out of the system altogether. And we are just beginning to place an emphasis on the need for counseling and assistance to minimize the detrimental effect of tracking on opportunities for minority group members.

Obviously, the total number graduating from high school is basic to the pool available for university education. In the university arena there is an increase in awareness of this interdependence between the public schools and universities. Programs to ease the movement from high school into postsecondary education are being developed.

While standards of performance are raised at the precollegiate level, the move toward "excellence" has been applied to the university community in the form of increased attention to admissions standards. Politicians have been looking for a "clean" measure to divide students for acceptance or rejection. They want a standard that they can explain to their constituents, that looks scientific, and that hopefully will see that educational opportunity at the collegiate level goes "to the most worthy." The Scholastic Achievement Test (SAT) and ACT provide a tidy hurdle. Unfortunately, such test scores correlate primarily with family income and show little or no correlation with collegiate completion. Blacks fare poorly when this arbitrary measure is used.

As the push to use SAT as a breakpoint intensifies, a number of us concerned about the appropriateness of an SAT standard for all students, and particularly its impact on minority students, have been looking for alternative ways to establish higher admissions standards. The move to reestablish high school course requirements for collegiate admissions is such an alternative. The very process of establishing course requirements adds to the national discussion of what body of information an educated person should master. Course requirements make explicit the expectations universities have of high schools, and tend to raise levels of performance. In the long run the fact that all students enter college at a more common starting point should assist minority students to gain full access to college training.

Within college one of our greatest difficulties is the unevenness of student preparation. One student will have read *Hamlet*, while the next may not have heard of Shakespeare. Most of our white students have completed three years of high school mathematics, but many of the black students entering college have not had precollegiate math after eighth grade. This difference in preparation not only compounds the problem of teaching college courses, but also makes it more difficult for students to pass successfully a legislatively required collegiate math test at the end of their sophomore year in order to get an Associate of Arts degree or enter the junior year.

Florida moved to establish course requirements for university admissions in 1981, with full implementation of those requirements in 1987, after one full generation of high school students had been warned. We hoped to give ourselves time enough to establish the supports needed to see that the course requirements were not a barrier to college admissions.

In Florida, the biggest debate that occurred during the establishment of the 1987 course requirements was in the area of foreign languages. When the board of regents originally established standards in 1981, it was found that eight school districts in the state did not teach any foreign language and a number offered only one year of a foreign language. Additionally, foreign language teaching in our universities was in a shambles. We decided 1990 would be a reasonable date to implement a foreign language requirement. The state legislature, in 1983, chose to include university admissions standards as a part of legislation and added two years of a foreign language as a part of the 1987 admissions requirements.

The establishment of collegiate entrance requirements places even greater emphasis on the need to examine high school counseling. We are establishing programs to try to meet counseling needs. It would appear we are gradually making progress. In 1983 and 1985 we surveyed the change in courses taken by graduating high school seniors. The results show a marked enhancement of the high school programs of college-bound students, with a decided dampening of differences between racial groups. Foreign language training is still the area of greatest disparity between blacks and others. The foreign language component of the admissions requirements was extended to 1989 by the legislature, but the Board of Regents began enforcing the new requirement for admission in fall, 1987. They did so without the benefit of policy analysis predicting the impact of the new rule upon minority enrollment. After a series of meetings with admissions directors, the Regents gained confidence that the requirement would have no negative impact upon total or minority enrollment. Consistent with this view, reportedly the University of Florida and Florida State University have achieved expected freshman enrollments for fall, 1987, but no data are available describing the impact of the new requirement on minority enrollment.

This foreign language problem raises the question of how long it will be politically viable to handle admissions concerns by exception. One ranking academic officer in Tennessee stated that the legislature has consistently made exceptions for blacks in a whole array of fields from standards to financial aid, and he sees much of the motivation of this policy as a way of building a structure that will fall of its own weight in the near future and thereby resegregate education.

Over time, similarity of courses should even test scores. The movement of black test scores in recent years in Florida supports this hypothesis. Between the 1982–83 and 1983–84 school years, the number of black Florida public-school seniors taking the SAT increased 3% while the number of white students taking the test increased 0.2%. The mean SAT composite score for black students increased 12 points, to 710, in a year's time, while the mean composite score for white students increased 2 points, to 922.

Though the courses offered for admissions officially are similar, we face the problem of whether they truly do provide an adequate base for collegiate work. The need for people within a given discipline to review course content is apparent in all disciplines, but is perhaps best illustrated by the field of chemistry. At the collegiate level every five years about one full year of course content is added to the information to be mastered by a chemistry major. With this kind of galloping expansion of expectation of the college students, one can imagine the increasing gap between high school experience and the expectations of the college faculty. Teachers, discipline by discipline, are coming together to see where the problems are and what the expectations are. The challenge is to integrate academically all education.

Along with increased admissions standards has come a move to place all remedial work in the community colleges, thus producing a truly two-tiered educational system. Questions about the ease of movement between universities and community colleges and the problems of stigma for students in the community college track have not been examined fully, and could also bring their toll on the minority presence in the university community in postsecondary education.

As mentioned before, the strong two-tiered system has caused Florida to create an examination of minimum competencies in the fields of communications and computation required for acceptance at the junior level in a state university or to receive an Associate of Arts diploma. Miami-Dade Community College proposed using a weighted combination of grade point averages and test scores for determining graduation. But as planned, the graduation tests are not rigorous; requirements for passing them are scheduled to rise over a short time period. Since the present plan clearly will have a negative impact upon blacks, the schedule for increasing the test requirements may be extended.

Along with standards of performance at the end of the sophomore year, careful records are being kept within the university system of retention by race and estimates of performance at the time of university graduation. The retention rate for blacks has improved markedly and is now slightly higher than that for whites, although attrition of all students is discouragingly low. In some professions such as teaching, an exam has been initiated for certification. In other fields, long-standing examinations for entrance to a profession, like the bar exam and the graduate record exam, are monitored closely for the first time. All of these standards and exams are a part of the same move to improve the quality of performance of the educational system. A student's prior educational opportunity continues to influence the results.

Although we as a state have looked at issues of quality, we have looked at issues of access only in terms of the expansion and placement of postsecondary institutions around the state. The general social, economic, and political implication for all citizens of limiting access to state-sponsored education through raised standards has seldom entered the debate.

Particularly troublesome for blacks is the fact that there has been little discussion of financial aid or tuition policy as it relates to minority students. In Florida, per capita income for blacks is about half that for whites. Nationally, nearly half of college-bound blacks come from families with annual incomes below $12,000 (*USA Today*, April 19, 1985, p. 1). "The number of minority students getting financial aid to attend public colleges dropped 12.4 percent between the 1981–82 and 1983–84 academic year" (*New York Times*, July 3, 1985, p. 14). Additionally, the federal policy of increasing loans works hardship on low-income and first-generation students. Job opportunities, particularly for black teenagers, have been dropping. Cost is the greatest barrier to entry. In Florida the issue of financial aid has been so far off the agenda that we do not even have an approximation of unmet student need. We have just gotten the university records in a position to know how we handle financial aid and what the total aid dollars are.

Although many examples are drawn from Florida, the quality movement is nationwide. If financial aid remains inadequate and stiffer admissions policies and performance standards are put into effect without care and adequate support, the negative impact on minority enrollment will overshadow any positive results from Title VI litigation.

4

Adams Litigation: One State's Unique Response for the Enhancement of Its Historically Black University

RAYMOND M. BURSE
Kentucky State University

Governor John Y. Brown, Jr. and the Commonwealth of Kentucky were delivered a Martin Luther King, Jr. birthday present on January 15, 1981. Kentucky's Governor received from the US Department of Education's Office for Civil Rights (OCR) a letter stating that the commonwealth had failed to eliminate the vestiges of its former *de jure* racially dual system of public higher education. The letter came as a result of a 1979 review of Kentucky public higher education under the authority of Title VI of the Civil Rights Act of 1964. OCR mailed letters of finding to the commonwealth and nine other states as required by the First Federal District Court in *Adams v. Richardson* (356 F. Supp. 92 [D.C.C. 1973]).

The Office for Civil Rights cited the commonwealth for failure to enhance its only traditionally black public institution, Kentucky State University; to desegregate the student body at all public higher education institutions; and to desegregate the faculty and staff at all public institutions of higher learning. Governor Brown delegated to the Kentucky Council on Higher Education the responsibilities, duties, and obligations for developing the commonwealth's response to the letter of January 15, 1981.

The Council on Higher Education, in its initial response to OCR, argued that Kentucky should not have received such a letter and cited several reasons why not. Regardless, Kentucky officials agreed to develop a plan addressing the deficiencies cited by OCR in accordance with federal guidelines developed to assist states, insisting at the same time that the commonwealth held no official responsibility to abide by them.

Reaching agreement between the Kentucky Council and the public institutions aimed at correcting two deficiencies—desegregating student enrollment, and faculty and staff—was easy compared to reaching consensus on the third—what to do about Kentucky State University. Many individuals felt that if Kentucky State had not existed, no letter of deficiency would have been sent. In similar situations the easy answer has been to blame the victim and then to propose his or her elimination. Many thought that eliminating KSU would quickly bring to a conclusion Kentucky's involvement with OCR. Thus what began as a relatively routine response by commonwealth officials became a year-long agony for Kentucky State University. What developed in Kentucky was an odyssey: a series of events that brought about a unique response regarding the enhancement of the commonwealth's traditionally black institution.

Many policy-makers and educators wanted KSU closed as a way of addressing the OCR problem, but others suggested downgrading KSU to a community college. Still others—largely black educators with past or current affiliations with KSU—wanted the institution upgraded and given a competitive place after decades of neglect in Kentucky public higher education. Finding a solution that was reasonable yet politically feasible was not an easy task.

One of Kentucky's first official acts in response to the desegregation problem was to ask OCR for an advisory opinion regarding a merger between the University of Louisville and Kentucky State University, a solution that would effectively abolish Kentucky State University as a viable institution. The Office for Civil Rights quickly ducked the issue of what to do about KSU, advising the Kentucky Council on Higher Education that it was not in the habit of providing advisory reports; but if the institution submitted a statewide desegregation plan, taking into account all aspects of the OCR's findings, a response would be forthcoming. Needless to say, the council's request generated a great deal of turmoil and served to heighten the emotions of many concerned groups and individuals, particularly those favoring enhancement of KSU.

Regardless of OCR's response, or perhaps because of it, merger of Kentucky State remained a policy for consideration during the process of developing a statewide desegregation plan. And many other proposals, good and bad, surfaced during the course of the year 1981, including the approach followed in most Title VI states in determining the future role of traditionally black institutions. A typical approach in other circumstances has been to add new high-demand instructional programs that are nonduplicative of others within the state. Such programs are believed to serve as a mechanism for the enhancement of the historically black institution that hopefully will lead to the enrollment of white students.

Examples of this strategy include transferring a doctoral program to

South Carolina State from the University of South Carolina, placement of degree programs in architecture and pharmacy at Florida A&M, and the placement of new doctoral programs at Grambling State University and Southern University in Louisiana. Results of such undertakings have been mixed. The placement of high-demand instructional programs at black campuses may constitute the best way to bring about both desegregation and enhancement, but in doing so very little attention typically has been placed upon more fundamental changes within institutions—changes that foster permanent improvement, growth, and self-perpetuation.

THE PROPOSALS

Applying standards of improvement, growth, and self-perpetuation, a determination of what to do with, to, or for Kentucky State was the toughest part of developing Kentucky's desegregation plan. The plan that emerged contained six proposals for the enhancement of Kentucky State. Each proposal is briefly summarized below.

Kentucky State University Proposal

Developed by top administrators at KSU, this proposal addressed what it considered to be the necessary elements for strengthening and continually renewing its existing undergraduate curriculum. The three elements were improvement of the university's human, physical, and fiscal resources. The university's academic enhancement would be directed at five specific academic areas plus the necessary research and academic support. The targeted broad academic areas were public affairs, business, applied mathematics, and education. The research programs would occur in a newly established Public Service Institute and a Center for the Study of Afro-American Life in Kentucky. Academic support would consist of faculty development and a comprehensive student development services program. The goal of this proposal was movement toward the university's rightful place as a full member of the higher education system of the Commonwealth of Kentucky.

Within the public affairs area the university wanted to strengthen its existing program, adding instruction in paralegal and international studies. In business, the university would develop an M.B.A. degree program, create an institute for small business administration, obtain American Assembly accreditation, create a word-processing center, and establish new programs in hotel and restaurant management, insurance, and real estate. In applied sciences and technology, the university would add five new programs in information science at the master's level; and aviation, power and transportation, graphic arts, and communication at the baccalaureate level. In the natural sciences and mathematics, the university's existing biology, chemistry, mathematics, and physics programs would be strengthened, while associated environmental studies programs were developed. In education, the university would add an atypically structured master's level program to certify K–12 teachers. The cost of these new instructional programs was estimated to be approximately $2 million excluding the cost for additional physical facilities.

William McCann Proposal

The Chairman of the Kentucky Council on Higher Education, William McCann, developed this proposal. It called for the continuation of Kentucky State University as a freestanding institution, but its mission would encompass the following characteristics:

1. KSU would serve as a public service institution.
2. KSU would expand its community college program in Franklin and surrounding counties.
3. In conjunction with other public institutions, KSU would host a graduate center that recognized and capitalized upon the needs of state government and the surrounding area.
4. The residential nature of KSU would be deemphasized.
5. A leadership and management system at KSU would have to display the ability and desire to implement the university's new image.
6. The implementation of the revised university mission would be accompanied by the critical evaluation and elimination of existing programs not compatible with the revised mission.
7. Extremely close ties to and strong support by state te agencies of the re the revised mission would be a necessity.
8. The land-grant status would be altered to support the revised KSU mission, or eliminated.
9. The proposal would support diversity in the Kentucky system of public higher education by assigning to KSU a mission that placed first priority on public service. This designation would be unique in the commonwealth.

Morton Holbrook Proposal

This proposal, developed by Morton Holbrook, a member of the Council, recommended merging Kentucky State University, the University of Louisville, and Jefferson Community College to form an urban, truly multicultural center for educational excellence. The KSU land grant function would be merged with the University of Kentucky's land grant function. The KSU campus in Frankfort would be made available to state government for other educational needs.

Raymond Burse Proposal

This writer developed his proposal while serving as a council member prior to being appointed president of KSU. It would continue Kentucky State University as a freestanding institution within the state system, but the undergraduate curriculum would be reviewed and courses that could not be justified on the basis of cost, demand, and necessity of a comprehensive program would be eliminated.

The University would be expected to give top priority to strengthening the undergraduate curriculum also by providing new instructional programs. New undergraduate programs designed to meet the expanding needs of state government—in particular state government's economic and international development goals—would be given priority for placement at KSU over a five-year period. The KSU mission statement would be revised to include the following:

1. Public affairs would remain a part of the mission.
2. KSU would be designated as a small institution within the Kentucky system.
3. KSU would be a selective admissions institution.
4. KSU would have a quality-limited comprehensive educational program.
5. KSU would maintain its land-grant status.

Kentucky State University Board of Regents Proposal

This proposal would continue KSU as a freestanding institution, eliminate weak programs, and strengthen the remaining ones. It also called for the addition of a few new instructional programs. There would be established on the campus a New College division, as an experimental program for nontraditional students. New programs were proposed in five broad categories: public affairs, business, applied technology, natural sciences, and education. The programs would offer associate, baccalaureate, and master's degrees. The proposal would include the Center for the Study of Afro-American Life in Kentucky. This plan was estimated to cost approximately $11.5 million over five years.

Robert Bell Proposal

Developed by Robert Bell, a council member, this proposal would maintain a public higher education presence in Frankfort but redirect the thrust of KSU's educational mission. Kentucky State University, as it existed, would be phased out. The four principal elements of the proposal were to phase out Kentucky State effectively at the end of the 1982–83 school year; create a capital community college as a part of the University of Kentucky Community College System for the 1983–84 school year; create an institute of government, effective July 1, 1983; and reallocate the financial resources expended at Kentucky State to programs designed to advance black student opportunities and black faculty and staff careers in state-supported institutions.

THE RESPONSE

During the period from April to November, 1981, a special committee of the Kentucky Council on Higher Education, charged with the development of a final and official Kentucky desegregation plan, studied and met often to come to grips with the six proposals. The political climate in which planning and decision-making occurred placed Kentucky State University in a very precarious position. Daily, the news media discussed the future of the university, and naturally many students and their parents questioned whether KSU would still be around at the end of the week. Many felt that one way to resolve the issue of whether the institution should be continued was to measure its value. Moreover, taking initiative to improve the institution demonstrated its worthiness to survive. Such concerns led to a critical review and evaluation of the entire institution from top to bottom.

Under any circumstances an institution placed under a microscope will reveal deficiencies—even the wealthiest, best-known, and most highly praised as well-managed, financially stable, and qualitatively sound. Not unexpectedly, then, during the period of developing the plan the University Board of Regents discovered deficiencies in the KSU community and subsequently voted to undertake an evaluation of the president's leadership.

A critical point in Kentucky State University's development occurred on November 11, 1981, when the council's Desegregation Implementation Plan Committee voted three to two to accept the Bell proposal. This decision involved converting Kentucky State University into a community college and creating on the university's campus an institute of governmental service similar to the one at the University of North Carolina at Chapel Hill. By adopting this plan as the one to be recommended to the full council, the Implementation Plan Committee of course rejected all the others.

Responding to the action by the committee, a small ad hoc group of Kentucky higher education policy officials submitted a second report offering a plan that consolidated all proposals advocating KSU's continuance as a freestanding, four-year institution. The consolidated proposal included the following prescriptions:

1. KSU's mission would be refined to establish the fact that KSU would serve the needs of state and local government and emphasize providing liberal arts, natural sciences, and occupational curricula for students in the surrounding areas.
2. A complete evaluation of existing academic programs would be completed, emphasizing improvement in current and anticipated academic program needs.
3. A corresponding evaluation anticipating subsequent reductions in faculty and staff should parallel the academic program review.
4. The master's program in public affairs would receive emphasis and become strengthened, and an interinstitutional graduate center would be established at Kentucky State.

Two dissenting members of the committee—a KSU regent and the council chairman—with assistance from the council staff, developed the consolidated proposal. It was submitted in the manner of providing the council with a well-developed alternative to the Bell proposal.

THE DECISION

December 3, 1981, is a day that will long be noted in the annals of the history of Kentucky State University and Kentucky public higher education. At a meeting on this date the full Council had to make a decision about the future of Kentucky State University. The December meeting marked a historic step in Kentucky public higher education in that the council, its progressive members having had their arms twisted politically and their opinions placed before the entire citizenry via the news media, decided to take unique action with regard to Kentucky State University. Rather than adding new high-demand, nonduplicative instructional programs, and simply infusing millions of dollars into physical plant improvements, the council chose to give to Kentucky State University a substantive new mission. KSU would become the Commonwealth's small public liberal studies institution. In other words, the council adopted with only minor modifications the consolidated plan. The decision reached by the council led to the following new KSU mission:

1. Kentucky State University shall serve as a residential institution with a range of traditional collegiate programs appropriate to its role as *the unique, small, liberal studies institution with the lowest student–faculty ratio in the state system* (emphasis added). The University shall focus on the needs of its student body, which includes but is not limited to full-time and part-time residential students, commuting students from its primary service area, and state governmental employees; and on the expanding instruction, applied research and service needs of state government. Associate and baccalaureate degree programs should be oriented toward liberal studies, selected career opportunities related to state governmental services and related human and public services.

2. At the master's-degree level, the University should emphasize public administration curricula to meet the needs of state government. These programs should be carefully articulated, with related doctoral programs offered by the doctoral-granting institutions in the system. Other graduate offerings should be provided through a multi-institutional graduate education center administered by Kentucky State University.

3. Kentucky State University, as one of the two land-grant institutions in the system, should carry out its responsibilities under federal law and participate fully in appropriate US Department of Agriculture programs, placing emphasis on activities that are in accord with the mission of the institutions.

4. Kentucky State University should strive to become a major repository for the collection of books, records, and artifacts relative to its history in educating black citizens of the Commonwealth and should make such materials available for casual and scholarly study.

From KSU's point of view and perhaps that of the council, the consolidated plan represented a unique and bold step. It gave Kentucky State a new lease on life, changing the basic fabric and consensus upon which the institution had been built. But the drama accompanying this decision notwithstanding, what the council did on that day was not inconsistent with earlier decision-making. In 1977 the council, on behalf of the commonwealth, had begun to develop a coherent *system* of public higher education. In contrast to the continuation of undisciplined growth and the decline of a disparate set of public institutions, a new approach emerged, in principle involving the establishment of a public system wherein several different kinds and types of institutions are supported in keeping with the needs of Kentucky citizens. Within such a system large and medium-sized institutions as well as small colleges are needed. Such a mix enables students to study in various academic and professional curricula in a variety of institutional environments. Kentucky State University became the new system's small liberal arts institution with the lowest student–faculty ratio in the commonwealth and an emphasis upon government affairs.

The decision-making environment out of which KSU's new identity emerged within the council at the start of the December 3rd meeting was evenly divided over the course of action to take. Out of 138 members of the Kentucky General Assembly (state legislature), 103 had earlier signed a petition to keep KSU open. Notably, the general assembly would have to ratify any decision reached by the council. Also the black community of the state had rallied to support "their" institution. But at the same time clear consensus existed that if KSU remained free-standing, strong action toward change was needed. With the diverse plans submitted and great variety of advice offered about the problem, the council needed a solution that would keep KSU a free-standing four-year institution, enhance its attractiveness to whites, radically change KSU's direction toward making it different from the other state institutions, and preserve the council's status on issues of higher education policy-making in state government. Agreement to accept the consolidated proposal seemed the best decision.

THE RESULT

The new mission for KSU that emerged from the December 3rd meeting not only resolved the short-term threat to merge or close down the institution, it also seemed to put KSU on a firm foundation for the future. In the public sector in Kentucky no true liberal arts institutions existed. All such institutions were located in the independent sector, following the pattern of most states. Attempts at inaugurating liberal studies curricula seem to have been tried at several other campuses around the country with limited success. But more closely viewed, prior attempts involved introducing liberal studies as a separate curriculum, not on an institution-wide basis. Most efforts failed in part due to competition with existing instructional programs that already included some liberal studies requirements. The lack of strong support, stemming in part from the interdisciplinary and therefore diffuse feature of many such programs, and also from the absence of a cadre of faculty believers, led to problems with faculty approvals over curricula, tenure decision-making, and other governance processes. The fate of liberal studies programs interjected into traditional academic settings particularly at large institutions is well known among educators. Not surprisingly, Robert Hutchins' idea of liberal education thrives today at only a handful of private institutions.

The KSU approach is different. It involves changing the entire institution to make it compatible with liberal studies goals, not simply adding a new instructional program. In changing the entire institution, KSU's experience is unique and potentially more successful than other more limited efforts at building a true liberal studies environment.

But describing a new mission on paper is easy compared to implementing it. The 1981 KSU catalog asserts that the university is "to achieve [its] aims by offering a curriculum in a regular four-year liberal arts program." To give meaning to its revised mission in 1983, members of the KSU community looked critically at the university's academic offerings toward the goal of developing a curriculum centered upon the humanities, and natural and social sciences. The key elements of the new curriculum program are:

1. A new liberal studies approach unique to Kentucky public higher education.
2. Establishment of the Whitney M. Young, Jr. College of Leadership Studies.
3. Establishment of a unique cooperative program with each of the state-supported professional schools for Kentucky State University students interested in entering medical, dental, or law school.
4. Achievement of the lowest student–faculty ratio among the commonwealth's public universities, thereby ensuring the enhancement of the quality of teaching and the capacity for individualized instruction.
5. Review of all existing academic programs and offerings to eliminate those unnecessary to the university's new mission and to add those supportive of it.

To carry forward this academic program, the president appointed a planning coordinator and a committee to study the core curriculum of the university. The Core Curriculum Committee spent the summer of 1981 in Colorado, in a workshop sponsored by the Lilly Foundation, reviewing in detail the composition of core liberal studies programs of several institutions. But in addition to the curriculum revision, by July, 1982 more than 53 other changes at the university were promised in the commonwealth's desegregation plan. These included an evaluation of the faculty and staff, a revised financial planning system, an assessment of physical facilities, a survey of state government employees' higher education needs, inauguration of student and faculty exchange programs with other public institutions in Kentucky, a revision of KSU's graduate program in public affairs and administration, and budget revision reallocating funds to areas of the university identified for expansion.

Leaders and members of the Kentucky State University community took seriously their mission of becoming the commonwealth's only four-year liberal studies college. A detailed critical review of instructional programs resulted in the voluntary suspension of 12 of them in early 1982. Since then four additional programs have been suspended. All of these suspended programs may be renewed by the university at a later date if appropriate, since rules of the commonwealth permit such actions at any time. The university continues today to review its programs, seeking to consolidate and improve all of the ones it chooses to keep.

The Curriculum Review Committee completed its review of the university's curriculum and proposed its principal liberal studies requirements in early 1983, one year ahead of schedule. The new liberal studies curriculum now includes typical offerings in communications, art, music, rhetoric and reasoning, the natural and physical sciences, foreign and computer languages, and the social and behavioral sciences. Unique in the new curriculum is a required, four-course, integrative studies sequence. This sequence of courses seeks to integrate broad subject matter areas including science, literature, and art into a cohesive whole, expanding the student's breadth of knowledge and his or her ability to analyze and synthesize information. The new curriculum is designed to result in graduates who not only know subject matter, but also know how to reason, to write well, to make decisions, and to question others' conclusions with discipline and sensitivity.

This new liberal studies curriculum constitutes the foundation for the kind of institution Kentucky State is to become. To help faculty members prepare to teach courses falling within the new curriculum, KSU has provided release time to at least five faculty members each term. The faculty on leave from teaching assignments prepare course materials and present them to a wider group of faculty members. The university has also sponsored a summer institute in which more than 20 faculty participated toward this same goal.

In addition to the new liberal studies requirements for all students, KSU started the Whitney M. Young, Jr. College of Leadership Studies. The college provides an alternative mechanism for implementing the university's new liberal studies mission by attracting outstanding students desiring to study in a unique learning environment. The Whitney Young College, based upon the "Great Books" approach of St. John's College in

Annapolis, requires students to assume a great deal of responsibility for planning and undertaking their own courses of study. They are enrolled in small classes that require a great deal of writing and result in considerable individual attention from faculty. Whitney Young College provides a new programmatic thrust at KSU, unduplicated within the Commonwealth of Kentucky. It epitomizes what a small liberal studies university can become, and it attract students from a wide variety of geographical areas and social backgrounds.

Whitney Young College not only improves the overall academic preparation of KSU students, it comes at a time when the university implemented a new selective as opposed to open admissions policy. The university's admission policy utilizes American College Testing Program (ACT) scores, high school grade point averages (G.P.A.s), and class rankings as criteria for granting qualified or unqualified admission. The policy went into effect in Fall, 1984, and the ACT score and G.P.A. requirements will continue to rise over the next three years. The new policy also involves identifying high-ability but underprepared students and providing them with remedial or developmental studies courses.

Seeking to provide more opportunities for its students, KSU developed agreements with other public institutions in the commonwealth to provide postbaccalaureate professional school admissions for KSU graduates. Today three percent of the entering classes in the commonwealth's medical, law, and dental schools are KSU graduates who are also Kentucky residents. Agreements resulting in this policy provide an added advantage to KSU alumni, who are "guaranteed" admission to a professional school if their undergraduate records are suitable.

Under provisions of the desegregation plan, KSU also established an interinstitutional graduate center at the campus through which three other state universities offer graduate courses and new degree programs. An interesting feature of the interinstitutional graduate center has been the agreement under which several participating universities provide teacher education courses, allowing students to earn a degree at any of the participating institutions regardless of which courses they enroll in at the center. In addition, the graduate center, through individual universities, offers degree programs ranging from social work and criminal justice to business administration and computer science. One outgrowth is that KSU will soon offer a master's degree in public affairs program at the graduate center at Northern Kentucky University.

The desegregation plan has not only brought new programs, it also has enhanced existing ones by strengthening course requirements, bolstering faculty qualifications, reordering course sequences, expanding student advising services, providing new classroom equipment, increasing library resources, and adding instructional laboratories and other support services.

To enhance programs without also providing opportunities for faculty to be retrained or renewed would have constituted poor implementation. KSU made available to all faculty members opportunities to return to graduate school to complete terminal degrees, renew old skills, and learn new ones suitable for use in some area of KSU's revised curriculum. In three years KSU has provided leaves to 20 faculty, three of whom completed their doctorates.

One important aspect of KSU's enhancement program involves streamlining and strengthening the university's financial operations. This change has also been undertaken successfully. In 1982, the second year KSU used a "big eight" accounting firm to conduct an audit of its financial procedures, the university received a "qualified opinion." In 1983 the same accounting firm gave an "unqualified opinion" on KSU's financial operations. The improvement occurred because members of the university community have been as serious about the quality of management of the institution as they have been about the quality of academic offerings and student support services.

Even more unusual amidst KSU's rebirth is the fact that changes from 1982 to 1984 came without any increase in state funding. To build its 1983–84 operating budget, meet all desegregation plan requirements, and fund the outlined enhancements, 41 administrative positions at the university were eliminated, providing, with other savings, almost $1 million that was reallocated to academic programs. KSU is not only operating in a manner that results in unqualified financial audits, it is also run efficiently. Attempts to enhance black colleges and universities in accordance with federal requirements for desegregation may not have always produced similar results. But doing so is clearly possible.

The programmatic enhancements of Kentucky State would not be complete without some physical facilities enhancement. Over a period of less than three years, the institution has spent approximately $12 million on renovation and maintenance of its campus facilities, including construction of a new cafeteria, complete renovation of two dormitories, installation of new roofs on approximately 90 percent of the university's buildings, repainting all campus buildings (in some instances for the first time in 20 years), and many other improvements. The university is presently spending approximately $12 million for additional renovations on campus. These physical enhancements coupled with academic changes place Kentucky State University in a unique role.

To borrow from Robert Frost's words, the Commonwealth of Kentucky:

> [S]hall be telling this with a sigh
> Somewhere ages and ages hence:
> Two roads diverged in a wood, . . .
> [And KSU] took the one less traveled by,
> And that has made all the difference.

5
Desegregation of Higher Education:
A Private/Public Cooperative Alternative

ISRAEL TRIBBLE, JR.
McKnight Programs in Higher Education,
Tampa, Florida

The intent of this chapter is to provide an anecdotal view and analysis of activities involved with desegregation in higher education. It is meant to be thought-provoking, not comprehensive, with respect to this issue. The chapter focuses specifically on state plans and their lack of success, but it also describes an alternate desegregation model established in Florida and explores the model's potential for achieving some of the stated as well as implied goals of desegregation policy in higher education.

For the past 11 years, I have been directly and indirectly involved with policy matters regarding desegregation of higher education. Over this period of time I have had a chance to look at this issue from several different and distinct vantage points, enabling me to provide a meaningful professional perspective. My experience suggests generalizations about some of the implementation problems and issues involved in desegregating higher education systems as well as insight about goals and objectives of state plans.

HISTORICAL BACKGROUND

The federal agency responsible for developing criteria and approving desegregation plans is the Department of Education (ED); in earlier years it was the Department of Health, Education and Welfare (DHEW). The agency received its direction from the US District Court for the District of Columbia in *Adams v. Richardson* (1973). The court's order required DHEW to enforce Title VI of the Civil Rights Act of 1964, particularly but not exclusively within the public higher education community.

Once the district court issued its order, DHEW held responsibility for developing guidelines that were to be used in implementing desegregation within higher education. *De jure* segregation was clearly manifested in the mere existence of a dual system of higher education, certain institutions having been established for the purpose of educating blacks and others for educating whites. Even though it was clear that the states no longer prevented black students from attending the schools established originally for whites, the institutions in question—in the opinion of the court—still enrolled in 1970 almost 100 percent of the group that they were originally founded to educate. Continuance of this kind of a dual system violates Title VI of the 1964 Civil Rights Law.

Notably, the federal district court directed DHEW to take a statewide approach to the problem of desegregation in higher education, despite the fact that a serious lack of viable statewide coordination existed where all issues of higher education policy were concerned. The premise that DHEW used to carry out the court's mandate was essentially that statewide planning is consistent with sound educational policy. If a statewide system of higher education was to be changed, then a mechanism was needed that would allow the proper planning and administration of that system, so that certain kinds of results could be uniformly obtained and later measured.

Since 1970 the process of desegregating higher education can best be characterized as a series of pulls and tugs, with political sand being thrown into the gears by successive leaders of the executive branch of federal government. The bottom line is that states managing to get approval for their desegregation plans in some form or another have five years within which to reach their goals. When OCR assessed progress at the end of successive five-year periods between 1973 and 1983, it found predictably poor results. No state has managed to achieve even a major portion of the goals included in its desegregation plan and, if anything, many have shown negative results. At this point, one would be hard pressed to substantiate region-wide achievement of even a single state's success at higher education desegregation.

Understanding why this is the case involves identifying and understanding the roles and constraints upon individual players in the implementation process. The most important are:

The NAACP Legal Defense Fund (LDF)
The Office for Civil Rights (OCR)
The First Federal District Court
Public higher education systems
Individual colleges and universities
State legislatures
Black and white students

A cursory look at this playbill leads to the observation that most actors in the desegregation drama arrived on the stage with varying view-
points and experiential backgrounds. Lack of background with the
problem accounts for mistakes that were made. For example, the NAACP
LDF brought suit to force DHEW to order desegregation, but in doing
so regrettably failed to see a fundamental contradiction of their legal approach. It is at best problematic to desegregate predominately white institutions while simultaneously enhancing traditionally black colleges and
universities in the same system. An unfortunate outcome of attempting
both goals is that predominately white institutions have successfully enrolled larger percentages of better-prepared black students within the
states involved in Title VI, at the same time reducing and changing the
student pool available for traditionally black colleges and universities.

Like LDF, OCR also had to be considered a rookie in 1969 when it
came to higher education. OCR staff had had little or no experience with
implementing public policy in higher education, having concentrated all
their efforts prior to 1969 on elementary and secondary education. Many
of the young lawyers on the OCR legal staff, trying to set forth arguments favoring elimination of the vestiges of dual higher education systems, were not knowledgeable about the intricate policies and practices
of public college and university systems. Even though all LDF and OCR
staff were from higher education, not many were of it!

When the federal court is considered, Judge Henry Pratt seemed to
understand clearly the dilemma that his decision would present. He recognized that there was no experiential foundation upon which to base the
actions of the federal government, and that there was little to be gained
from the experience of desegregating public primary and secondary school
systems. On the other hand, the state legislatures involved in desegregation were not surprisingly less supportive and knowledgeable about successful methods. Arguably, legislators have tended to be self-serving and
to hold basic beliefs and opinions fostered through years of segregated
education. The response received from elected law-making bodies regarding desegregation and statewide plans was rather predictable. Legislatures have done little that adversely affects their "alma maters" or the
broader status quo within higher education.

In hindsight it seems reasonable that those most knowledgeable about
the domain of higher education were representatives of the public higher
education systems themselves. Acknowledging this fact leads to the suggestion that many states have not very successfully accomplished desegregation goals probably because higher education officials know what is
possible, and allow state government and other officials to set forth plans
that do not have a high probability of success.

Perhaps the clearest example of this problem exists where enhancement of traditionally black institutions occurs. One of the insurmountable hurdles in desegregation planning is that of establishing the proper mission and scope of traditionally black colleges and universities. Most state policy-makers view traditionally black institutions as undergraduate, open admissions colleges with limited graduate offerings mostly at the master's level and in the field of professional education. The existence of or potential for offering doctoral-level programs goes largely undiscussed. If such improvements are considered, doctoral offerings in education are promoted initially, despite the fact that under Title VI allowing the mission of traditionally black institutions to remain unchanged is unconstitutional and clearly disparages the intent of the federal court.

In most state systems, the pecking order for colleges and universities is a very sensitive issue. Therefore any substantive change in mission for the traditionally black institution constitutes a challenge to many of the other institutions. To change a mission and thus require the assignment of new programs, or the transfer of programs from traditionally white institutions, is a prospect very carefully scrutinized by other colleges and universities.

Still, changing the racial identity of a higher education system is very hard to accomplish without a mission change. And in some cases where programs were reassigned to emphasize a mission change, the strategies backfired and enrollment decreased at the traditionally black institution. In Florida, for example, when programs were realigned at predominantly white Florida State University (FSU) and predominantly black Florida A&M University (FAMU), white students changed their majors and remained at FSU, while black students left FAMU and enrolled at FSU. Consequently, FSU experienced an enrollment gain.

Changing the mission of black colleges and universities can also involve the equally challenging notion of eliminating duplicate degree programs at black and white institutions in the same geographical area. The intent of the federal court was to use the elimination of program duplication as a tool for creating greater desegregation. Underlying the court's order is an understanding that few state systems in the 1980s hold sufficient resources to justify similar instructional programs at two institutions, one black and one white, in some instances located around the corner from one another. Such circumstances appear wasteful and therefore unacceptable to the public during periods of extreme sensitivity to tax increases.

The "Revised Criteria Specifying the Ingredients of Acceptable Plans to Desegregate State Systems of Public Higher Education," provided by OCR as a guide for states preparing plans, requires the state desegregation plan to indicate:

[S]pecific steps to eliminate educationally unnecessary program duplication among traditionally black and traditionally white institutions in the same service area. To this end, the plan shall identify existing degree programs, (other than core curricula) among institutions having identical or overlapping service areas and indicate specifically with respect to each area what steps the state will take to eliminate such program duplication. The elimination of such duplication shall be carried out consistent with the objectives of strengthening the traditionally black colleges. (*Federal Register*, 1978)

The guidance offered by the amended criteria is at best confusing. Among other factors, the history of public institutions in a given state suggests that making comparisons of apparently similar entities is very difficult if not impossible. In a sense comparing an instructional program at a traditionally black institution with that at a traditionally white institution in the same service area always amounts to comparing apples and oranges. Mission, scope, program breadth, and resource base differ greatly between the two institutions.

It is hard to judge the impact of past legal segregation upon the growth and development of traditionally black institutions. Difficult-to-measure historical elements, though not required by the desegregation guidelines, have to be considered (or should have been) in the process of drawing comparisons. Moreover, the academic program and faculty of an institution constitute its essence. Not unexpectedly, then, elimination of program duplication meets with stiff resistance wherever and whenever it is seriously attempted. Eliminating duplicative programs became such a difficult and controversial undertaking that during the Carter Administration Secretary Hufstedler declared this strategy unacceptable.

In the final analysis, improvement of campus physical facilities may be the area that has shown the most success in the desegregation process. Instructional program enhancement has occurred in just about every state; but unfortunately, adding new programs and bolstering old ones have been severely handicapped by the constraints of mission and scope. Few traditionally black institutions ventured forth in the direction of requesting substantially elaborate and complex new instructional programs. Those that did seem to have made greater strides than those that did not.

Students enrolled at a particular institution seem little affected except where improvements in facilities have occurred. This judgment is supported by the fact that traditionally black institutions and predominantly white ones remain wedded to the same student populations that they served prior to Title VI regulation. A few such institutions like Kentucky State may constitute an exception. KSU's new mission includes responsibility for serving employees of state government, an assignment that substantially increased its white enrollment. However, the new white students attend primarily in the evening, and the racial status quo prevails throughout the daytime program.

Similarly, gains in the employment of faculty and administrative staff have been modest at best. New employment "ghettos" have developed in the student affairs domain of college administration and in colleges of education at predominantly white institutions. Stronger gains have occurred in lower-level job categories at predominantly white institutions, but these changes are marginal when the total employment picture is taken into account.

In summary, the federal government has not been very effective in desegregating public higher education because it was ill-prepared for the task, lacked sufficient understanding of the problems encountered, and lacked sufficient clout for undertaking the job in the first place. National political trends over the past 10 years—particularly in the South—signal the resurfacing of traditional conservative policy-making. Southern conservatism has always been marked by antagonism toward strong centralized federal authority, a feature of today's politics that has been extended to include many other regions of the country. The OCR incursion represents another infringement as viewed by many southern citizens. Therefore, most states respond with minimum compliance, while some refuse to act at all.

THE McKNIGHT PROGRAMS IN FLORIDA

Yet despite the generally negative picture, some grounds for hope are discernible. As a result of approximately one year of meetings, discussions, and travel around Florida, Russell V. Ewald, Executive Vice President of the McKnight Foundation in Minneapolis, presented to the Florida Association of Colleges and Universities (FACU) a unique and historic proposal. At the September 30, 1983 annual FACU meeting he presented the outline of a grant award program for Florida to be administered by FACU. Speaking at the concluding session, Mr. Ewald explained that approximately $16 million would be committed to a "private/public partnership" designed to help educators in Florida address some of their major concerns related to higher education. The private funding of the program involved money awarded by the foundation, while the public aspect he proposed would consist of matching funds from the government of Florida. He challenged the state to match with one dollar every two dollars that the foundation agreed to put into a new higher education fund. He proposed in this way to fund perpetually at least two fellowship phases of his proposed grandiose project.

His speech constituted a truly historic occasion for Florida. To the best of anyone's knowledge, his proposed private/public effort had never been undertaken anywhere else in the nation. His proposal reflected the realization that black access to higher education, black faculty employment, and black faculty development were important enough issues to fund in perpetuity.

The participative process used by the foundation to arrive at its offer to fund programs for increased black participation in Florida's higher education system involved discussions with educators from both the private and public sectors, the governor and his staff, leaders of the legislature, the chancellor of the state university system and her staff, as well as officers and directors of FACU. Five community college presidents, the presidents of four private universities, and seven presidents of state universities were also interviewed. This kind of a process allowed for the expression of a broad range of concerns and for the emergence of a consensus. The consensus occurred around areas of greatest concern preventing Florida from continued movement toward an exemplary status in public higher education. The foundation adopted the approach of responding to the expressed needs of Florida educators and citizens as opposed to telling the state what it wanted to do.

In Mr. Ewald's address to FACU, he noted that three major needs stood out in his discussions as priority considerations:

> The lack of access to quality education for minorities, especially blacks, in the State of Florida; the inadequate representation of black Americans in postsecondary education degree programs that will provide them with skills necessary to succeed in a fast-changing employment market; the disproportionate number of black adults who are functionally illiterate. (Ewald, 1983)

He went on in his address to present a three-phase program summarized as follows:

1. The McKnight Black Doctoral Fellowship Program, designed to increase dramatically the numbers of qualified black faculty in the colleges and universities of Florida. This program would provide up to $1 million annually for a three-year period for 25 fellowships for black Floridians.

   The McKnight Junior Faculty Development Fellowship Program

would provide up to $300,000 per year for a three-year period for fellowships primarily for nontenured assistant professors, with priority given to black and female candidates. This program is designed to encourage excellence in both teaching and research. The fellowships would allow selected faculty to spend one academic year pursuing academic interests.

Up to five centers of excellence would also be funded for a maximum of $500,000 per year ($100,000 for each center) over a three-year period. Centers would formulate plans to expand the minority student applicant pools and subsequently improve race relations in Florida.

Up to $150,000 per year for a three-year period was to be provided to establish communication and cooperation between secondary and higher educational institutions in Florida. This fourth step would allow support of activities involving educators from secondary and postsecondary education in discussion of ways to meet the needs and aspirations of Florida high school and college students and the demands of the world of work.

2. A fifth area would involve creating an endowment designed to ensure at a minimum the life of two of the four programs described under phase one. By December 31, 1986, a challenge grant of $10,000,000 by the foundation would have to be met by a gift of $5,000,000 by the state if the endowment was to be completed.

3. The last proposal called for the establishment of a group based on what Ewald described as the "public/private partnership." Funding had not yet been designated and the broad purposes of the group established in this phase of the project would include viewing and evaluating existing programs, identifying educational needs, and initiating new programs to alleviate educational problems. Basic to this sixth proposal would be the identification of foundations and corporations willing to provide further financial support of higher education.

At the McKnight Programs there are currently 42 black doctoral fellows and 33 Junior Faculty Fellows. The five centers of excellence are funded, staffed, and operational. Four articulation and cooperation projects are funded and being implemented. The legislature in its 1984 session established the Florida Endowment Fund for Higher Education. In 1985 it appropriated $2.5 million and the same amount in 1986 for a total of $5 million. Consequently by July 1, 1987 the McKnight Programs became fully funded.

Collectively, the McKnight Programs address very critical equity issues: faculty hiring, faculty development leading to promotion and tenure, increasing the quality of preparation and the quantity of prepared students in the academic pipeline, and improved decision-making about equity problems through greater communication among all levels of education and with the employment community. Undergirding this entire effort is the concept of empowerment. The foundation has gone beyond simply making a generous grant for a period of time. Instead, it is making it possible for the state, on behalf of its black citizens in particular, to build a number of institutions that will hopefully become permanent.

The McKnight Programs have been well received at all levels of education as well as within numerous black and white communities. The broad-based support received is attributable to good timing and the commitment of private resources for support. At the moment, resistance from the growing legions of antigovernment activists has not materialized. Excellence is the theme that runs through the two fellowship programs. Self-help and community leadership on behalf of black youngsters is the foundation upon which the centers of excellence are established. The centers require a coming together of various elements of the black community to improve the educational attainment of its youth. They do not reject assistance from public schools, but their leadership recognizes that there are some values and expectations for black youth that must remain the responsibility of adults within black communities.

It has quickly become prestigious to hold a McKnight Doctoral or Junior Faculty Fellowship at a university or college in Florida. Hosting a center of excellence in a given community promises hope at a time when the future for black children seems rather hopeless. The prognosis looks good for accomplishing important goals that hold long-term benefits for the citizenry and the state.

REFERENCES

Adams v. Richardson 356 F. Supp. 92 [D.D.C. 1973]
Ewald, Russell V. Speech delivered at the Annual Meeting of Florida Association of Colleges and Universities, Sept. 30, 1983.
Federal Register, 1978 *43*(32), 6659.

PART II

Problems and Prospects

6
Initiation of Desegregation Litigation: A Majority or Minority Responsibility

CHARLES V. WILLIE
Harvard University

"Legal history does not tell the 'whole story' of slavery." So states A. Leon Higginbotham, Jr. (1973, p. 3). Neither does it tell the whole story of segregation and discrimination in higher education. "Though the . . . Thirteenth, Fourteenth, and Fifteenth Amendments significantly expanded the actual rights and options of blacks, . . . the legal process failed to effectuate the full potential of the rights intended . . . under the constitutional amendments" (Higginbotham, 1973, p. 1). According to Frederick Douglass, the early American legal process brought slavery to blacks and liberty to whites (Higginbotham, 1973, p. 3). In addition to knowledge of the law, one must examine the legal process and how the law is implemented to determine whether the outcome is likely to be liberating or enslaving.

Title VI of the 1964 Civil Rights Act demonstrates this point about the legal process and its significance. When the NAACP Legal Defense and Education Fund (LDF)* filed a class-action suit in 1970, charging that the federal government had failed to enforce Title VI by withholding federal funds from 10 state systems that were guilty of operating dual or segregated systems of higher education, the National Association for Equal Opportunity in Higher Education, a collectivity of public and private predominantly black colleges and universities, requested in a friend-of-the-court brief that the suit be dropped. Why would a black-controlled association oppose a lawsuit that is for the purpose of enforcing what has been called by Schlei and Grossman (1978, p. 209) "the most important civil rights legislation of this century"?

Assisting in this case with the LDF, which at that time was headed

---

*This is a separate organization from the National Association for the Advancement of Colored People (NAACP). LDF was started by the NAACP and then separated from it.

by Jack Greenberg, a white civil-rights lawyer, was another white liberal lawyer, Joseph L. Rauh Jr., of the Washington, D.C., law firm of Rauh, Silard, and Lichtman. Earlier, Rauh had lobbied for passage of the 1964 Civil Rights Act (Rosenbaum, 1985). Jack Greenberg, of course, was on the staff of the LDF when it was headed by Thurgood Marshall, "whose record of success as a civil-rights lawyer . . . turn[ed] him into a legend" (Kluger, 1976, p. 18). Marshall became a US Supreme Court Justice. Rauh, early in his career, was law clerk to Justice Benjamin N. Cardozo and to Justice Felix Frankfurter of the US Supreme Court (Rosenbaum, 1985). Clearly the legal leadership of plaintiffs in the case of *Adams v. Richardson* (1973) had expert and liberal credentials. Nevertheless, the National Association for Equal Opportunity in Higher Education filed a second *amicus curiae* brief in 1976 opposing the Legal Defense Fund's action on the basis that the remedy, in the opinion of the association, would require merger of traditionally black institutions of higher education into traditionally white institutions.

Mr. Adams of Mississippi, a black man and the father of six children, claimed that the rights of his offspring under Title VI were violated and that Secretary of Health, Education, and Welfare Eliot Richardson defaulted in execution of his responsibilities under the law (Dentler et al., 1983). The objective of Title VI is to ensure that federal departments and agencies do not provide financial assistance to grant recipients that engage in discrimination. It covers, for example, education grants, public housing grants, and funding for highways and mass transit. An administrative charge filed on behalf of a person alleging discrimination by a grant recipient will prompt a federal agency investigation. The federal agency, following the investigation, makes a finding that the grant recipient either is in compliance or is in noncompliance with Title VI. According to E. Richard Larson and Laughlin McDonald, many federal agencies have had a poor reputation for enforcing Title VI (1979).

The *Adams v. Richardson* case was filed to end the practice of making a finding of discrimination but not enforcing the law by granting relief to the plaintiff. Although the Department of Health, Education, and Welfare ruled in 1969 that 10 states operated a dual system of segregated institutions of higher education, it had not taken any action against the states that had submitted unacceptable higher education desegregation plans. The National Association for Equal Opportunity in Higher Education was against segregated education; but also it was against abolition of the black experience in higher education. The association assumed that acceptable plans would require the merger of black colleges into white colleges, and not the other way around. Sociologist C.U. Smith reports that "when the press reports on the feasibility and functioning of black and white institutions in the same city, the stories almost invariably state or imply a threat to the survival and development of the *black* school only" (Smith, 1978, p. 209). More forcefully, Benjamin Mays, a former black college president, argued that "if America allows black colleges to die, it will be the worst kind of discrimination and denigration known in history" (Mays, 1978, p. 27).

The issue of this analysis is not whether Jack Greenberg and Joseph Rauh were right or wrong in filing a class-action suit on behalf of their plaintiff and other minorities similarly situated. Also it is not known whether the National Association for Equal Opportunity in Higher Education was right or wrong in filing a friend-of-the-court brief against the suit and urging that it be dropped. A more fundamental issue of analysis is this: Who has the responsibility to initiate action for the liberation of a population—members affiliated with the oppressed class or members affiliated with the oppressor class? This question is raised often with reference to the law: Who has "standing"?—that is, the "right to bring a law suit because [one] is directly affected by the issues raised" (Fischer, Schimmel, & Kelly, 1981, p. 285). But it seldom is raised outside a court of law. The determination of who has a fundamental or compelling interest in developing the process of legal action or strategy for liberation is a social as well as a legal matter.

At issue is who stands to suffer if the wrong issue has been raised or if the right issue has been raised but the wrong remedy proposed. Because the *Adams v. Richardson* case was filed as a class action, the outcome would affect Mr. Adams and other blacks similarly situated. In a class-action suit, the help or harm of the principle established or the remedy implemented is generalized, not limited. Because several black educators suspected that the remedy of Mr. Adams' victory against segregation in higher education might result in the abolition of predominantly black public colleges and universities and a diminishing of the black experience in the public sector of higher education, they opposed litigation of the case. Mays said that the diminishing of the black experience in education "would be a damnable act" (1978, p. 27). Thus, blacks could win the class-action *Adams* case and nevertheless lose if the remedy abolished predominantly black colleges.

Two cases of 20th-century vintage demonstrate the validity of concern about who is responsible for initiating litigation for liberation. The *Brown v. Board of Education* (1954) decision established a legal principle that was the anticipated outcome of a deliberate legal strategy developed by Charles Houston and other black lawyers he had trained or with whom he was associated at Howard University and the NAACP. While the ultimate goal was to outlaw segregated public education, Houston and his black legal colleagues believed that "the Supreme Court was not ready in the 1930s to repudiate the doctrine of 'separate but equal'" proclaimed in the *Plessy v. Ferguson* (1896) decision. By developing a litigation process that yielded "immediate benefits" for blacks such as equalizing teacher salaries and elimination of other major disparities, the black lawyers of the NAACP hoped to demonstrate the financial harm of attempting to maintain racially separate schools not only for blacks but also for whites. The strategy was to hold off on pushing ultimately for the elimination of separate schools until sufficient victories had been won to equalize financial provisions for the segregated institutions so that whites could recognize that segregation was "financially intolerable" (Hastie, 1973, pp. 22–25); blacks meanwhile would experience some beneficial outcomes from the accumulative court cases that erased disparities between the races.

In this connection, the NAACP assured plaintiffs that it would represent them with counsel but would not initiate litigation in a state or other locality unless "individual black teachers, students, and parents . . . were willing to risk economic reprisal and even violence by bringing suit" (Hastie, 1973, p. 25). The final decision whether to litigate or not to litigate was left to the locals to make. Thus, each case from the 1930s through the early 1950s became, as it were, a building block that was sanctioned by the people who had decided to cease cooperating in their own oppression.

William Hastie reported that "lawyers committed to the overall campaign were carefully avoiding the presentation of this ultimate issue [of the separate but equal doctrine] to the Court" (1973, p. 28). During the argument of a case against racial segregation for interstate passengers on buses, a Supreme Court justice "invited counsel to argue the constitutionality of the separate but equal doctrine." But, according to the litigation plan, "the invitation was declined" (Hastie, 1973, p. 28). The black lawyers had determined that the 1896 "separate but equal" doctrine resulted largely because the issue had been carried to the Supreme Court prematurely, that sufficient evidence had not been placed on the record in lower courts showing the consequences of imposed racial segregation. Hence, the Supreme Court in *Plessy v. Ferguson* (1896) had no way of anticipating the effects of its ruling and remedy. The black lawyers believed it was a mistake to ask the Supreme Court to rule on a matter as important as segregation without an accumulation of evidence on the record of the effects of segregation. That *Plessy v. Ferguson* went before the Supreme Court prematurely was a litigation mistake, in the opinion of the black lawyers who planned the civil rights legal strategy. They had decided that this mistake would not be repeated. Thus they refrained from presenting the ultimate issue of segregation (even though a white Supreme Court Justice invited them to do so) until in their judgment the time was ripe (Hastie, 1973, p. 28).

After the *Sweatt v. Painter* (1950) case in which "the Supreme Court decided in substance that for the state to impose segregated legal education upon its black citizens was to deny them the constitutionally guaranteed equal protection of the laws," the black lawyers believed the court had given a clear signal that it was willing "to reexamine the fundamental question of the constitutionality of imposed racial segregation without predisposition in favor of the rationale of *Plessy v. Ferguson*" (Hastie, 1973, p. 30). With this belief and the evidentiary base of lower court litigation and past victories, the NAACP lawyers revised the strategy that had guided and governed their civil-rights litigation for nearly two decades and argued the ultimate issue, the unconstitutionality of state-imposed racial segregation. Because of the evidence placed on the record during the 20-year legal campaign, "an equalitarian legal order" was the only decision left for the Supreme Court to make (Hastie, 1973, p. 30). This was the decision it rendered in *Brown v. Board of Education* (1954), which "scholars have assigned . . . a high place in the literature of liberty" (Kluger, 1976, p. x). Richard Kluger said, "The decision marked the turning point in America's willingness to face the consequences of centuries of racial discrimination" (Kluger, 1976, p. x). In the *Brown* decision, the Supreme Court stated in unequivocal language that "separate educational facilities are inherently unequal." The litigation strategy of Charles Houston and his associates was effective.

In the *Brown* case and those leading up to it, a happy outcome for all blacks was obtained, first, because the NAACP initiated litigation only when local blacks were willing to suffer the consequences of such action, and second, because a litigation process had been devised by black people who had fundamental or compelling interest in the outcome and who stood to suffer if the wrong principle was established or the wrong remedy was implemented.

The *Bakke v. Board of Regents of the University of California* (1978) case was one such case in which the fundamental or compelling interest of the University of California as litigant was an issue. Derrick Bell calls the *Bakke* case "a classic instance of litigation without representation" (Bell, 1978, p. 19). Allan P. Sindler observed that "minorities had the greatest stake in the outcome of the case, but they had no direct role as participants because the parties to the law suit were a white and the university" (Sindler, 1978, p. 237).

The University of California revealed in its petition to the California Supreme Court that it had "a strong interest in obtaining a review by the US Supreme Court of . . . whether the special admissions program . . .

[is] . . . unconstitutional" (Sindler, 1978, p. 84). Indeed, the University of California classified this interest as "more important." A number of minority organizations such as the Urban League requested the university not to appeal *Bakke* to the US Supreme Court. The NAACP wanted the case remanded to a lower court so that "more evidence could be presented" (Sindler, 1978, p. 237). The minorities believed that without a well-documented record such as preceded the *Brown* case too many options were available to the Supreme Court, some of which could be harmful to them.

Although the minorities had a fundamental or compelling interest in the outcome of the case as one that would validate the 1964 Civil Rights Act and its affirmative action procedures, their pleas were ignored by the University of California. Minorities were not involved in fashioning the legal strategy.

Minorities, of course, have a fundamental or compelling interest in remedying the effects of societal discrimination and in institutionalizing affirmative action. Justice Powell's opinion that resulted in the court's majority vote that outlawed the special minority admissions program of the medical school of the University of California at Davis said the University's program did not meet the test of a "compelling interest" in these matters that are so important to minorities (Sindler, 1978, p. 320). It is doubtful that such a statement could be made, if blacks or other minorities had been the litigants and if information had been placed on the record about the discriminatory effects of admissions programs in most colleges and universities that do not deliberately recruit minorities.

Indeed, the University of California's response to the court's decision that outlawed the UC-Davis medical school's special program for minorities demonstrated that its fundamental interest and that of minorities were different. The *Amsterdam News* of the black press declared that blacks had lost in the *Bakke* case because of the court's decision. But the University of California's president said it was "a great victory for the university" (Sindler, 1978, pp. 317–318).

The litigation initiated by the University of California in appealing lower-court decisions to the Supreme Court resulted in a doctrine on race that now is public policy: "Government may take race into account . . . to remedy disadvantages cast on minorities by past racial prejudice . . . when appropriate findings have been made by judicial, legislative, or administrative bodies. . . ." (Sindler, 1978, p. 321). According to this doctrine, statistical measures of underutilization alone are insufficient evidence of discrimination. There must be "appropriate findings" of discrimination by "appropriate and competent bodies" (Sindler, 1978, p. 321). Moreover, the Supreme Court in its *Bakke* opinion "provided no settlement of the question of how far a remedy could go once discrimination had been proven" (Sindler, 1978, p. 322). One could say that the *Bakke* decision "was as much an escape from affirmative action as a confirmation of it" (Sindler, 1978, p. 320).

All of this suggests that the issues raised in the *Bakke* case came to the attention of the highest tribunal in the land prematurely. The premature presentation of these issues resulted from litigation on behalf of minorities that was initiated by people affiliated with the majority who did not have a fundamental or compelling interest in the outcome of the case. They therefore could claim a victory for a decision against a special affirmative action program that minorities identified as a loss. In effect, the *Bakke* decision placed in jeopardy the affirmative action gains by minorities under Title VI that intended to ban employer discrimination (Sindler, 1978, p. 23).

Having been harmed by the *Bakke* case litigated by whites on behalf of minorities, blacks are disinclined to let others who do not have a compelling or fundamental interest in desegregation outcomes represent their interests again without their permission. Consequently, opposition to continuing litigation began in 1970 when the *Adams v. Richardson* case first emerged. "The broad base of support for the work of [the Legal Defense Fund] narrowed severely in the aftermath of *Adams*," according to Robert Dentler, an expert witness in the North Carolina case on enforcement of *Adams* (Dentler et al., 1983, p. 10). He said, "Jack Greenberg . . . and Joseph Rauh by 1975 were working in relative isolation," as black college presidents warned that "their campuses would 'slowly fade to white' " (Dentler, 1983, p. 11) if some of the remedies proposed were implemented. They conjectured that the *Adams* "desegregation strategy could prove fatal" (Dentler, 1983, p. 11). As blacks sized up the matter, the *Adams* case was not the next step that should be taken toward a just and permanent solution to segregated education. The legal strategy underlying *Adams* was more similar to *Bakke* than to *Brown*. Having been harmed once by liberal white intercessors, they were not about to risk such harm again. This accounts for their reluctance to give broad-based support to the lead the white lawyer litigants were taking in *Adams*.

Dominant people of power have difficulty comprehending the limitations that they should place upon themselves in initiating change in behalf of subdominants. The Civil Rights Act of 1964 not only authorized federal departments and agencies to withhold federal aid to grant recipients after a determination of racial discrimination had been made but also authorized the Justice Department, an agency of the dominant people of power, to intervene in schools cases. According to Gary Orfield, "the law . . . shifted the burden of initiating cases from private groups" (Orfield,

1978, p. 279). Eventually, the Justice Department, especially during the Nixon and Reagan administrations, began to settle out of court on partial plans that did not fully redress the grievances of minorities. An intercessor who has the power and authority to litigate in behalf of others has the authority to terminate such litigation in behalf of others whether or not they approve. Orfield is correct in his assessment that civil rights groups lacked the resources to counter all the opposition tactics and to pursue appeals when an adequate remedy was not provided by a lower court (Orfield, 1981, p. 31). Yet federal government, an agent of the dominant people of power, lacks the fundamental and compelling interest to fashion remedies through litigation in behalf of subdominants. There is no substitute for self-determination, for a group to identify the goals and objectives for which members are willing to sacrifice and suffer.

Despite limitation of resources, one group cannot assign to another a responsibility that only it must assume. When and how to sacrifice or suffer for the attainment of a goal such as justice is a decision that should be made only by those who have elected to risk sacrifice and suffering. No group—dominant or subdominant—has the right to offer up another for sacrifice. The decision when or whether to sacrifice is a personal and in-group decision and should not be made by external agents.

This means that the initiation of desegregation litigation is uniquely a responsibility of those who are oppressed by segregation. It is a burden to initiate such litigation, but it is a burden that cannot be shifted to others without risking the possibility of unfortunate consequences. Those who would not suffer a wrong outcome may be too quick or too slow to compromise. They may initiate action when the time is not ripe. They may delay action until after an opportunity has been lost. Self-determination is an important component in community organization and should be recognized and emphasized whenever possible. In summary, those who are responsible for the initiation of desegregation litigation are the people with a fundamental and compelling interest in the outcome.

Members of black minority groups in the United States followed this approach in designing an effective litigation strategy to achieve the national legal principle that segregation in public education is unlawful. What remains to be done is for subdominants to develop a new legal and legislative strategy for implementation of this policy. The strategy for the achievement of the legal policy resulted in great sacrifice and suffering but had a beneficial outcome, and so will a strategy for implementing the policy if it is self-determined by subdominants.

REFERENCES

Bell, Derrick. "The High Price of Non-Representation." *Phi Delta Kappan* (Winter, 1978).

Dentler, Robert A., D. Catherine Baltzell, and Daniel J. Sullivan. *University on Trial*. Cambridge, MA: Abt Books, 1983.

Fischer, Louis, David Schimmel, and Cynthia Kelly. *Teachers and the Law*. New York: Longman, 1981.

Hastie, William H. "Toward an Equalitarian Legal Order, 1930–1950." *The Annals* 407 (May 1973), pp. 18–31.

Higginbotham, A. Leon, Jr. "Racism and the Early American Legal Process, 1619–1896." *The Annals* 407 (May 1973), pp. 1–17.

Kluger, Richard. *Simple Justice*. New York: Knopf, 1976.

Larson, E. Richard, and Laughlin McDonald. *The Rights of Racial Minorities*. New York: Avon, 1979.

Mays, Benjamin E. "The Black College in Higher Education," in C.V. Willie and R.R. Edmonds (eds.), *Black Colleges in America*. New York: Teachers College Press, 1978, pp. 19–28.

Orfield, Gary. "Why It Worked In Dixie: Southern School Desegregation and Its Implications for the North," in Adam Yarmolinsky, Lance Liebman, and Corinne S. Schelling (eds.), *Race and Schooling in the City*. Cambridge, MA: Harvard University Press, 1978, pp. 24–44.

Orfield, Gary. *Must We Bus?* Washington, D.C.: The Brookings Institution, 1981.

Rosenbaum, David E. "Joe Rauh: 50 Years, and Counting, of Doing Good." *New York Times* (Jan. 8, 1985), p. A16.

Schlei, Barbara L., and Paul Grossman. *Employment Discrimination Law*. Washington, D.C.: Bureau of National Affairs, 1983.

Sindler, Allan P. *Bakke, DeFunis, and Minority Admissions*. New York: Longman, 1978.

Smith, Charles U. "Teaching and Learning the Social Sciences in the Predominantly Black Universities," in C.V. Willie and R.R. Edmonds (eds.), *Black Colleges in America*. New York: Teachers College Press, 1978, pp. 195–215.

7

Trends in Black Enrollment and Degree Attainment

WILLIAM T. TRENT
University of Illinois, Urbana-Champaign

JOMILLS H. BRADDOCK, III
Johns Hopkins University

Despite recent evidence reporting educational, economic, and political gains for blacks, substantial race differences remain throughout the educational pipeline. Inequality in higher education attainment among different racial groups remains a critical problem. Population demographics suggest cause for increased concern about race differences in higher education attainment.

A recent report by the National Institute of Independent Colleges and Universities presents a challenging scenario for education in the 1990s. Posing the question, "Guess Who's Coming to College?" the report gives a portrait of the current student population for the next decade that should entail substantial numbers of minority and female students at the postsecondary level. In the words of the report:

> The conclusion for higher education is inescapable: There is no alternative but to accept the fact that American public schools are now very heavily enrolled with minority students, large numbers of whom will be college eligible. Private elementary and secondary schools do not enroll enough students (mostly white) to alter this trend. Previous policies like "benign neglect" seemed reasonable to some when the percentage of minorities was 10–12%, but what state can neglect 40–45% of its youth?
>
> Thus, out of sheer self-interest, it behooves the higher education community to do everything to make sure that the largest possible number of minority students do well in public schools and thus become college eligible. If this is not done . . . the potential decline in the college cohort would not be 24% for the nation in 1990, but could be twice that. (Hodgkinson, 1983)

Often identified as "education pipeline" concerns, underpreparation, differential opportunities, limited financial resources, and differential dropout and graduation rates predispose minority students to lower rates of entry to college (Astin, 1982). Even when access and persistence are achieved, the problem of black and other minority underrepresentation in scientific, technical, and related fields of study remains at both graduate and baccalaureate levels.

We explore two pipeline issues in this chapter: (1) postsecondary enrollment; and (2) degree attainment at the bachelor's, master's, and doctoral levels. We compare both initial access and degree-attainment rates at two timepoints, allowing for approximation of short-term trends in these two indicators of black participation at the postsecondary level.

The enrollment data are reported for 1976 and 1982, while the degree-attainment data are for the 1975–76 and 1980–81 academic years. Both the enrollment and degree-attainment data represent the first and most recent periods for which statistics are reliable by race and gender for the nation's colleges. Enrollment data are reported for blacks and whites. Since enrollment patterns and problems differ by gender, we report enrollment and degree attainment separately for males and females in each racial group. Availability of data at two timepoints provides for longitudinal comparison of each enrollment and attainment measure. Our analysis begins with a consideration of first-time enrollment among specific populations and then analyzes degree-attainment trends.

Enrollment is presented for standard geographical regions, the entire nation, and states found in violation of Title VI. In addition we report degrees earned by blacks from both predominantly black and predominantly white colleges. Throughout our analysis we focus on changes in enrollment and degree attainment. Our discussion of trends in degree attainment is couched in terms of parity—representation commensurate with either the population or availability pools, both of which are defined below.

DATA AND METHODS

This chapter reports tabulations from the national surveys of opening fall enrollment and earned degrees collected every two years by race from all colleges in the nation as part of the federal government's Higher Education General Information Survey (HEGIS). The enrollment tabulations reported are for fall 1976 and fall 1982. The earned degrees data cover bachelor's, master's, and doctoral degrees for the 1975–76 and 1980–81 school years. In addition to reporting enrollment by full-time and part-time status, by degrees conferred for each major field for race, and by ethnic and gender groups, the HEGIS files also contain data on institutional characteristics including the predominant race of each institution's student body, the region in which it is located, public or private status, and level of program offerings. For the following analyses, the predominant race of the student body is reported for predominantly black and white institutions. The enrollment data reported here are for first-time freshmen only. Unclassified students are omitted as well as students continuing their enrollment beyond the first year.

Assessing equity in attainment depends fundamentally on parity between blacks and whites, or representation equal to an appropriate base at all levels of education. *Current Population Reports, Series P–20* (US Census Bureau, 1973a, 1973b, 1975, 1977, 1981), which reports socioeconomic characteristics of students, have been used to develop two separate measures of a base from which we can assess progress toward parity for blacks at the bachelor's degree level. The first is a population age cohort identifying the number of persons in the traditional college-aged population (18 to 24 years old) by race and gender who could be 1975–76 and 1980–81 bachelor's degree recipients. We have identified this age-cohort base for 1974 and for 1979, the years immediately preceding the awarding of bachelor's degrees reported here. The second baseline measure involves the availability pool of persons age 14 to 24 who had completed four years of high school by March 1972 and March 1977, respectively, and who would therefore be eligible for 1975–76 and 1980–81 college graduation. Using this base, parity is defined as a percentage of bachelor's degrees awarded to blacks that equals the percentage of blacks who are high school graduates.

Long-standing debate over the appropriateness of both measures hinges on the fact that blacks continue to graduate from high school at a lower rate and with weaker preparation than whites (ACE, 1983). The contention is that the availability pool measure has a built-in racial bias that, if ignored, would suggest parity based on a smaller proportion of blacks than the population pool measure and could lead to an overstatement of progress toward parity (ISEP, 1981). In effect, this view suggests that black-white parity based on the high school graduate availability pool proportions could be achieved, but that it might still not be equitable. We examine the use of both measures and assess differences in their implications. Arguably the availability pool measure may underestimate progress to the extent that on average the academic credentials of blacks are not equivalent to their nonminority counterparts. We examine the use of both measures and discuss the implications of using each one.

The basis for parity at the doctoral level is somewhat less precise. We use an availability pool measure based on the percentage of 20- to 34-year-olds in the population who had completed at least four years of college in 1970 and 1976, five years prior to the 1975–76 and 1980–81 school years, respectively, in order to determine an expected proportion of black doctoral recipients in those latter two years. These baseline measures are presented for blacks and whites. It should be added that this measure may also be affected by an inherent racial bias to the extent that blacks and whites differ in average time to degree completion.

RESULTS

Table 7.1 presents black and white first-time freshman enrollments, part-time and full-time, in two- and four-year colleges by gender and geographic region. The figures reported are 1976 and 1982 opening fall enrollments.

The data show that the six-year period from 1976 to 1982 provided occasion for the development of different enrollment patterns for black and white males and females. Males show a precipitous decline in absolute and relative terms. For black males, the 1982 freshman enrollment total is 4% less than the 1976 total. White males show a corresponding decline of 2%. By contrast, both black and white female enrollment improved. The 1982 total black female enrollment is 4% greater than 1976 enrollment figure, and the corresponding increase for white females is 9%. The general pattern of improvement for first-time freshman women illustrated by these data is consistent with the trends since 1970 (National Center for Education Statistics, 1982).

The data also show different racial trends in freshman enrollment. Both black males and females suffer in relation to whites. Compared to white males, black first-time freshman male enrollment declined at a faster rate; and compared to white females, black female enrollment increased at a lower rate.

Similarly, the distribution of freshman enrollment across two- and four-year institutions and by full- and part-time enrollment status follows a consistent pattern for all student subgroups, with increases occurring in the part-time, two-year college category. Concentration of blacks in the colleges characterized as least likely to enhance further college attainment has been increasing.

In the bottom panel of Table 7.1, we present 1976 to 1982 first-time freshman enrollment nationwide for blacks and whites. The trends illustrate that first-time freshman enrollments for both races peaked in 1980. Recent enrollment declines have affected all students; however, the black

TABLE 7.1. Percentage of First-Time Freshmen in Part-Time, Full-Time, Two-Year, Four-Year Enrollment[1]

By Gender, Race, and Region, 1976 and 1982

Race/Gender / Enrollment Status	North[2] 1976	North[2] 1982	Midwest[3] 1976	Midwest[3] 1982	South[4] 1976	South[4] 1982	West[5] 1976	West[5] 1982	Nation 1976	Nation 1982
Black Male (N=)	(14,898)	(18,051)	(26,561)	(21,281)	(55,230)	(53,092)	(16,679)	(16,625)	(113,368)	(109,049)
PT-2 Yr.	13.5	15.7	28.4	26.5	15.0	16.3	43.6	55.5	22.1	24.2
PT-4 Yr.	7.8	4.6	4.3	5.1	5.4	7.2	2.2	2.2	5.0	5.6
FT-2 Yr.	35.1	28.5	31.0	29.4	32.2	30.6	40.3	30.0	33.5	31.6
FT-4 Yr.	43.6	41.2	36.3	39.0	47.4	45.9	13.9	12.3	39.4	38.6
White Male (N=)	(204,785)	(205,061)	(285,638)	(285,366)	(259,645)	(257,061)	(208,147)	(193,510)	(956,215)	(940,998)
PT-2 Yr.	9.5	11.0	22.9	23.9	18.0	21.5	38.2	42.4	22.1	24.2
PT-4 Yr.	7.1	6.7	3.7	3.3	4.4	4.1	3.3	3.0	4.5	4.2
FT-2 Yr.	29.1	29.9	24.2	25.9	29.2	27.5	30.1	26.7	27.9	27.4
FT-4 Yr.	54.2	52.3	49.2	46.9	48.4	46.9	28.4	28.0	45.5	44.2
Black Female (N=)	(22,768)	(27,865)	(34,441)	(27,638)	(69,349)	(71,555)	(17,558)	(19,357)	(141,154)	(146,415)
PT-2 Yr.	13.0	17.3	31.2	28.3	13.6	17.9	45.7	58.7	22.1	25.1
PT-4 Yr.	8.0	5.7	5.1	6.8	5.3	6.3	2.4	2.3	5.4	5.8
FT-2 Yr.	31.4	38.4	29.0	28.0	31.4	31.4	35.4	24.5	32.0	31.0
FT-4 Yr.	47.6	38.6	34.7	36.9	49.7	44.4	16.5	14.5	40.5	37.9
White Female (N=)	(201,819)	(229,887)	(282,662)	(305,665)	(253,026)	(286,564)	(213,094)	(216,027)	(950,601)	(1,038,143)
PT-2 Yr.	10.6	15.8	27.5	30.0	21.4	27.0	44.7	48.5	26.2	29.9
PT-4 Yr.	8.0	7.7	4.7	4.4	5.3	4.8	3.2	3.0	5.2	4.9
FT-2 Yr.	29.0	28.7	21.5	22.6	25.1	25.4	25.3	23.1	24.9	24.8
FT-4 Yr.	52.4	47.8	46.3	43.0	48.2	42.8	26.8	25.4	43.7	40.4

[1] Enrollment is included only for the 50 states and the District of Columbia. Enrollment figures do not include unclassified students.
[2] North: ME, NH, VT, MA, RI, NJ, NY, PA, CT
[3] Midwest: IL, IN, IA, KS, MI, MN, MO, NE, ND, OH, SD, WI
[4] South: AL, AR, DE, DC, FL, GA, KY, LA, MD, MS, NC, OK, SC, TN, TX, VA, WV
[5] West: AK, AZ, CA, CO, HI, ID, MT, NV, NM, OR, WA, WY

TABLE 7.1. (*continued*)

	By Race Nationally, 1976 to 1982			
	1976	*1978*	*1980*	*1982*
Black (N =)	(254,522)	(259,728)	(279,705)	(255,464)
PT–2 Yr.	22.1	24.5	24.5	24.7
PT–4 Yr.	5.2	5.4	6.1	5.7
FT–2 Yr.	32.6	31.2	31.1	31.3
FT–4 Yr.	40.0	38.9	38.3	38.3
White (N =)	(1,906,816)	(1,925,666)	(2,068,146)	(1,979,141)
PT–2 Yr.	24.1	25.5	27.6	27.2
PT–4 Yr.	4.9	4.8	4.4	4.6
FT–2 Yr.	26.4	25.1	25.4	26.0
FT–4 Yr.	44.6	44.5	42.6	42.2

decline between 1980 and 1982 of about 9% is more than double the white decline of about 4%. From Table 7.1 it is also clear that compared to whites, a greater percentage of blacks are enrolled in part-time programs at the two-year level. By 1982 black enrollment declined to near-1976 levels despite increases by black females. The national and regional enrollment trends show an overall pattern of declining black participation except among part-time, two-year college entrants, where the average student's chances for eventually earning a four-year degree or better are very slim.

Table 7.2 presents 1976 and 1982 enrollments at public four-year colleges and universities in Title VI states. Black student enrollment statistics in these Title VI states follow national trends of stagnation in the levels of black participation in higher education. These data also show major enrollment shifts among black students away from predominantly black institutions toward predominantly white ones, even though increases in total black enrollment have not taken place. The shift between 1976 and 1982 involves nearly a 100% increase in black full-time freshman enrollment in predominantly white colleges. By 1982 total freshman enrollment at predominantly black colleges amounted to just 66% of their 1976 total.

These freshman enrollment trends give little cause for optimism. The declining numbers, concentration of blacks into two-year programs, and concommitant reductions in full-time four-year enrollment give clear evidence of major obstacles to the attainment of equity. Not unreasonably, many educators, students, and policy-makers expected greater progress in states affected by Title VI; but little appears to be taking place.

Table 7.3 presents the overall summaries for degrees by degree level, race, and gender across relevant time periods.

Examining overall degree attainment in Table 7.3, only at the bachelor's degree level did an increase take place in the total number of degrees awarded. Compared to five years earlier, 12,654 (1.3%) more degrees were awarded at the bachelor's level in the 1980–81 year. By contrast, a modest decrease occurred in the number of master's and doctoral degrees earned. For the master's degree, 14,945 (4.8%) fewer were awarded in the 1980–81 year. The corresponding decrease at the doctoral level was 393 degrees or approximately 1%.

Data in Table 7.3 suggest widespread improvement in degree attainment among females. Nearly all of the increase in total degrees awarded at the bachelor's level is attributable to advances by black and white females. At the doctoral level, females of both races increased their degree totals, nearly offsetting the overall decrease in earned doctorates among males. Between the 1975–76 and 1980–81 years females increased their

TABLE 7.2. First-Time Black Freshmen Student Enrollment[1] in Four-Year Public Institutions in Adams States[2] by Full- or Part-Time Status and Year

Freshmen Enrollment	1976		1982	
	N	%	N	%
Part-Time				
Predominantly Black College	1,584	7.9	334	1.6
Predominantly White College	226	1.1	914	4.5
Full-Time				
Predominantly Black College	13,055	65.0	8,671	42.3
Predominantly White College	5,281	26.0	10,581	51.6
	20,083	100%	20,500	100%

[1]Enrollment figures do not include unclassified students.
[2]Only Adams States with accepted plans as of 8-5-83 are included: AR, FL, NC, OK, VA, GA, WV, SC, MO, DE, TX, KY, PA.

share of degrees at each level by no less than 4%. Only at the master's degree level, and mainly for black females, did a departure take place from this general pattern of gain. Over this period, black females experienced a decrease of 1326 degrees or 10.8% of their 1975–76 total.

Despite general improvements for females, approximating parity (50% of earned degrees) at the bachelor's and master's levels, the gender disparity at the doctoral level remained 2 to 1 (66 to 33%) in the 1980–81 year favoring males. This is the case despite a 37% increase in earned doctorates between 1976 and 1981 for females. After a 37% increase for females at the bachelor's level in the 1980–81 year, and given comparability between males and females at the bachelor's and master's levels, the continuing gender disparity at the doctoral level appears more striking.

The patterns of change for each racial group in Table 7.3 require careful interpretation, especially when gender is considered and when viewed in the larger context of overall change. Blacks increased their share of earned bachelor's degrees by the 1980–81 year by 0.2%. Whites increased their actual bachelor's degree count by a 0.6% increase, but received a small decrease (0.7%) in their share of all bachelor's degrees awarded.

Blacks experienced both a lower actual count and a lower share of master's degrees in the 1980–81 year compared to five years earlier: 2779 fewer degrees, constituting a 14% decrease and a 0.6% smaller share of all earned master's degrees. This substantial decrease stands in sharp contrast to the overall 4.8% decrease in earned master's degrees among all races. Among blacks, the decrease occurred among males both in actual numbers (1453 versus 1326) and in percentage terms (19.1 versus

TABLE 7.3. Race and Sex Distribution of Bachelor's, Master's, and Doctoral Degrees[1] Awarded in 1975–76 and 1980–81

Race/Sex Group	Year	Number of Bachelor's Degrees Awarded	Percent of Total	Percent within Sex	Number of Master's Degrees Awarded	Percent of Total	Percent within Sex	Number of Doctorate Degrees Awarded	Percent of Total	Percent within Sex
Males										
Black	1975–76	25,301	2.7	5.0	7,611	2.4	4.6	743	2.2	2.8
	1980–81	24,511	2.6	5.2	6,158	2.1	4.2	694	2.0	3.1
White	1975–76	441,191	47.8	87.7	136,366	43.9	81.8	20,281	59.1	77.7
	1980–81	406,185	43.4	86.4	115,562	39.1	78.6	17,310	51.0	76.4
TOTAL[2]	1975–76	503,254	54.6	100%	166,649	53.6	100%	26,099	76.0	100%
	1980–81	469,898	50.2	100%	147,046	49.7	100%	22,651	66.7	100%
Females										
Black	1975–76	32,952	3.6	7.9	12,301	4.0	8.5	426	1.2	5.2
	1980–81	36,162	3.9	7.8	10,975	3.7	7.5	571	1.7	5.1
White	1975–76	361,608	39.2	86.3	120,375	38.7	83.6	6,363	18.5	77.3
	1980–81	401,149	42.9	86.2	125,654	42.5	84.5	8,598	25.3	76.2
TOTAL	1975–76	419,253	45.4	100%	144,039	46.4	100%	8,235	24.0	100%
	1980–81	465,263	49.8	100%	148,697	50.3	100%	11,290	33.3	100%
Both Sexes										
Black	1975–76	58,253	6.3		19,912	6.4		1,169	3.4	
	1980–81	60,673	6.5		17,133	5.8		1,265	3.7	
White	1975–76	802,799	87.0		256,741	82.6		26,644	77.6	
	1980–81	807,334	86.3		241,216	81.6		25,908	76.3	
TOTAL	1975–76	922,507			310,688			34,334		
	1980–81	935,161			295,743			33,941		

[1]Degree counts presented in this table are for colleges and universities located in the 50 states and the District of Columbia.
[2]Totals include Hispanics, Native Americans, Asian and Pacific Islanders, and nonresident aliens.

10.8%). Whatever the factors contributing to substantial reductions for blacks' master's degree attainment, the results are considerably more deleterious for black males as a group.

A similar pattern of race-specific gender differences exists among blacks at the doctoral level. Like white males, black males earned more doctoral degrees than their female counterparts in the 1980–81 year. However, the gender disparity favoring black males decreased by nearly two-thirds, from 27.2% in 1975–76 to 9.8% in 1980–81. Because black females earned 145 more doctorates in 1980–81 (a 34% increase) compared to five years earlier, and black males earned 49 fewer doctoral degrees (a 7% decline), the overall increase in earned doctorates among blacks is clearly attributable to gains by black females. In fact, black males earned about the same share of degrees at each level compared to five years earlier.

Among whites the pattern of change in earned degrees is straightforward, and the gender differences are clear and consistent: White females increased their actual count and their share of earned degrees at each level, while the reverse was true for white males. Actual gains in degrees earned by white females were 39,541 (10.9%), 5279 (4.4%), and 2235 (35.1%), respectively, for bachelor's, master's, and doctoral categories. Nonetheless, in 1980–81 white males still received 50.3% of all bachelor's degrees, 47.9% of all master's degrees, and 66.8% of all doctoral degrees earned by whites. Thus, very notable increases on the part of white females, combined with substantial declines for white males, produced approximate gender equity by the 1980–81 year at the lower degree levels, but left a substantial, unchanged gap in female–male attainment at the doctoral level.

These changes in degree attainment are informative, but a more complete assessment of equity depends upon measuring parity between blacks and whites. Reflecting the methods described earlier, Table 7.4 shows that blacks fail to approach parity on either measure at the bachelor's degree level, and this is especially clear for black males.

Black females, on the other hand, made gains toward parity between 1976 and 1981. Overall, the black population age cohort was 12.1% in 1974 and 12.6% in 1979, but blacks received only 6.5% of bachelor's degrees awarded in 1975–76 and 6.7% five years later. The difference between the population cohort percentage and the degree-attainment percentage widened during the five-year period. The increase in the black population within the age cohort (0.126 − 0.121, or 0.005) was greater than the increase in blacks' bachelor's degree attainment (0.067 − 0.065, or 0.002), constituting a net decrease in progress toward parity.

By contrast, the black proportion of the availability pool was 10.9%

TABLE 7.4. Comparisons of College-Age Population and Available Pool Distributions with Degree-Attainment Distributions for Blacks and Whites by Sex for Degrees Awarded in 1975–76 and 1980–81

BACCALAUREATE

	Percent of College-Age (18–24) Population (in 1000s)		Percent of Available Pool (in 1000s) (H.S. Grads 19–24)		Percent of Baccalaureate Degrees Received	
	1974	1979	1972	1977	1975–76	1980–81
GRAND TOTAL (N=)	(25,670)	(27,974)	(11,354)	(12,702)	(922,507)	(935,161)
Male	48.0	48.5	43.8	47.1	54.7	50.4
Female	52.0	51.5	56.2	52.9	45.3	49.6
BLACKS (N=)	(3,105)	(3,511)	(1,237)	(1,398)	(58,253)	(60,673)
% of Total	12.1	12.6	10.9	11.0	6.3	6.5
Males (N=)	(1,396)	(1,577)	(515)	(634)	(25,301)	(24,511)
% of Total	5.4	5.6	4.5	5.0	2.7	2.6
% of Sex	11.3	11.6	10.4	10.6	5.0	5.2
% of Race	45.0	44.9	41.6	45.4	43.4	40.4
Females (N=)	(1,709)	(1,934)	(722)	(764)	(32,952)	(36,162)
% of Total	6.7	6.9	6.4	6.0	3.6	3.9
% of Sex	12.8	13.4	11.3	11.4	7.9	7.8
% of Race	55.0	55.1	58.4	54.6	56.6	59.6
WHITE (N=)	(22,141)	(23,895)	(9,999)	(11,095)	(802,807)	(801,441)
% of Total	86.3	85.4	88.1	87.3	87.0	85.7
Males (N=)	(10,722)	(11,721)	(4,388)	(5,233)	(441,191)	(406,185)
% of Total	41.8	41.9	38.6	41.2	47.8	43.4
% of Sex	87.1	86.4	88.3	87.5	87.7	86.4
% of Race	48.4	49.1	43.9	47.2	55.0	50.7
Females (N=)	(11,419)	(12,174)	(5,611)	(5,862)	(361,616)	(395,256)
% of Total	44.5	43.5	49.4	46.2	38.2	42.3
% of Sex	85.5	84.5	87.9	87.2	86.3	85.0
% of Race	51.6	50.9	56.1	52.8	45.0	49.3

DOCTORAL

	Percent of Ages 20–34 in the Population (in 1000s)		Percent of Available Pool (in 1000s) (Persons Completed at Least 4 Yrs. of College Ages 20–34)		Doctoral Degrees Awarded	
	1970	1976	1970	1976	1975–76	1980–81
GRAND TOTAL (N=)	(40,458)	(49,959)	(3,606)	(6,073)	(34,334)	(33,941)
Male	48.1 (19,442)	49 (24,463)	51.4 (1,852)	51.8 (3,145)	76.0 (26,099)	66.7 (22,651)
Female	51.9 (21,016)	51 (24,496)	48.6 (1,754)	48.2 (2,928)	24.0	33.3
BLACKS (N=)	(4,477)	(5,425)	(188)	(346)	(1,169)	(1,265)
% of Total	11.1	10.9	5.2	5.7	3.4	3.7
Males (N=)	(2,092)	(2,413)	(81)	(132)	(743)	(694)
% of Total	5.2	4.8	2.2	2.2	2.2	2.0
% of Sex	10.8	9.9	4.4	4.2	2.8	3.1
% of Race	46.7	44.5	43.1	38.2	63.6	54.9
Females (N=)	(2,385)	(3,012)	(107)	(214)	(426)	(571)
% of Total	5.9	6.0	3.0	3.5	1.2	1.7
% of Sex	11.3	12.3	6.1	7.3	5.2	5.1
% of Race	53.3	55.5	56.9	61.8	36.4	45.1
WHITES (N=)	(35,475)	(43,508)	(3,331)	(5,483)	(26,644)	(25,908)
% of Total	87.7	87.1	92.4	90.3	77.6	76.3
Males (N=)	(17,103)	(21,583)	(1,725)	(2,893)	(20,281)	(17,310)
% of Total	42.3	43.2	47.8	47.6	59.1	51.0
% of Sex	88.0	88.2	93.1	92.0	77.6	76.4
% of Race	48.2	49.6	51.8	52.8	76.1	66.8
Females (N=)	(18,372)	(21,925)	(1,606)	(2,590)	(6,363)	(8,598)
% of Total	45.4	43.9	44.5	42.6	18.5	25.3
% of Sex	87.4	89.5	91.6	88.5	77.3	76.2
% of Race	51.8	50.3	48.2	47.2	23.9	33.2

in 1974 and 11.0% in 1979; thus the increase in the availability pool (0.1%) was less than the increase in degree attainment (0.2%), indicating that a slightly larger percentage of those blacks who completed high school in 1977 also completed college in 1980–81, compared to their 1972–73 and 1975–76 counterparts.

Blacks are a demographically younger population than whites, with higher concentration in this college-eligible age range. Although the black–white gap in high school completion rates is closing (Mare, 1981), it continues to be substantial. Completion of high school is a prerequisite for college entry, and until that gap closes or in fact until blacks graduate from high school and college at a greater rate than whites, there can be little progress in closing the total population-based parity gap.

In addition to between-race differences, there are also intra-gender differences. Among males, the parity issue is most severe for blacks. Although black males increased as a percentage of both bases (by 0.2% and 0.5%, respectively), they decreased as a proportion of degree recipients (by 0.1%) over the five-year period. White males also increased somewhat as a proportion of both bases and declined as a percentage of degree recipients. Unlike black males, though, white males continue to receive a larger share of all degrees than either their population or availability pool proportions would predict.

For blacks, the parity issue at the doctoral level is quite complex. Compared to the population base, blacks made very small progress toward equity: They gained in degree shares, but lost a 0.2% share of the population. Compared to the availability pool, however, blacks did not keep pace. They constitute a 0.5% share of the 1976 pool, but only a 0.3% share of 1980–81 doctorates, for a net decrease in parity of 0.2%. The situation is very different for males and females. Black males are closer to parity using the population base than are black females at either time-point, and black males are at or near parity using the availability pool base. Black females, on the other hand, are at less than 50% of parity using the 1980–81 availability pool base, despite an increased share of doctorates. These comparisons yield two major implications. First, gender gaps in degree attainment are dramatic at the doctoral level regardless of race. Second, if blacks—especially black males—were closer toward parity earlier in the pipeline (bachelor's and master's), substantial increases in equity could occur at the doctoral level.

One unexpected result of using these census data population and availability pool measures to assess black–white parity is the relative distribution of postsecondary education between black males and black females. Examining the 1974 and 1979 population bases, males constitute in both years a smaller proportion of the 18-to-24-year-old age group (45 and 44.9%) than females. The comparable availability pool base—1972 and 1977—shows that black males constitute an even smaller share of the availability pool (41.6 and 45.4%). Similarly disturbing is the continuing downward trend in black males' share of college credentials. In 1976 black males earned 43.4% of bachelor's degrees awarded to blacks, but by the 1980–81 year they earned only 40.4% of black baccalaureates. When we extend the population age range to 20- to 34-year-olds (Table 7.4) and examine both the population base and availability pool base for 1970 and 1976, we observe a similar pattern of black male disadvantage. In 1970, males constituted 43% of all blacks with at least four years of college, and by 1976 only 38%, a 5% decrease compared to a 2% decrease in population percentage over the same period. When we consider bachelor's degrees awarded to blacks in the 1975–76 and 1980–81 years, we see that a larger proportion goes to black females. This evidence suggests that at stages in the education pipeline when blacks as a group fare well, black males are disproportionately unsuccessful.

Table 7.5 presents 1975–76 and 1980–81 black student distributions by major field of study for bachelor's, master's, and doctoral degrees, respectively. Separate distributions are presented for males and females.

In general, black males are more likely than females to earn degrees in scientific, technical, and business fields, and females continue to show an advantage in education and the health services professions. Second, all blacks show shifts out of social sciences and education into more math- and science-related areas. These patterns are evident at each degree level, but gender differences that are very clear at the bachelor's degree level are much less so at the doctoral level.

Education and business degrees earned provide good examples of these general patterns. In education at the bachelor's level, males earned about half as many degrees as their female counterparts in both 1976 and 1981 (15 and 10.6% for males compared to 31.7 and 19.1% for females in 1976 and 1981, respectively). In business the reverse was true: Males earned from twice as many degrees in 1976 to one and one-half times as many in 1981 as their female counterparts (23 and 26.5% for males compared to 10.9 and 19.1% for females in 1976 and 1981, respectively).

Even with the declining percentages of earned degrees in education for all blacks at each degree level, black males earn at least 15% fewer degrees in education compared to black females at any degree level. Conversely, even with substantial increases in the proportion of earned degrees in business at each degree level, males earned at least 1½ times as many degrees in business as females. At both the master's and doctoral levels, the male advantage was about 3 to 1 in 1981 (25.2 to 7.3% at the master's level and 3.7 to 1.1% at the doctoral level).

TABLE 7.5. Major Field Distribution of Bachelor's, Master's, and Doctoral Degrees Earned by Black Males and Females in 1975–76 and 1980–81

Major Field	Males B.A. 1976 (25,301)	B.A. 1981 (24,511)	M.A. 1976 (7,611)	M.A. 1981 (6,158)	Ph.D. 1976 (743)	Ph.D. 1981 (694)	Females B.A. 1976 (32,952)	B.A. 1981 (36,162)	M.A. 1976 (12,301)	M.A. 1981 (10,975)	Ph.D. 1976 (426)	Ph.D. 1981 (571)
Agriculture	1.0	1.1	.9	.9	2.2	2.0	.1	.3	–	.2	.5	.2
Architecture	1.0	.9	1.8	1.2	.5	.7	.1	.2	.9	.4	.2	.2
Area Studies	.2	.1	.2	–	.5	.9	.2	.1	.1	.1	1.2	0
Biological Sciences	4.0	3.9	1.4	1.3	4.3	5.2	3.4	3.6	.8	.8	2.8	4.9
Business	23.0	26.5	15.8	25.2	2.2	3.7	10.9	19.1	2.5	7.3	0	1.1
Communications	2.0	4.0	1.1	1.1	.8	.4	2.0	3.9	.7	1.1	.5	1.2
Computer Sciences	1.0	1.6	.6	.8	0	.1	.4	1.1	.1	.2	0	0
Education	15.0	10.6	47.6	33.5	51.3	41.6	31.7	19.1	70.3	60.0	66.4	56.9
Engineering	5.0	8.2	2.5	3.6	2.4	3.3	.2	1.2	.2	.3	0	.2
Fine Arts	3.0	3.3	1.9	2.4	1.5	1.7	2.9	2.8	1.0	1.1	1.9	.9
Foreign Languages	.5	.3	.5	.2	.4	.6	1.2	.6	.6	.2	.9	.9
Health Professions	1.0	1.8	2.2	3.2	1.5	1.3	6.9	8.8	3.6	6.3	1.2	3.0
Home Economics	.3	.3	.1	.2	0	.4	3.0	2.9	.8	1.1	1.2	1.1
Law	.1	–	.2	.4	0	.1	–	–	–	.1	0	0
Letters	3.0	2.7	1.8	1.2	4.2	4.0	5.0	3.6	2.4	1.6	6.6	4.9
Library Science	–	–	.9	.5	.1	.4	.2	.1	2.9	1.7	.7	1.1
Mathematics	1.0	1.1	.9	.5	.9	.9	1.3	.9	.4	.3	.2	.5
Military Sciences	.2	–	0	0	0	0	0	–	0	0	0	0
Physical Sciences	1.7	2.5	1.2	1.3	3.9	4.0	.6	.8	.3	.3	.7	.7
Psychology	4.5	4.2	2.5	2.7	5.9	8.9	6.1	6.3	1.8	2.4	4.0	9.5
Public Affairs	5.9	7.0	8.5	11.6	2.4	2.7	5.5	8.7	7.6	10.8	2.3	5.8
Social Sciences	22.2	15.1	6.2	5.1	10.6	9.5	15.6	12.3	3.1	2.8	7.7	6.0

In view of their complexity, these general patterns deserve a closer look. Table 7.6 enables a more focused consideration of these patterns.

The central focus of Table 7.6 is major field concentrations for black males and females and the extent of disparity in concentrations. It is often assumed that race alone is the critical factor, but these data provide clear evidence that gender exerts still further influences. We present here the 10 fields in which black males earned the highest proportion of their bachelor's degrees in 1976 and the five fields in which they received the highest proportion of their master's and doctoral degrees in 1976. These serve as the references to which we compare 1981 black male degree concentration to identify shifts and to which we compare 1976 and 1981 black female concentrations to identify similarities and differences in concentrations and shift patterns.

For black males, at each degree level there is substantial consistency in the rankings of the fields at each timepoint despite some notable shifts in percentages for given fields. At the bachelor's level nine of the 1976 fields are still in the top 10 in 1981, and four retain their 1976 ranking. At the master's level, the top four 1976 fields are the same in 1981; likewise in the top three doctoral fields. Even more interesting, these 10 fields account for about 89% of all black male bachelor's degrees in 1976 and about 72% in 1981. At the master's level, the five fields account for 66 and 78% of black males' degrees in 1976 and 1981, respectively. The comparable figures at the doctoral level are 76.3 and 69.2%. At each degree level, then, black males are concentrated in a relatively small number of fields, at rates ranging from 66 to 90%. These concentrations are particularly crucial at the postbaccaulaureate levels, where four of the five are social science and education fields.

Contrasting the black female rankings with those for black males, several patterns appear. First, at least eight of the 10 top fields for male bachelor's degrees are also among the top 10 for females. The major field similarities are even more comparable at each succeeding degree level. At the master's level four of the fields are in the top five; depending upon years compared at the doctoral level, the top five male fields in 1976 are the same for females in both 1976 and 1981.

Differences in the rankings of the major fields for males and females mainly at the bachelor's degree level are also more apparent in 1976 than in 1981. At the master's and doctoral levels, the rankings are more comparable, and by 1981 the rankings of the major fields are also more similar. These fields also account for the vast majority of degrees earned by black females in each year and at each degree level. The appropriate percentages are: bachelor's, 84 and 80%; master's, 85.3 and 83.3%; doctoral, 87.5 and 82.2%.

TABLE 7.6. Comparison of Major Field Concentrations for Black Males* and Females at the Bachelor's, Master's, and Doctoral Levels, 1976 and 1981

Major Field	Males				Females			
	1976	Rank	1981	Rank	1976	Rank	1981	Rank
BACHELOR'S DEGREES								
Business	23.0	(1)	26.5	(1)	10.9	(3)	19.1	(1)
Social Science	22.2	(2)	15.1	(2)	15.6	(2)	12.3	(3)
Education	15.0	(3)	10.6	(3)	31.7	(1)	19.1	(1)
Public Affairs	5.9	(4)	7.0	(5)	5.5	(6)	8.7	(5)
Engineering	5.0	(5)	8.2	(4)	.2	(17)	1.2	(13)
Psychology	4.5	(6)	4.2	(6)	6.1	(5)	6.3	(6)
Biological Science	4.0	(7)	3.9	(9)	3.4	(8)	3.6	(8)
Interdisciplinary	3.3	(8)	4.1	(7)	2.8	(11)	3.5	(10)
Fine Arts	3.0	(9)	3.3	(10)	2.9	(10)	2.8	(12)
Letters	3.0	(10)	2.7	(11)	5.0	(7)	3.6	(8)
MASTER'S DEGREES								
Education	47.6	(1)	33.5	(1)	70.3	(1)	60.0	(1)
Business	15.8	(2)	25.2	(2)	2.5	(6)	7.3	(3)
Public Affairs	8.5	(3)	11.6	(3)	7.6	(2)	10.8	(2)
Social Science	6.2	(4)	5.1	(4)	3.1	(4)	2.8	(5)
Psychology	2.5	(5)	2.7	(7)	1.8	(8)	2.4	(6)
DOCTORATES								
Education	51.3	(1)	41.6	(1)	66.4	(1)	56.9	(1)
Social Science	10.6	(2)	9.5	(2)	7.7	(2)	6.0	(3)
Psychology	5.9	(3)	8.9	(3)	4.0	(4)	9.5	(2)
Biological Science	4.3	(4)	5.2	(5)	2.8	(5)	4.9	(5)
Letters	4.2	(5)	4.0	(7)	6.6	(3)	4.9	(5)

*The leading major fields for black males in 1976 serve as the reference base at each degree level.

High overall, similarly concentrated enrollment in a relatively few fields for both males and females occurs in 1976 (89 and 84%) at the bachelor's degree level. In 1981 at the bachelor's degree level and for each year at the master's and doctoral levels, females are more heavily concentrated than are males. Mainly, females' greater proportions of education degrees, especially at the master's and doctoral levels, accounts for their concentration. Taken together, the slightly lower male concentration and the higher female proportions in education are evidence of the gender disparity among all major fields for blacks.

Next we examine the predominant race of the student body at colleges from which blacks receive their degrees. Two issues are explored: (1) the relative black degree productivity of predominantly black and predominantly white colleges, and (2) degree distributions by major field for predominantly black and predominantly white colleges.

Tables 7.7 and 7.8 present data showing the relative degree productivity of predominantly black and predominantly white colleges. We focus upon the extent to which each type of institution is under- or overrepresented in certain fields given the overall percentage of degrees awarded by each. Based on HEGIS data, predominantly black colleges comprise about 10% of the nation's baccalaureate-granting schools. These institutions account for roughly 33 percent of all bachelor's degrees awarded to blacks. In certain fields where blacks have traditionally been underrepresented, predominantly black colleges also contribute disproportionately to black degree attainment. Tables 7.7 and 7.8 show the representation of predominantly black colleges for each major field for males and females, respectively, at the bachelor's and master's degree levels for two academic years.

The first four columns of Tables 7.7 and 7.8 give the within-field share of bachelor's degrees awarded to black males and females, respectively, in 1975–76 and 1980–81. For black males (Table 7.7), predominantly black colleges accounted for 37% of total 1975–76 bachelor's degrees; and in the fields of agriculture, biological sciences, business, education, mathematics, physical sciences, and theology, black colleges awarded shares ranging from 38 to 57%, taking all degrees awarded to blacks into account. By the 1980–81 year, black colleges and universities awarded just 33% of all bachelor's degrees to black males, but bachelor's degrees to blacks from these same institutions were overrepresented in the fields just identified and in engineering. Interestingly, in math, where the total number of degrees declined, the share awarded by predominantly black colleges increased.

Predominantly black colleges also accounted for a disproportionate share of the bachelor's degrees awarded to black females at each time pe-

TABLE 7.7. Total Number of Earned Bachelor's and Master's Degrees in Each Major Field Awarded and Percentage Awarded by Predominantly Black Colleges[1] to Black Males in 1975–76 and 1980–81

Major Field	Bachelors				Masters			
	1975–76		1980–81		1975–76		1980–81	
	N^2	%	N^2	%	N^2	%	N^2	%
Agriculture	230	57	259	57	71	54	53	21
Architecture	210	19	210	23	140	11	74	18
Area Studies	43	2	20	0	14	0	2	0
Biological Sciences	1,120	42	954	42	106	23	82	34
Business	5,858	44	6,503	37	1,201	10	1,554	14
Communications	586	15	980	24	81	5	65	15
Computer Sciences	201	32	394	34	47	2	52	12
Education	3,669	54	2,587	49	3,622	30	2,061	29
Engineering	1,268	35	2,020	36	188	1	222	10
Fine Arts	736	24	811	25	143	8	140	3
Foreign Languages	117	24	76	11	38	8	10	30
Health Professions	378	27	436	27	106	5	197	3
Home Economics	66	24	83	55	5	0	11	55
Law	19	11	9	0	13	0	27	30
Letters	732	23	666	24	140	6	72	7
Library Science	3	100	2	50	71	44	33	24
Mathematics	373	51	276	53	66	17	33	30
Military Sciences	44	0	5	40	0	0	0	0
Physical Sciences	440	38	613	40	93	28	79	35
Psychology	1,128	23	1,040	23	193	10	164	17
Public Affairs	1,495	23	1,726	23	646	12	713	13
Social Sciences	5,611	35	3,696	29	474	19	311	15
Theology	130	54	142	44	38	5	58	0
Interdisciplinary	844	13	1,003	8	55	4	136	2
TOTAL	25,301	37%	24,511	33%	7,611	21%	6,158	19%

[1]Predominantly black colleges are those reporting in 1980–81 that blacks constituted the larger proportion of enrolled students.
[2]Total of degrees earned in the respective major field.

TABLE 7.8.   Total Number of Earned Bachelor's and Master's Degrees in Each Major Field Awarded and Percentage Awarded by Predominantly Black Colleges[1] to Black Females in 1975–76 and 1980–81

	Bachelors				Masters			
	1975–76		1980–81		1975–76		1980–81	
Major Field	N[2]	%	N[2]	%	N[2]	%	N[2]	%
Agriculture	37	54	121	57	6	33	20	10
Architecture	47	13	90	20	53	0	48	21
Area Studies	65	0	47	0	11	0	12	0
Biological Sciences	1,115	46	1,315	40	100	38	89	42
Business	3,604	56	6,897	41	310	19	805	21
Communications	648	15	1,425	24	89	8	122	21
Computer Sciences	121	49	392	47	7	0	18	0
Education	10,440	55	6,907	48	8,646	30	6,584	24
Engineering	62	45	429	29	21	0	38	3
Fine Arts	952	22	429	29	21	7	98	3
Foreign Languages	394	23	217	12	71	14	23	0
Health Professions	2,268	22	3,167	27	444	4	692	2
Home Economics	988	44	1,042	36	97	28	121	24
Law	7	0	13	0	5	20	11	0
Letters	1,650	37	1,314	25	292	29	178	22
Library Science	72	33	28	25	353	29	183	28
Mathematics	412	49	308	52	52	19	34	38
Military Sciences	0	0	1	100	0	0	0	0
Physical Sciences	197	50	293	46	33	30	28	50
Psychology	2,007	27	2,268	26	218	13	260	11
Public Affairs	1,797	34	3,143	29	932	15	1,180	16
Social Sciences	5,144	39	4,433	30	384	23	304	15
Theology	18	39	24	17	16	25	13	0
Interdisciplinary	907	12	1,264	11	40	—	94	2
TOTAL	32,952	43%	36,162	35%	12,301	23%	10,975	21%

[1]Predominantly black colleges are those reporting in 1980–81 that blacks constituted the larger proportion of enrolled students.
[2]Total of degrees earned in the respective major field.

riod (43 and 35%, respectively) and, as was true for males, a pattern of overrepresentation emerges in agriculture, biological sciences, business, education, math, and physical sciences. Also for black females, predominantly black college graduates are overrepresented in the field of computer science. On the other hand, in engineering—where black females increased their degree count by a factor of almost 7 (from 62 to 429)—the percentage of degrees awarded by predominantly black colleges declined substantially, from 45 to 29%.

The distribution of degrees awarded by predominantly black colleges at the master's level depicted in the last four columns of Tables 7.7 and 7.8 is quite similar to baccalaureate degree patterns for both males and females. For males (Table 7.7), predominantly black colleges accounted for 21 and 19% of master's degrees in 1975–76 and 1980–81. For black females (Table 7.8) the comparable figures are 23 and 21%. Again, however, in the biological and physical sciences especially, predominantly black colleges accounted for nearly twice the proportion of degrees one would expect based on their overall 1980–81 degree production.

These figures highlight the essential role of predominantly black colleges in producing black degree holders. Predominantly black colleges constitute less than 10 percent of all four-year colleges and universities, but award a disproportionate percentage of degrees earned by blacks especially in so-called "nontraditional" fields. Predominantly black colleges' track record in awarding degrees to blacks suggests that access to and, more important perhaps, retention within predominantly white colleges remain unresolved issues.

Although not shown in Tables 7.7 and 7.8, in the 1975–76 year predominantly black colleges accounted for 35 (3%) of all doctorates earned by blacks, and 20 were in education. Five years later, predominantly black colleges and universities accounted for 69 (5.5%) of all doctorates earned by blacks, with only eight in education. Twenty-one were in biology, nearly half of the 1980–81 doctorates earned by blacks in this field.

The implications are quite clear: Predominantly black colleges continue to contribute substantially to both the quantity and diversity of blacks' postsecondary credentials. Perhaps much can be learned by examining factors resulting in three predominantly black institutions producing the same number of black biology doctorates as the 100 or more predominantly white institutions that offer a Ph.D. in biology.

CONCLUSION

The data reported here describing enrollment and attainment are institutional data, not reports on individuals. As a consequence, questions about the role of students' high schools, family backgrounds, and personal attributes in producing enrollment trends can only be inferred. These data do not allow us to identify unique institutional features that contribute to the observed patterns of enrollment and degree attainment. For these reasons we are limited in any attempt to identify causes of the patterns observed in this research that might consist of individual, group, or institutional factors. Nonetheless, the patterns presented do describe a national phenomenon of limited progress by blacks with respect to enrollment and degree attainment. Both nationally and in Title VI states, the data also demonstrate among blacks clear differences between males and females on a variety of education pipeline issues.

The inconsistency of enrollment patterns across regions suggests that the causal factors may not be pervasive throughout the nation. In the South, where nearly all of the predominantly black colleges are located, the 1976 and 1982 total headcount enrollments are virtually unchanged. Equally important, the proportion of black, full-time, four-year enrollment shows a substantial decline in the South, where historically black four-year colleges have traditionally kept this enrollment proportion comparable to that of whites. In the same region, decline occurs in blacks' share of full-time, four-year total enrollment for both females and males, despite overall gains in first-time, numerical enrollment for black females.

The combination of virtually no change in total black first-time enrollees in the South, and the redistribution of total black enrollment by level and full- or part-time status is particularly serious, since nearly one-half of all black first-time enrollees live in the South, and since the range of institutions there has been most conducive to sustaining and increasing black enrollment. In short, if gains are not occurring in the South, then the causal structure for remedying low black enrollment is indeed complex.

Overall black enrollment in the North and West show some improvement, but like the South, a redistribution by college level and enrollment status towards two-year colleges and part-time status is taking place. The net result is slower and lower rates of baccalaureate and graduate degree attainment, reflecting low transfer from two- to four-year colleges. We can only speculate that these trends and redistribution patterns are caused by traditional barriers: underpreparation at the high school level and limited financial means. It is easy to argue that recent public policy and public opinion have not been supportive of blacks' educational aspirations and needs, especially in these areas. The recent abundance of higher education reform recommendations include references to quality, including increased use of standardized testing and adding more required high school courses. Currently, fewer black students take the appropriate mix of college preparatory courses compared to their white peers. At every level of education, at each critical transition point in the education pipeline—from ability group and track placement through admissions testing—disproportionate reductions in black student populations occur. Enrollment in general and vocational curriculum tracks, poor quality schooling, and low achievement test performance do not lead to growth in the pool of blacks eligible for selection into four-year colleges.

Government retrenchment has been characterized by funding shortages and changes in funding priorities. Although the budget dilemmas of the 1976–80 Carter Administration compelled debate over program priorities, the Reagan Administration emphasized reduced spending on social programs, including educational intervention projects and enforcement of affirmative action practices. More pertinent to enrollment, the Reagan Administration set a clear policy of shifting the burden of higher education costs from government onto students and their families, and of restructuring limited forms of federal assistance available to pay college costs.

A further socioeconomic issue also influences enrollment figures for black students. Fully one-third of all black students attend public elementary and secondary schools in seven major metropolitan areas. These seven centers also show the highest rates of black unemployment, which constricts the funding of public education in their communities and further limits municipal government's ability to fund continuing education. At the same time, the cost of a college education is increasing, with regular tuition increases at state institutions. It is also important to note that the policy orientations and financial constraints that define and accompany retrenchment are sufficiently pervasive to influence national and regional patterns of educational opportunity as well as individual perceptions and expectations regarding educational opportunity.

The net effect of these demographic factors, policy shifts, and reductions in government support may well have been to alter fundamentally the real and perceived cost of postsecondary education. Under such circumstances, minority students especially become far more cautious in deciding whether and at what level to enter postsecondary education.

In light of the data presented in this chapter, it is important to recognize that many of the same barriers to attainment of educational parity identified in the 1960s and early 1970s continue to restrict black attainment in the 1980s. This is not to suggest that blacks have made no progress. Indeed, both the 1976 and 1982 first-time enrollment figures are substantially larger than black representation in higher education in 1970. Nevertheless, tangible and impressive gains among blacks have not led to racial parity, and data do not support an optimistic view of prospects for doing so. Under these circumstances renewed efforts to reduce the negative effects of the traditional barriers to increased black enrollment and degree attainment are called for.

REFERENCES

American Council on Education. *Status of Minorities in Higher Education, 1982–83.* Washington, DC: ACE, 1983.

Astin, Alexander W. *Minorities in American Higher Education.* San Francisco: Jossey-Bass, 1982.

Hodgkinson, Harold L. *Guess Who's Coming to College?—Your Students in 1990.* Washington, DC: National Institute of Independent Colleges and Universities, 1983.

Institute for the Study of Educational Policy. *Equal Educational Opportunity Scoreboard: The Status of Black Americans in Higher Education, 1970–1979.* Washington, DC: Howard University Press, 1981.

Larson, E. Richard and Laughlin McDonald. *The Rights of Racial Minorities.* New York: Avon, 1979.

Mare, Robert D. "Trends in School." *The Annals,* Jan. 1981, pp. 96–122.

National Center for Education Statistics. *Fall Enrollment in Colleges and Universities, 1976.* Washington, DC: US Department of Health, Education and Welfare, 1977.

National Center for Education Statistics. *Fall Enrollment in Colleges and Universities, 1978.* Washington, DC: US Department of Health, Education and Welfare, 1979.

National Center for Education Statistics. *Fall Enrollment in Colleges and Universities, 1980.* Washington, DC: US Department of Education, 1981.

National Center for Education Statistics. *Fall Enrollment in Colleges and Universities, 1982.* Washington, DC: US Department of Education, 1983.

National Center for Education Statistics. *Higher Education General Education Survey of Earned Degrees, 1975–76.* Washington, DC: US Department of Health, Education and Welfare, 1977.

National Center for Education Statistics. *Higher Education General Education Survey of Earned Degrees, 1980–81.* Washington, DC: US Department of Education, 1982.

US Bureau of the Census. *Current Population Reports, Series P-20, No. 243. Educational Attainment, March, 1972.* Washington, DC: US Government Printing Office, 1973a.

US Bureau of the Census. *Current Population Reports, Series P-20, No. 250. Persons of Spanish Origin in the United States, March, 1971 and 1972.* Washington, DC: US Government Printing Office, 1973b.

US Bureau of the Census. *Current Population Reports, Series P-20, No. 286. School Enrollment—Social and Economic Characteristics of Students. Oct. 1974.* Washington, DC: US Government Printing Office, 1975.

US Bureau of the Census. *Current Population Reports, Series P-20, No. 314. Educational Attainment, March 1977 and 1976.* Washington, DC: Government Printing Office, 1977.

US Bureau of the Census. *Current Population Reports, Series P-20, No. 360. School Enrollment—Social and Economic Characteristics of Students, October, 1979.* Washington, DC: US Government Printing Office, 1981.

US Bureau of the Census. *Current Population Reports, Series P-20, No. 250. Persons of Spanish Origin in the United States, March 1971 and 1972.* Washington, DC: US Government Printing Office, 1973b.

8
The Educational Attainment
Process among Black Youth

EDGAR G. EPPS
University of Chicago

KENNETH W. JACKSON
University of Houston

The Carnegie Commission on Higher Education (1971) estimated that to achieve educational equality black student enrollment in higher education would have to increase to about 1 million in 1980 and to about 2 million by the end of this century. In the fall of 1982, the National Center for Education Statistics reported that 611,000 black students were enrolled in four-year institutions and 483,000 were enrolled in two-year institutions, for a total enrollment of 1,094,000. This comprised 8.87% of the total population. It should also be noted that blacks comprised 8.0% of enrollment in four-year institutions and 10.3% of enrollment in two-year institutions. In the states affected by Title VI regulation of higher education, black undergraduates constituted 13.6% of total enrollment, while the black college-age population in these states was almost 20% of the total (Brazziel & Brazziel, 1980; American Association of University Professors, 1983). These figures suggest that there is still considerable room for improvement in educational attainment among blacks.

The research reported here examines the process by which educational attainment is generated in the black population. Specifically, our efforts are to determine the mechanism that generates educational mobility among black Americans. The basic theoretical orientation for our analysis is the Wisconsin model of status attainment (Sewell, Haller, & Portes, 1969). This model and its variants, in their "traditional" form, have not worked very well in terms of their explanations of the black educational attainment process (see Hout & Morgan, 1975; Kerckhoff &

This chapter is based upon research funded by the Southern Education Foundation, Atlanta.

Campbell, 1977). We contend that this problem is due primarily to a status attainment model. That is, the Wisconsin model and its variants are basically social-psychological models emphasizing the primary role played by social-psychological influences. These factors, usually measured in terms of influential others and aspirations, serve as key mediators of the effects of earlier social circumstances such as one's school career or family history.

The model is summarized below:

> [T]he model . . . assumes that predetermined social structural and psychological factors—that is, socioeconomic status and mental ability—affect the youth's academic performance and the influence significant others have on him; that the influence of significant others and possibly his own ability affect his levels of educational and occupational aspirations; and that levels of aspiration affect educational and occupational status attainment. Thus, the model provides a causal argument linking social origins and ability with educational and early occupational status attainments by means of intervening behavioral mechanisms (Sewell, Haller, & Ohlendorf, 1970, p. 1015).

We contend that social-psychological factors are not as central to the generation of educational attainment for blacks as they are for whites. We hypothesize that the school dimension is of considerably more importance than the social-psychological dimension for blacks.

In this research, we attempt to modify the traditional status attainment model. This modification consists primarily of a respecification of the school dimension, with the other dimensions (background and social-psychological) remaining basically unchanged. The rationale for respecifying the school dimension is that this component may represent a very critical aspect of the status attainment process for blacks. If our hypothesis concerning the importance of the school dimension is correct, a respecification of this dimension should increase the explanatory power of the model for blacks. The results could also provide a basis for making recommendations about schooling that could help to increase black participation in higher education.

PREVIOUS RESEARCH

Studies of status attainment among blacks will be presented in the following order: socioeconomic background, demographic characteristics, school-related characteristics, students' personal characteristics, and significant others' influence. In examining the research results, the focus will be on the way these sets of variables function in the prediction of educational aspirations and attainment.

Socioeconomic Background

Most studies find positive and significant relationships between family social status and students' educational aspirations (Allen, 1980; Epps, 1969; Howell & Frese, 1979; Hout & Morgan, 1975; Thomas, 1979). However, there are some exceptions. DeBord, Griffin, and Clark (1977) and Kerckhoff and Campbell (1977) report that socioeconomic background has little effect on educational aspirations or expectations of black students.

Studies that have looked at educational attainment have usually found socioeconomic level of family of origin to have an important influence on the amount of education attained by respondents (Kerckhoff & Campbell, 1977; Portes & Wilson, 1976; Thomas, 1979). Wilson (1979) reported that socioeconomic level of students' families was more strongly related to black students' educational attainment in integrated schools than in segregated schools.

Demographic Characteristics

Two demographic variables have been identified in previous research that influence aspirations and educational attainment among black Americans; these are northern versus southern region of residence and size of school district. Little research on school district size has been done with black students, although the typical finding for other populations is that urban students have higher aspirations than rural students (Cosby, 1969; Kuvlesky & Ohlendorf, 1969). It has also been suggested that sources of aspirations for urban students are more strongly influenced by parents while rural students' aspirations are more strongly influenced by peers (Picou & Carter, 1978). It remains to be demonstrated that these generalizations are applicable to blacks.

Northern vs. southern residences. Bachman (1970) and Epps (1969) found that important information may be lost when black students are studied as a single group. Background variables appear related to aspirations and expectations in a different manner for northern and southern students. For example, Epps (1969) found that northern males were the only subgroup (among southern males, northern females, and southern females) for which father's education was a stronger predictor of aspirations and educational expectations than mother's education. Additional evidence for the importance of region and school district size in the status attainment process among blacks is reported by Crain and Mahard (1978). Using data from the National Longitudinal Study of 1972, these researchers found that region interacts with school racial composition on both achievement and college attendance among blacks. They also report that school district size is positively associated with achievement in the North but not in the South, and that attending integrated schools has a stronger positive effect on achievement in the North than in the South. Using data from the 1962 and 1973 Occupational Changes in a Generation surveys, Hogan and Featherman (1977) found that northern blacks have higher educational attainments than southern blacks, but that this advantage is decreasing. The northern advantage is, in their opinion, at least partially attributable to the larger proportion of southern men who have farm origins. They also contend that the status attainment process for northern blacks more closely approximates that of whites than does that of southern blacks. The decreasing advantage of northern blacks referred to by Hogan and Featherman is probably attributable to the increased urbanization of southern blacks.

School-Related Characteristics

Among the school-related characteristics that have been found to have important effects on aspirations and educational attainment of blacks are: student body racial composition (Bachman, 1970; Coleman et al., 1966); social class of student body (Coleman et al., 1966); classroom racial composition (McPartland, 1969); curriculum placement or academic track (Alexander, Cook, & McDill, 1978; Rosenbaum, 1980; Thomas, 1979); and school academic climate (Brookover et al., 1979). Wilson's study (1979) found that the negative effect of disciplinary problems on black students' educational attainment is almost three times as great in racially mixed schools as in segregated schools. This reinforces the notion that it is important to take school characteristics into consideration when studying educational attainment.

Students' Personal Characteristics

Ability and aptitude frequently have been found to have a strong positive influence on aspirations and educational attainment of black students (DeBord, Griffin, & Clark, 1977; Epps, 1969; Kerckhoff & Campbell, 1977; Porter, 1974; Thomas, 1980). There are, however, some inconsistencies in the research results. Portes and Wilson (1976) found the effect of aptitude on educational aspirations to be trivial, while Hout and Morgan (1975) found the effect of ability on educational expectations of black males to be mediated entirely by grades, although there was a direct effect of ability on the educational expectations of black females.

Ability and aptitude are also related to almost all other variables included in studies of mobility processes. Thus, aptitude affects curriculum placement (Rosenbaum, 1980), disciplinary problems (Kerckhoff & Campbell, 1977), and time spent on homework (Page & Keith, 1981). Generally, the relationship of achievement test scores to aspirations and attainment parallels the results for ability and aptitude.

Several studies have found grades or high school rank to be strongly related to educational aspirations and expectations (Allen, 1980; Hout & Morgan, 1975; Kerckhoff & Campbell, 1977; Portes & Wilson, 1976). There are, however, some inconsistencies in the results. For example, Kerckhoff and Campbell (1977) found senior high school grades to be the strongest predictors of educational expectations among black students. Porter (1974), in contrast, found no direct relationship between high school grades and educational attainment among blacks in his sample. Portes and Wilson (1976) contend that grades from black segregated schools are systematically discounted by admissions officers at traditionally white colleges and universities, therefore weakening the relationship between grades and educational attainment among blacks. Measurement differences may also contribute to the inconsistencies among results. Some studies use self-reports of grades while others use grades obtained from school records. The official grades contain less error, and should therefore be better predictors of aspirations and attainment than student self-reports of grades.

Achievement attitudes may be considered the motivational component of the social mobility process. Among the frequently studied achievement-related attitudes are self-esteem, academic self-concept, and sense of control over the environment. Positive attitudes toward achievement are thought to be predictive of later attainments. Previous research has demonstrated that the self-perception and control orientation variables are positively and significantly related to academic achievement and educational expectations (Coleman et al., 1966; Epps, 1969). Portes and Wilson (1976) found self-esteem to be second only to educational aspirations and stronger than socioeconomic status and mental ability in predicting educational attainment among black males.

Aspirations and expectations are also considered to be achievement attitudes (Allen, 1980). There is considerable evidence that educational aspirations and expectations are highly predictive of actual later attainment (Portes & Wilson, 1976; Thomas, 1979; Wilson, 1979). We view aspirations and expectations as intervening variables dependent upon social background, aptitude, and influential others. However, when we look at sophomores involved in the High School and Beyond (HSB) study, aspirations are treated as outcome variables.

Significant Others' Influence

Most studies of the attainment process include measures of parental, peer, teacher, or counselor influence. For example, DeBord, Griffin, and Clark (1977) obtained student reports of teacher, parent, and peer influence. They found that mothers' encouragement affects the aspirations of black girls while peer group plans affect the aspirations of black boys. Porter (1974) found a composite measure of significant others' influence to be a strong predictor of conformity to middle class values among blacks which, in turn, is a strong predictor of ambition, grades, and educational attainment. The relationship between significant others' influence and aspirations is to some extent the result of the fact that student self-reports are used to assess both types of variables. Students' reports of the amount of influence or encouragement they receive are certain to be influenced by the students' own aspirations; in other words, students' perceptions of the way others see them probably reflect the way students view themselves. In spite of this measurement problem, student reports of encouragement by influential others have been found to be strongly related to educational attainment (Thomas, 1977).

DATA FOR THE PRESENT STUDY

The data for this analysis were taken from the 1972 National Longitudinal Study (NLS) and its 1980 follow-up, and the 1980 HSB study and its 1982 follow-up. Both are national samples selected so as to be representative of high school seniors in the United States at the time the data were collected. The analyses reported in this research are based on the following sample size: HSB males, 259; NLS males, 167; HSB females, 324; NLS females, 319.

The estimation techniques used in the analyses are those found usually in status attainment research. These strategies, commonly referred to as path analytic techniques, have proven to be quite informative with respect to understanding the dynamics of educational attainment.

The basic dynamics of the model are assumed to be as follows: Background factors (socioeconomic status and ability) are those crucial elements that the individual brings to the attainment process; they then are assumed to have a direct impact on those school factors (track, semesters of coursework completed, and grades) that are relevant for subsequent attainment. The effects of these school factors are then mediated by the social-psychological factors (influential others and aspirations) which, in turn, have a direct impact on status. As we view the process for blacks, the social-psychological component should have a relatively weak mediating effect on school factors. Descriptions of variables are provided in the Appendix to this chapter.

RESEARCH FINDINGS

National Longitudinal Study (NLS) Males.   The model accounts for about 31 percent of the variance in educational attainment in this cohort of black males. The significant direct influences were ability, track, influential others, and aspirations. Except for track the school component, contrary to our expectations, did not exert much influence on educational attainment. Ability was by far the most important determinant of educational attainment ($b = 0.353$), while the aspirations variable ($b = 0.196$) was second in importance. The pattern observed here is similar to that usually found for white males. That is, social-psychological factors, net of ability, tend to mediate the effects of background and school factors.

NLS Females.   The model was slightly more successful for females than for males, accounting for just over 34 percent of the variance in educational attainment. We also find that the school component tends to be more significant for females. Both track ($b = 0.195$) and grades ($b = 0.105$) have substantial direct effects on educational attainment. As was the case for males, however, ability and aspirations stand out as the most important determinants of educational attainment ($b = 0.275$ for ability, 0.331 for aspirations).

Since aspirations are the most crucial determinant of educational attainment, we asked which factors are most important in the generation of aspirations. We find that the only important determinants of aspirations are the school factors (grades, semesters of coursework taken, and track). It is of interest to note that the only school variable that had a significant effect on aspirations for males was grades, with most of the important determinants being related to the background of the student. On the other hand, for females the school factors mediate both background and ability and also have direct influences on educational attainment. Thus, our hypothesis is at least partially supported for NLS females.

High School and Beyond (HSB) Males.   We find that the model explains approximately the same amount of variance in educational attainment for HSB males, 29 percent, as for NLS males, 30 percent (Figure 8.1).

However, there are differences in the effects of certain variables.

FIGURE 8.1. Male Status-Attainment Model Using High School and Beyond Data

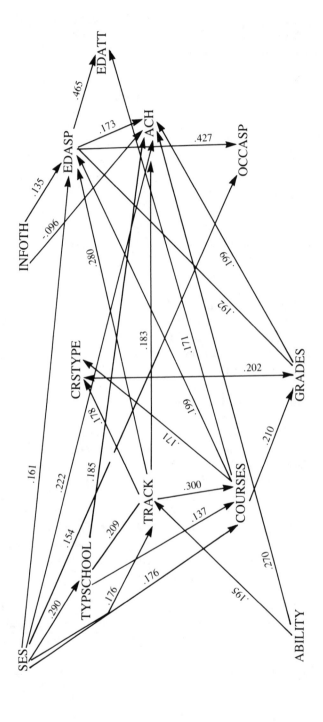

FIGURE 8.2. Female Status-Attainment Model Using High School and Beyond Data

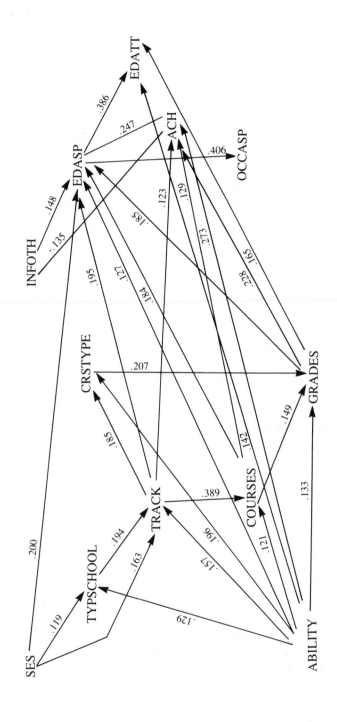

146 PROBLEMS AND PROSPECTS

Unlike NLS males, for HSB males educational attainment is influenced considerably more by school factors. For NLS males, background and social-psychological factors were more important. For HSB males, however, the background factors had no direct impact on educational attainment, while only aspirations among the social-psychological variables had any significant effect. On the other hand, although aspirations had the strongest effect ($b = 0.448$), both track ($b = 0.123$) and semesters of coursework ($b = 0.166$) also had significant direct effects on attainment. It should be noted that the pattern for HSB males is similar to that for NLS females. Grades, semesters of coursework taken, and track were all significant determinants of aspirations. The differences observed for the two male cohorts suggest the possibility that a very fundamental shift in the generation of educational status may have occurred between 1972 and 1980. If this is indeed the case, it would appear that the attainment of high levels of education has become less dependent on individual ascriptive or motivational factors and more dependent on institutional or school factors.

HSB Females. With respect to educational attainment for females, we do less well with the HSB cohort, 25 percent of variance explained, than with the NLS cohort, 34 percent of variance explained (Figure 8.2). As was the case for the NLS females, two school factors (track and grades) have rather substantial direct influences on educational attainment. Only semesters of coursework taken was unimportant among this group of school factors. However, coursework does affect educational attainment indirectly through its effect on aspirations. Aspirations, as was the case for NLS females, had the strongest direct influence on educational attainment ($b = 0.334$).

The factors responsible for the generation of educational aspirations are substantially different for HSB and NLS females. For NLS females, the principal influences were all school factors. In the HSB cohort, not only were school factors important, but background (both socioeconomic status and ability) also exerted a significant direct effect on this variable. This finding implies a slight shift away from the more institutional factors observed in the NLS cohort to an emphasis on the more ascriptive or motivational individual components in the HSB group. This is not to imply that school factors are unimportant; they still have a significant impact on aspirations. However, they are not sole determinants of aspirations for the HSB females as is the case for the NLS females.

We find, then, that for the HSB females there has also been a shift in the process by which educational attainment is generated, although it has not been as substantial as the general tendency in recent years for background factors to increase their influence. The fact that we account for no more than 34 percent of the variance in educational attainment for NLS females and only 25 percent for HSB females suggests that other factors (presumably unmeasured) are also contributing to the variance in educational attainment. That is, we suspect that the variables typically included in this type of research are becoming less influential, and that perhaps some previously unidentified variables are becoming more important.

Adding Analyses.   In an effort to see if early attainment processes differ from the pattern observed for HSB seniors, we applied our model to HSB sophomores. We can only look at the generation of aspirations for this cohort (rather than educational attainment). For sophomore males, school factors tend to dominate in terms of their influence on aspirations (Table 8.1). In fact, all three school variables entered into the model (track, courses taken, and grades) directly influence aspirations. Socioeconomic status and influence of significant others also had strong direct effects on aspirations. What is different about the sophomore male results, however, is the decreased importance of ability. For senior males, ability had a significant direct influence on all relevant dependent variables except educational attainment. For the sophomores, ability directly influenced only grades and track, and in neither case was it the most important influence.

For sophomore females, socioeconomic status, track, courses taken, grades, and influential others all have significant direct effects on aspirations (Table 8.2). For senior females, the only difference was that ability also had a significant direct effect and grades did not. Socioeconomic status had a stronger impact on subsequent variables for sophomore females than for any other cohort. This tends to provide additional support for our contention that there seems to be a general trend, especially among females, away from the more structurally oriented dimensions such as school factors and toward the more individually oriented background characteristics. This is not an indication that school factors have diminished in importance. Rather our results seem to indicate that socioeconomic status is becoming a more salient factor in the generation of success among black American females.

In an attempt to improve the specification of the school component, we conducted an analysis in which additional school variables were added to the model and occupational and educational aspirations were entered as separate variables rather than as a composite. This analysis involved the HSB senior cohort. Three additional variables were added to the model: the type of school the student attended (public or private), whether or not the student had taken remedial or advanced courses, and achievement as

TABLE 8.1. Nonzero Paths for HSB Males: Alternate Model

	Dependent Variables									
	EDATT	ACH	OCCASP	EDASP	INFOTH	GRADES	CRSTYPE	COURSES	TRACK	TYPSCH
SES	—	.222	.154	.161	—	—	—	.176	.176	.290
ABILITY	—	.270	—	—	—	—	—	—	.195	—
TYPSCH	—	.185	—	.280	—	—	.178	.137	.209	—
TRACK	.171	.183	—	.199	—	.210	.171	.300	—	—
COURSES	—	—	—	—	—	.202	—	—	—	—
CRSTYPE	—	—	—	—	—	—	—	—	—	—
GRADES	—	.199	—	.192	—	—	—	—	—	—
INFOTH	—	-.096	—	.135	—	—	—	—	—	—
EDASP	.465	.173	.427	—	—	—	—	—	—	—
OCCASP	—	—	—	—	—	—	—	—	—	—
ACH	—	—	—	—	—	—	—	—	—	—
R^2	.306	.552	.241	.326	—	.100	.078	.199	.153	.081

TABLE 8.2. Nonzero Paths for HSB Females: Alternate Model

	Dependent Variables									
	EDATT	ACH	OCCASP	EDASP	INFOTH	GRADES	CRSTYPE	COURSES	TRACK	TYPSCH
SES	—	—	—	.200	—	—	—	—	.163	.119
ABILITY	.142	.273	—	.127	—	.133	.196	.121	.157	.129
TYPSCH	—	—	—	.195	—	—	.185	.389	.194	—
TRACK	—	.123	—	.184	—	.149	—	—	—	—
COURSES	—	.129	—	—	—	.207	—	—	—	—
CRSTYPE	—	—	—	—	—	—	—	—	—	—
GRADES	.165	.228	—	.185	—	—	—	—	—	—
INFOTH	—	-.135	—	.148	—	—	—	—	—	—
EDASP	.386	.247	.406	—	—	—	—	—	—	—
OCCASP	—	—	—	—	—	—	—	—	—	—
ACH	—	—	—	—	—	—	—	—	—	—
R^2	.273	.420	.162	.323	—	.107	.083	.182	.109	.031

measured by standardized tests. A different measure of ability was also used (the combined scores of a picture and number test, a mosaic comparison test, and a visualization test instead of the math, reading, and vocabulary tests).

The inclusion of the additional variables does not greatly alter our results. Although differences were observed, the basic findings remain unaltered. For males, we find that courses taken and educational aspirations are the only two variables that have any significant direct effect on educational attainment. This differs from the original specification only in that track also had a significant direct effect which does not show up now. The amount of variance in educational attainment explained by the model only increased from 29 to 31 percent. It is interesting to note that in this specification we are able to account for over 55 percent of the variance in achievement for black males. This is quite substantial given other attempts at explaining achievement.

We also note that our ability to predict aspirations in the original case was due almost exclusively to our ability to predict educational aspirations. In fact, almost all of the influential determinants of aspirations in the original model are attributable to educational aspirations. The major difference between the two models is with respect to the influence of background factors. In the original model, ability had a strong direct effect on aspirations; in the alternate model, socioeconomic status influences aspirations along with the school factors (track, courses, grades, and achievement).

For females, the results are similar to those for males. There is only a slight improvement in accounting for the variance in educational attainment (27 compared to 25%). However, unlike the male results, ability has a significant direct effect on educational attainment along with grades and educational aspirations. Educational aspirations are predicted by socioeconomic status, ability, track, courses taken, grades, and influential others. We also do a good job of predicting achievement among females, accounting for 42 percent of the variance. It is interesting to note that for both sexes achievement does not influence educational attainment. Our basic conclusion for the results of the alternate specification is that the overall pattern observed in the original specification is not substantially changed.

SUMMARY

Our analysis has revealed that the relative importance of school factors tends to vary depending on which cohort one is observing. We found that for NLS males school factors were relatively unimportant, with social-psychological factors being more important. Although doing a respectable job of accounting for educational attainment, we found that for NLS males our assumptions were not correct. School factors, even after being specified in a more representative manner, did not dramatically increase our understanding of the generation of educational attainment for the NLS males.

We also found that this pattern did not generalize to the HSB sample. Using the HSB data to estimate a similar model, we found that school factors contributed significantly more to explanations of educational attainment than any of the other dimensions considered. This finding indicated that a major shift away from the individual background factors had taken place. In other words, what goes on in schools seems to matter considerably more for black males in the 1980s than it did in the early 1970s.

Our analysis indicated for females that the generation of educational attainment was already based on the more institutionally related school factors in the early 1970s. School related factors were by far the most critical elements in this process for females. Thus, the process found for the 1980 cohort of males was similar to that found for females in the early 1970s.

This process, however, has not remained stable. Our analysis revealed a slight shift for females over time. That is, background factors tended to be more important in the 1980s than they were in the 1970s for females. This is not to say that school factors decreased in importance. The analysis revealed that school factors continued to be important, but that the background factors increased in importance for the 1980 HSB females.

Thus, given the relative stability of the school factors for the two female cohorts as well as the shift toward an emphasis on school factors among males, it is likely that the pattern observed for females tends to be the pattern that males will follow at a later point in time. If this assessment is correct, we can expect that background factors will also become more relevant for black males in the future.

It is of interest to note that the alternate model using HSB data does a good job of predicting achievement as measured by tests. The variables that had a positive effect on achievement for males were socioeconomic status, ability, type of school (public or private), track, grades, and educational aspirations. For females, ability, track, courses taken, grades, and educational aspirations were positive influences. What is somewhat puzzling in this analysis is the fact that achievement appears to be unrelated to educational attainment. This is contrary to expectations and provides clear support for the notion that aspirations may be more important for educational attainment among blacks than measured achievement. One possible explanation for this seeming anomaly is the well-known fact that achievement tests do not measure blacks' accomplishments very well. Thus, the students' personal ambitions tend to be somewhat more important than achievement in predicting actual attainment. However, this interpretation must be viewed with caution, because of one major limitation of the HSB data. HSB students have been out of high school only two years. This means that our measure of educational attainment is constrained by the fact that students have not had sufficient time to complete their education. Future follow-up surveys may find that with additional variance in educational attainment better prediction is possible. This limitation does not apply to the NLS data to the same extent, because students in that cohort had been out of high school for eight years.

What we can say is that the model we used permits us to identify, to a certain degree, the basic pattern associated with the generation of educational attainment. Also, we can point out that there is support for our contention that as things now stand, the more institutionally relevant school variables are among the critical elements in the educational attainment process for both black males and black females. These factors have a profound influence on educational attainment in terms of both direct and indirect effects. Aspirations are very important, but they serve primarily as mediators of school factors since they are almost wholly generated by these institutional influences.

DISCUSSION

The research presented here addresses the issue of access to higher education for black Americans. The issue is of major concern for blacks in Title VI states where blacks continue to be underrepresented in postsecondary education. The data analyzed for this study are representative of blacks nationally at two periods in time: a 1972 cohort and a 1980 cohort. While the results from this study are suggestive for blacks in the Title VI states, analyses addressed to a sample of southern blacks may yield information that is more directly applicable to youth in the southeastern region.

The discussion that follows is based upon this analysis and other relevant studies of black status attainment processes. Most studies, including this one, find that socioeconomic status (SES) of family of origin has little direct influence on educational attainment. However, SES does have a substantial direct influence on educational aspirations. Of the factors included in studies of educational attainment, educational aspirations is the variable that has the strongest direct influence on educational attainment. Therefore, it is important to understand the determinants of educational aspirations. In addition to SES, ability influences educational aspirations directly for NLS and HSB females, but not for males. Ability also influences aspirations indirectly: Ability influences track placement which, in turn, influences educational aspirations. Ability also influences the number of academic courses taken for females, but not for males. A substantial relationship also exists between achievement and aspirations. In our model, we assume that aspirations influence achievement. However, some researchers contend that achievement influences aspirations or that the two variables have a reciprocal effect. Significant others' influence also has a direct effect on aspirations for the HSB sample, although this is not true for the NLS cohort.

Which school variables that we hypothesized should be more important for blacks than for whites? Track placement has a strong direct effect on educational attainment in some samples (e.g., NLS males), and a significant direct effect on educational aspirations for both males and females in the NLS and HSB cohorts. SES influences track placement, thus having an indirect influence on aspirations through track. The number of math, English, science, and foreign language courses taken is directly related to both educational aspirations and educational attainment in the HSB sample, and is directly related to educational aspirations in the NLS sample. High school grades also have a direct influence on aspirations in addition to serving to mediate the effect of academic courses taken for both males and females. Grades also mediate the effect of ability for females.

What this suggests in terms of policy implications is that the school factors that might prove responsive to manipulation are related to academic course requirements. Other research (Coleman, Hoffer, & Kilgore, 1982) suggests that school climate, including discipline and academic expectations, is important. Although this research is merely suggestive for southern populations, it does provide some hints about directions for further exploration.

APPENDIX: METHODOLOGY

Sample

The data for this analysis were taken from the 1972 National Longitudinal Study (NLS) and its 1980 follow-up, and the 1980 High School and Beyond (HSB) study and its 1982 follow-up. Our samples, for both NLS and HSB, were first stratified with respect to sex. Research has indicated that the status generation process may differ in important ways for males and females (see Alexander & Eckland, 1974; Hout & Morgan, 1975). Thus, if our sample were pooled, estimates based on the total sample would be less accurate and less informative than estimates based on separate analyses for males and females. The analyses reported in this research are based on the following sample sizes: HSB males, 259; NLS males, 167; HSB females, 324; NLS females, 319. The HSB sample of high school sophomores was also used in one analysis. The sophomore sample included 203 males and 289 females.

The specific indicators used to represent each dimension in the model employed in this study are described below.

Background Variables

Socioeconomic status (SES) was measured by five indicators: father's occupation, mother's occupation, mother's education, father's education, and parental income. The SES measure used in the analysis was a weighted linear combination of the five indicators. The weights were determined by regressing each factor on the ultimate dependent variable, occupational attainment. The SES indicators for the HSB sample were identical to those used for the NLS data with the exception of parental income. For HSB the income categories ranged from less than $7000 to more than $38,000, while for NLS the income categories ranged from less than $3000 to more than $18,000.

Ability, for both the NLS and HSB data sets, was measured by three tests designed to tap the individual's general ability in three areas: reading (20 items), vocabulary (15 items), and mathematics (20 items). The ability measure used was a simple linear combination of these three tests. Weights were not employed because each test exerted comparable influence on occupational attainment.

School–Related Variables

Track was measured by a single indicator of the student's high school program: academic, general, or vocational. This variable was recoded to produce an ordinal scale with vocational program scored low and academic program scored high. The measure is identical for both HSB and NLS.

The *courses* variable was measured by four indicators: total semesters of foreign language, total semesters of English, total semesters of science, and total semesters of mathematics. The information was obtained directly from school records for the NLS data set. The NLS courses variable is a weighted linear combination of the above four areas. The weights were determined by regressing each one on the dependent variable, occupational attainment.

For the HSB data set there were two major differences: first, the data were obtained from student self-reports; second, the foreign language component for HSB consisted of a combination of the total semesters in French, German, and Spanish. These areas, along with mathematics, English, and science, were then combined in a weighted linear fashion to yield the HSB courses variable.

Grades were taken directly from school records for NLS respondents. The grades obtained yielded a 14-category measure ranging from below F to a high of A+. This variable was also measured in a different manner for the HSB sample. Grades were obtained from HSB student self-reports. The resulting measure was an eight-category indicator ranging from a low of mostly below D or a numerical average of 60, to a high of mostly A's or a numerical average of 90 to 100.

Social-Psychological Variables

Influential others (INFOTH) was measured by nine indicators for the NLS sample. Each asked respondents how much the following person(s) influenced their plans for after high school: parents, relatives other than parents, guidance counselor, teacher, principal, clergyman, state employment officer, other adult, and friends. Responses to each were based on a three-category Likert scale: not at all, somewhat, and a great deal. The measure used here was a simple linear combination of each, conceptually designed to measure the degree to which outcomes are influenced by other individuals. The resulting measure had a theoretical range of 0 to 18.

For the HSB sample, INFOTH is a fundamentally similar variable with a few differences in the particular individuals to which the basic stem question is addressed. For the HSB sample, the relevant individuals for whom responses were solicited were: father, mother, guidance counselor, teachers, friends or relatives, military recruiters, and college recruiters. Preliminary analyses indicated that the differences in the way this variable is measured in the two samples do not substantially affect the overall validity of this concept. Consequently, we employed a similar combination strategy to yield a composite indicator ranging from a low of 0 to a high of 18.

Aspirations (ASP) was measured by two indicators—educational aspirations and occupational aspirations. For educational aspirations the respondent was asked to indicate the highest level she or he would like to attain. Categories ranged from a low of less than high school to a high of graduate or professional school. For occupational aspirations the respondent was asked to indicate the area of work she or he planned to enter. These areas were then recoded using Duncan (1961) socioeconomic index (SEI) scores. The resulting aspiration measure was a weighted linear combination of these two indicators. Weights were determined by regressing each on the dependent variables on occupational attainment. This variable is identical for the HSB sample.

Outcome Variables

Educational attainment (EDATT) was measured by three variables: years in vocational or trade school, highest level to college, and kind of degree earned. These were combined and recoded to create a single categorical variable consisting of eight categories ranging from a low of no college or vocational training to a high of advanced degree for the NLS sample. The major difference in EDATT for the HSB sample is that these respondents have been out of high school only two years. Thus, we can expect that the HSB measure will be less representative of the ultimate attainment process than the NLS measure. With this in mind, the actual measure used for the HSB sample consists of three indicators: whether or not the respondent completed high school, number of years in vocational or trade school, and highest level of college attained. These three indicators were combined and recoded to create a single 10-category variable ranging from a low of "did not complete high school" to a high of "one or more years of college."

Occupational attainment (OCCATT) was measured by a single indicator, the job the NLS respondent held as of the 1980 follow-up. The responses were then coded based on census classifications and then recoded using Duncan SEI scores. Occupational attainment was not assessed for the HSB sample because these respondents were too recently graduated from high school to make such an assessment meaningful.

Data Analysis

The basic dynamics of the model are assumed to be as follows: Background factors are those crucial elements that the individual brings to this process; they then are assumed to have a direct impact upon those school factors that are relevant for subsequent attainment. The effects of these school factors are then mediated in some respects by the social-psychological factors which, in turn, have a direct impact on status. As we view the process for blacks, we feel that the social-psychological component should have less of a mediating effect on school factors. As a result, school factors should have a more direct effect on status.

The particular estimation techniques used in the analyses are those usually found in the status attainment literature. These strategies, commonly referred to as path analytic techniques, have proven to be quite informative with respect to understanding the dynamics of status attainment (for a discussion of these strategies see Goldberger & Duncan, 1973; Hanushek & Jackson, 1977; Pedhazur, 1982). Each coefficient appearing in a table had to be significant at the .025 level in order to be retained. Following this, each coefficient had to have a tolerance level of at least .05 to remain in the equation. Thus, all variables appearing in the tables meet these requirements. *Where blanks appear, the variables did not meet these requirements.* There are no unmeasured variables in the model. Residual paths are not included in the path diagrams because we did not wish to complicate the presentation. They are easily interpretable from the table of nonzero paths. There the R^2 value for each dependent variable is given, and the error component associated with each is simply $1-R^2$.

Some scholars have questioned the assumption that the status attainment process can be explained satisfactorily by a recursive model. They suggest that there are reciprocal effects that should be taken into consideration. We contend that, in a theoretical sense, the use of reciprocal models is only important when one is actually concerned about estimating their effects. In this case, that is not our basic concern. Also, we do not believe that our recursive estimation is unrealistic. Although Pedhazur (1982) mentions both motivation and aspirations in this vein, it is our contention that only an estimation that involved motivation directly would create unrealistic estimates. It is our position, in other words, that aspirations do not function in the same reciprocal fashion as does motivation, especially given the particular measurement of aspirations used here. In addition, we compensate in some sense for aspirations being based on performance by the use of grades as a predictor of aspirations and then using aspirations as a predictor of achievement measured in terms of educational attainment. Such a situation would have the result of at least producing statistically reliable (if not statistically consistent) results, and would also be in line with the argument raised by Pedhazur. Our assumptions aside, when residuals were plotted against predicted scores for the full model, there did not appear to be any serious violations of the regression assumptions.

REFERENCES

Alexander, K.L. and B.K. Eckland. Sex differences in educational attainment process. *American Sociological Review*, 1974, 39, 668–682.

Alexander, K.L., M. Cook, and E.L. McDill. Curriculum tracking and educational stratification. *American Sociological Review*, 1978, 43, 7–66.

Allen, W.R. Preludes to attainment: Race, sex and student achievement orientations. *The Sociological Quarterly*, 1980, 21, 65–79.

American Association of University Professors. *Footnotes*, 1983, 1 (fall).

Bachman, J.G. *Youth in transition, Vol. 2: The impact of family background and intelligence on tenth grade boys.* Ann Arbor: Survey Research Center, Institute for Social Research, 1970.

Brazziel, W. and M. Brazziel. *Recent college and university enrollment patterns of black students in states affected by Adams-Califano litigation.* Atlanta: Southern Education Foundation, 1980.

Brookover, W.B., et al. *School social systems and student achievement.* New York: Praeger, 1979.

Carnegie Commission on Higher Education. *From isolation to mainstream: Problems of the colleges founded for negroes.* New York: McGraw-Hill, 1971.

Coleman, J.S., et al. *Equality of educational opportunity.* Washington, DC: US Government Printing Office, 1966.

Coleman, J.S., T. Hoffer and S. Kilgore. *High school achievement: Public, Catholic and private schools compared.* New York: Basic Books, 1982.

Cosby, A.G. The disadvantaged student, goal blockage, and the occupational aspirations of southern youth. Paper presented at the Association of Southern Agricultural Workers Meeting, 1969.

Crain, R. and R. Mahard. School racial composition and black college attendance and achievement test performance. *Sociology of Education*, 1978, 51, 81–100.

DeBord, L., L. Griffin, and M. Clark. Race and sex differences in the schooling process of rural and small town youth. *Sociology of Education*, 1977, 42, 85–102.

Duncan, O.D. A socioeconomic index for all occupations. In A. Reiss (ed.), *Occupations and social status.* New York: Free Press, 1961.

Epps, E. Correlates of academic achievement among northern and southern Negro students. *Journal of Social Issues*, 1969, 25 (3), 55–70.

Goldberger, A. and O.D. Duncan. *Structural education models in the social sciences.* New York: Seminar Press, 1973.

Hanushek, E.A. and J. Jackson. *Statistical methods for social scientists.* New York: Academic Press, 1977.

Hogan, D.P. and D.L. Featherman. Racial stratification and socioeconomic change in the American North and South. *American Journal of Sociology*, 1977, 83 (1): 100–126.

Hout, M. and W.R. Morgan. Race, sex and educational attainment. *American Journal of Sociology*, 1975, 81, 365–394.

Howell, F.M. and W. Frese. Race, sex and aspirations: Evidence for the "race convergence" hypothesis. *Sociology of Education*, 1979, 52, 34–46.

Kerckhoff, A. and R. Campbell. Black-white differences in the educational attainment process. *Sociology of Education*, 1977, 50, 15–27.

Kuvlesky, W.P. and G.W. Ohlendorf. A rural/urban comparison of the occupational status orientations of Negro boys. *Rural Sociology*, 1969, 33 (2), 141–152.

McPartland, J. The relative influence of school and of classroom desegregation on the academic achievement of ninth grade Negro students. *Journal of Social Issues*, 1969, 25 (3), 93–102.

Page, E.B. and T. Keith. Effects of U.S. private schools: A technical analysis of two recent claims. *Educational Researcher*, 1981, 10 (7), 7–17.

Pedhazur, E.J. *Multiple regression in behavioral research*. New York: Holt, Rinehart & Winston, 1982.

Picou, J.S. and M.T. Carter. Significant other influence and aspirations. *Sociology of Education*, 1976, 46:12–22.

Porter, J. Race, socialization, and mobility in early occupational attainment. *American Sociological Review*, 1974, 39, 303–316.

Portes, A. and K. Wilson. Black–white differences in educational attainment. *American Sociological Review*, 1976, 41, 414–431.

Rosenbaum, J.E. Track misperceptions and college plans. *Sociology of Education*, 1980, 53, 74–88.

Sewell, W.H., A.O. Haller, and G.W. Ohlendorf. The educational and early occupational attainment process: Replication and revision. *American Sociological Review*, 1970, 35, 1014–1027.

Sewell, W.H., A.O. Haller, and A. Portes. The educational and early occupational attainment process. *American Sociological Review*, 1969, 34, 82–92.

Thomas, G.E. *Race and sex effects on access to college*. Baltimore, Maryland: Center for Social Organization of Schools. Johns Hopkins University, 1977.

Thomas, G.E. Influence of aspirations, achievement and educational expectations on black–white post-secondary enrollment. *Sociological Quarterly*, 1979, 20, 209–222.

Wilson, K. The effects of integration and class on black attainment. *Sociology of Education*, 1979, 52, 84–98.

9

Black and White Students' Academic Performance in Majority White and Majority Black College Settings

MICHAEL T. NETTLES
Educational Testing Service
Princeton, New Jersey

On February 15, 1978, the US Department of Health, Education, and Welfare (DHEW) published "Criteria Specifying the Ingredients of Acceptable Plans to Desegregate State Systems of Public Higher Education" (*Federal Register* 1978, 43[32], 6658–6664). The criteria set forth the requirements for effectively planning desegregation of public colleges and universities in 19 southern and border states. These states had been found guilty of unconstitutionally operating *de jure* segregation prior to 1954. The criteria pertain to admitting, recruiting, and retaining students; starting new academic programs; enhancing black colleges; changing the racial composition of college faculties; and appointing blacks to administrative and lay leadership roles in colleges and universities.

This chapter is concerned with the criterion requiring states to eliminate the dual system of higher education by increasing the percentage of black students attending white universities and the percentage of white students attending black universities. The chapter examines effects that attending the two types of universities (predominantly white and predominantly black) exert upon students' performance, attitudes, and behaviors. It also examines the predictors of black and white students' performance at each of the two types of universities.

The tendency for blacks and whites to enroll in higher education institutions where they are in the minority racial group has increased steadily over the past two decades. Census data on enrollment of blacks in predominately black institutions show that in 1964, the majority (51%) of black students were in predominately, mostly historically, black colleges. Since that time, the proportion of black students in predominately black colleges has declined. In 1966, almost one half (48%) of the blacks enrolled in higher education were in black colleges. Ten years later, only 18 percent of all blacks were enrolled in black colleges (National Advisory Committee on Black Higher Education and Black Colleges and Universities, 1978, p. 13). Similarly, the 44,828 white students enrolled in black colleges represented only 0.04 percent of all white college students enrolled in higher education in 1982 (NCES, 1985), but this modest rate constitutes a notable increase over prior generations. The increasing attendance of blacks and whites in opposite-race institutions is largely attributable to pressure by federal judges upon both black and white colleges and universities to recruit, admit, and retain greater numbers of minority students.

Examples of judicial pressure have emerged in a variety of federal court cases. For example, in *Adams v. Richardson* (1973) a federal judge required 19 state governments to assure greater recruitment, admission, and retention of minority students in both black and white colleges. In *Hunnicutt et al. v. Burge* (1972) a different federal judge directed the state of Georgia to enroll a majority of white students in the state's historically black colleges. In *Geier v. Alexander* (1984) yet another federal judge signed a legal settlement that contained a commitment from leaders of both black and white public universities to admit and facilitate the enrollment of a greater percentage of minority students on their campuses. In the *Geier* case the judge went so far as to order a quota of 50 percent white enrollment at Tennessee's only black public university by 1990.

In response to pressure from the federal courts, colleges and universities have instituted recruitment programs to achieve greater minority enrollments. Bellamy (1982) describes how one black college in the state of Georgia has responded by instituting substantial financial aid programs for white students and by staffing many of its chief administrative positions (previously held by blacks) with white professionals as a means of attracting and retaining white students. These actions typify measures recently taken by both black and white colleges and universities throughout the South to attract "other-race" students. But curiously, despite the advent of such procedures, very little is known about the retention rates, progression rates, and academic performance of black and white students when they are in the minority compared to majority racial groups on campus (US Department of Education, 1982). Even less is known about their backgrounds, attitudes, and behaviors, and about how these characteristics affect their college performance. Comparisons of this kind are important for illustrating the challenges that lie ahead for both black and white institutions to achieve genuine racial integration beyond merely admitting "other-race" students.

PREVIOUS RESEARCH

Prior to the 1964 Civil Rights Act, characterizing the enrollments of institutions in most states constituted a simple task. Blacks generally attended black colleges, and whites generally attended white colleges. Black colleges and universities have historically been characterized as enrolling students less prepared academically and financially than students at white institutions (Hills, Klock, & Lewis, 1963; McGrath, 1965; Jaffe, Adams, & Meyers, 1968). One effect of higher education desegregation upon black institutions has perhaps been to heighten this tendency. For example, as early as 1968, only 14% of 938 black finalists for the National Achievement Scholarship Program chose to attend a black college or university (Blumenfeld, 1968). Similarly, a more recent study of black freshmen in North Carolina's predominantly white colleges reported that students of higher academic achievement and higher income were attracted to the predominantly white universities (Davis & Borders-Patterson, 1973).

In the North Carolina study and others like it in recent years, the reasons given by black students for attending white universities include their perception of white universities as offering higher-quality facilities and academic programs and culminating in degrees with greater market value than those of traditionally black institutions (Davis & Borders-Patterson, 1973). Although a variety of other factors may also contribute to this enrollment trend, the existing research literature is devoid of comparative data on the background characteristics of black students at black and white colleges beyond their SES, academic ability, and their reason for attending a black or white institution.

There is also limited published research on the characteristics of white students at black institutions. The few available studies characterize white students on black campuses as commuter students, older than the average student on campus, and not very involved in campus activities outside the classroom (Brown & Stein, 1972; Nettles et al., 1985). Unlike comparative studies of black students, studies of white students tend to provide little information on the socioeconomic status and academic achievement of white students at black campuses as compared to whites at white campuses.

Research on the predictors of students' performance at black and white institutions is also very limited. Using the 1972 National Longitudinal Survey (NLS) data base to predict black students' grades at four two-year and four-year black and white colleges, Braddock and Dawkins (1981b) found that high school grades were stable predictors of black students' performance at all colleges, while Scholastic Aptitude Test scores were significant at only one of the two-year black colleges. Braddock also found that noncognitive factors such as study habits, social class, and prior desegregation experiences inconsistently affect students' grades, and that these effects did not appear to vary by type or predominant race of the institution. Comparing students' performance at black and white institutions, Ayres (1983) found that after controlling for entering aptitude of college students, both black and white students attending white colleges and universities in North Carolina performed better on the National Teachers Examination (NTE) than black and white students attending black colleges and universities.

On the other hand, Anderson and Hrabowski (1977) discovered no difference in the graduate school performance of black students with undergraduate degrees from black colleges as compared to white colleges. And similarly, Baratz and Ficklen (1983), in a study of black college graduates of both black and white institutions, found no overall difference in the employment and graduate school attendance rates of the two groups. Absolutely no studies appear in the literature comparing the relationship of background, college attitudes, and experiences to white students' performance at black as compared to white colleges.

The dearth of research characterizing the backgrounds and college experiences of black and white students and the relationship of these characteristics to performance severely weakens our ability to explain the qualitative effects of desegregation in higher education. This study will attempt to begin filling that void by comparing black and white students on black and white college campuses, illustrating some of their similarities and differences and predicting their college grade point averages using a variety of cognitive and noncognitive precollege and in-college variables.

METHODOLOGY

This study is based upon a survey of 4944 students attending 12 predominantly white and six predominantly black public colleges and universities located in 10 southern and mid-Atlantic states. The students were randomly selected from the sophomore, junior, and senior classes at their universities in the fall of 1982. The sampling procedure was designed to select 300 students from each of the 18 institutions—50 black and 50 white students from each of the sophomore, junior, and senior classes—for a total of 5400 students. However, on several campuses there were too few "other-race" students to select 50 from each class. In these cases, all sophomores, juniors, and seniors in the minority group were selected, resulting in an original sample size of 4944 students. The sample size of 2636 for the analyses in this chapter represents a return rate of 53%.

TABLE 9.1.   Students in the Sample

	Number of Students		
	Black	*White*	*Total*
Black public universities	891	194	1,098
White public universities	496	1,042	1,538
TOTAL	1,387	1,241	2,636

Two types of institutions are included in this paper: black and white public universities. The number of black and white students in the sample are shown in Table 9.1.

Each student in the sample received a survey instrument entitled, "The Student Opinion Survey" (SOS), which was designed to collect various personal, academic, demographic, and attitudinal data. The SOS was developed for the study entitled "The Causes and Consequences of Students' College Performance: A Focus Upon Black and White Students Retention Rates, Progression Rates and Grade Point Averages" (Nettles et al., 1985). The SOS contains 109 questions about students' academic and personal backgrounds, opinions and perceptions about various aspects of their university, college performance, attitudes and behaviors in college, and aspirations. Published instruments useful in developing the SOS include Educational Testing Service's College and University Environmental Scale (CUES II) and the Higher Education Evaluation Kit of the Center for the Study of Evaluation at the University of California, Los Angeles (Pace, 1975).

Because the sampling procedure involved selecting equal numbers of black and white students at each institution, a weighting scheme was applied to the data analyses to control for oversampling of students in the minority (whites at black institutions and blacks at white institutions) at each campus. The formula used to weight each student response is shown in Figure 9.1.

FIGURE 9.1.   Weighting Formula

$$\text{Weight} = \frac{\text{\% of students at the institution who are of respondent's race}}{\text{\% of institutional sample who are of respondent's race}} \times \frac{\text{\% of total student population who attend respondent's institution}}{\text{\% of total sample who attend respondent's institution}} \times \frac{N}{N}$$

The analyses used in this chapter serve the following three purposes: (1) to compare the background, attitudinal factors, and performance characteristics of black and white students on black and white college campuses; (2) to illustrate the significant predictors of black and white students when in the majority as compared to the minority racial group on their campus; and (3) to compare the significant predictors of black and white student performance at both black and white colleges and universities.

Duncan's Multiple Range Test is used to compare the four groups of students—blacks on white campuses, blacks on black campuses, whites on white campuses, and whites on black campuses—on background, attitudinal factors, and performance variables. Analyses of variance (ANOVA) is used to illustrate the significance of the differences among the four groups on each variable. Pearson product moment correlations are employed to illustrate the direct relationships between interval-level student variables and students' cumulative college grade point averages. Finally, four stepwise multiple regression analyses are used to illustrate the significant predictors of black and white students' college grade point averages at black and white colleges and universities. Stepwise regressions are used in order to allow all variables to be entered concurrently into the equation, in this way isolating the independent effects of each predictor variable with all others in the model statistically controlled. Variables are considered statistically significant if they contribute to the model at the .05 level of significance.

Dependent Variable.   The dependent variable in this study is students' cumulative college grade point average (CCGPA) representing students' overall college performance. This was self-reported by students on the SOS, which requested students to indicate their letter grade equivalent GPA by choosing one grade from a list of nine. The nine-point scale is as follows:

1 = A	4 = B	7 = C
2 = A−	5 = B−	8 = C−
3 = B+	6 = C+	9 = D or less

These grades are analyzed statistically by using the nine-point ordinal scale.

Independent Variables.   Seventeen independent variables are analyzed in this chapter. These variables represent many of the students' academic, personal attitude, and behavioral characteristics before and during college. The five precollege characteristics are high school grade point average, type of high school attended, racial composition of high school, composite Scholastic Aptitude Test (SAT) score, and socioeconomic status (SES). The in-college attitudinal and behavioral characteristics are factor scales developed through a factor analysis of 72 items from the SOS. The seven factor scales describing students' in-college attitudes and behaviors are (1) academic integration, (2) feelings that the university is racially discriminatory, (3) student satisfaction, (4) peer group relations, (5) interfering problems, (6) study habits, and (7) socioeconomic status. Socioeconomic status includes parents' income, educational attainment, and occupation.

Six additional variables that are analyzed include age, sex, marital status, transfer status, number of miles between a student's permanent home and his or her high school, and degree aspirations.

Findings

The statistical analyses conducted in this study reveal grave differences among the four groups of students as well as important differences in the predictors of their college performance. The comparative analyses are discussed first, followed by the multivariate predictive analyses.

Tables 9.2 and 9.3 illustrate the Duncan's multiple range test analyses showing the relationship between minority students and majority students on both black and white campuses using a variety of performance, attitudinal, and behavioral characteristics. These tables reveal no consistent patterns along racial lines nor by institutional type for the performance variables, but there are some patterns in terms of the attitudinal and behavioral variables. In general, students are more similar to other students on their same campus than they are to students of the same race at a different type of institution.

Academic Performance Comparisons.   Table 9.2 illustrates the comparisons of black and white students on black and white campuses in terms of both precollege and in-college academic performance. The performance measures include SAT scores, high school grade point averages (HSGPA), college cumulative grade point averages (CCGPA), and college progression rates. White students on white college campuses exhibit higher levels of performance than the other three groups on two of the four performance variables. Specifically, whites on white campuses have the highest average composite SAT scores and fastest progression rates among the four groups. The average composite SAT scores reported by white students on white campuses is 1010.3; followed in descending order by

TABLE 9.2.   Relationship Between Academic Performance Variables and Minority and Majority Students on Black and White College Campuses

Dependent Variable	Analysis of Variance (F-Model)	Grouping	Mean	Race of Student and University
SAT	359.36[1]	A	1010.3	Whites on white campuses
		B	949.4	Whites on black campuses
		C	864.4	Blacks on white campuses
		D	759.8	Blacks on black campuses
High School GPA	50.66[1]	A	3.08 (B+)	Whites on white campuses
		A	3.29 (B+)	Blacks on white campuses
		B	4.10 (B)	Whites on black campuses
		B	4.18 (B)	Blacks on white campuses
College GPA	28.71[1]	A	4.14 (B)	Whites on black campuses
		B	4.50 (B)	Whites on white campuses
		C	5.19 (B−)	Blacks on black campuses
		D	5.95 (C+)	Blacks on white campuses
Progression Rate (credit hours)	54.74[1]	A	15.61	Whites on white campuses
		B	14.72	Blacks on white campuses
		C	13.52	Blacks on black campuses
		D	11.90	Whites on black campuses

[1]Significant at .001 level (degrees of freedom = 4).

whites on black campuses, 949.4; blacks on white campuses, 864.4; and blacks on black campuses, 759.8. In terms of progression rates, white students on white campuses have the fastest progression rates, at 15.6 credit hours per term; followed by blacks on white campuses, 14.7; blacks on black campuses, 13.5; and whites on black campuses, 11.9. Each group is significantly different from all others on both the SAT and progression rate variables. White students on white campuses also report the highest high school grade point averages, but not significantly higher than blacks on white campuses.

Whites at black colleges exhibit significantly higher college grade point averages than the other three groups, but they have the slowest college progression rates with 11.9 average credit hours per term of enrollment. White students on black campuses exhibit superior college grade performance (CCGPA of B+), and relatively average performance on the SAT (949.4) and HSGPA (B).

Black students on white campuses have relatively high high-school grades (B+), but rank third in terms of SAT scores (864.4), rank second in terms of progression rates (14.7), and have the lowest college grade point averages among the four groups. Black students on black campuses, on the other hand, report the lowest high school grades, lowest SAT scores, next to lowest college progression rates, and next to the lowest college grade point averages. However, black students on black campuses have significantly higher CCGPAs than black students on white campuses.

Overall, the group comparisons on the academic variables indicate that white students on white campuses have the best precollege preparation as shown by their high school grades and SAT scores, and black students on black campuses are least prepared prior to entering college. By contrast, black students on white campuses appear well prepared for college in terms of high school grades, but have relatively low composite SAT scores. White students on black campuses appear to have average overall preparation for college, and they are better prepared than black students on the same campus. Whites on black campuses have roughly the same high school GPA (B+) as blacks on the same campuses, but their composite SAT scores are nearly 200 points higher. However, the average composite SAT score of white students on black campuses is 60 points below that of white students on white campuses.

These data suggest that in terms of academic preparation and performance, the "best" black students attend white institutions along with the "best" white students. Since this trend certainly did not exist until recently, desegregation may have had the effect of attracting the best prepared black students away from black colleges into white institutions, and relatively average white students into black colleges. At the same time, however, the better prepared black students who attend white colleges have lower college grades than their black counterparts attending black colleges. The regression analyses presented later will help to explain some of the probable causes for the lower grades of blacks attending white colleges. In terms of academic performance in college, the lower progression rates of white students on black campuses (11.9 credit hours per term) suggest that many white students at black colleges attend on a part-time basis; therefore, while black colleges have succeeded in attracting greater numbers of white students, it appears that the new arrivals are not traditional college-aged individuals. They are likely older, nonresidential students (Nettles et al., 1985).

Attitudinal and Behavioral Comparisons. Table 9.3 illustrates the comparisons among the four groups on nine attitudinal and behavioral characteristics that represent measures of quality of the college experience or factors that are found to influence college performance. A major goal of higher education desegregation should be not only to enroll greater numbers of minority students, but also to assure that minority and majority students have equally high quality college experiences. In addition, such factors as students' satisfaction with their university, peer group relations, academic integration, study habits, interfering problems, degree aspirations, and feelings of racial discrimination have been found to be consistent predictors of students' college performance (Astin, 1982; Nettles et al., 1985).

Table 9.3 shows that among the four groups, white students on white campuses experience significantly greater satisfaction with their university, have more satisfactory peer group relations, good study habits, very low feelings of being racially discriminated against, and very few problems that interfere with their school work. In stark contrast, whites on black campuses are the least satisfied with their universities among the four groups, report high feelings of racial discrimination, have the poorest peer group relations, and show only average study habits. Whites on black campuses, as well as whites on white campuses, have relatively low aspirations for pursuing a degree beyond the baccalaureate degree. They also do not experience many problems that interfere with their school work. White students on black campuses are more likely than the other three groups to be married (49.7% are married students compared to 12% of whites on white campuses and 8% of blacks on both white and black campuses). White students on black campuses have high academic integration (signaling favorable relationships with faculty) while whites on white campuses have relatively low academic integration. It appears that students in general have higher academic integration at black colleges than at white institutions; this academic integration is probably more closely associated with institutional rather than students' background or academic characteristics.

Blacks on white campuses and blacks on black campuses appear to be more similar to each other attitudinally and behaviorally than the two groups of white students. However, there are some differences. Blacks on white campuses, surprisingly, indicate being substantially more satisfied with their university than blacks on black campuses. However, among the four groups, blacks on white campuses feel more racially discriminated against and among the four groups are the least academically integrated into their campus environments. By contrast, while blacks on black campuses exhibit relatively low satisfaction with their university, they experience relatively low racial discrimination, and have the highest academic integration among the four groups. Both groups of black students indicate having equally good peer group relationships and equally high aspirations for pursuing degrees beyond the baccalaureate. But they also indicate having more problems that impede their academic efforts than

TABLE 9.3. Relationship Between Academic Performance Variables and Minority and Majority Students on Black and White College Campuses

Dependent Variable	Analysis of Variance (F-Model)	Grouping	Mean	Race of Student and University
Student satisfaction with university	95.72[1]	A	.277	Whites on white campuses
		B	.068	Blacks on white campuses
		C	−.468	Blacks on black campuses
		D	−.822	Whites on black campuses
Peer group relations	26.48[1]	A	.024	Whites on white campuses
		A	.020	Blacks on white campuses
		A	−.029	Blacks on black campuses
		B	−.974	Whites on black campuses
Academic integration	39.12[1]	A	.374	Blacks on black campuses
		A	.242	Whites on black campuses
		B	−.017	Whites on white campuses
		C	−.334	Blacks on white campuses
Study habits	30.07[1]	A	.134	Whites on white campuses
		A	.056	Blacks on white campuses
		B	.205	Whites on black campuses
		B	.242	Blacks on black campuses
Interfering problems	45.09[1]	A	.339	Blacks on white campuses
		B	.140	Blacks on black campuses
		C	−.270	Whites on black campuses
		C	−.301	Whites on white campuses
Degree aspirations	12.45[1]	A	.786	Blacks on black campuses
		A	.715	Blacks on white campuses
		B	.589	Whites on white campuses
		B	.558	Whites on black campuses
Feelings of racial discrimination	159.74[1]	A	.786	Blacks on white campuses
		B	.487	Whites on black campuses
		C	−.353	Blacks on black campuses
		C	−.366	Whites on white campuses
Marital status	40.24[1]	A	.497	Whites on black campuses
		B	.124	Whites on white campuses
		C–B	.089	Blacks on black campuses
		C	.070	Blacks on white campuses
Miles from permanent home	63.30[1]	A	3.44	Blacks on white campuses
		B	3.20	Whites on white campuses
		C	2.67	Blacks on black campuses
		D	2.04	Whites on black campuses

[1]Significant at .001 level (degrees of freedom = 4).

white students. While blacks on white campuses appear to have relatively good study habits, the study habits of black students on black campuses are the weakest among the four groups. Blacks on white campuses are more likely than the other groups to attend college a greater distance from home.

Effective desegregation plans might reasonably address the differential quality of experiences of students attending both black and white institutions. Of particular concern are the high feelings of racial discrimination of minority students attending both black and white institutions (blacks on white campuses and whites on black campuses). Some of the differences between minority and majority students appear to be due to differences in the operations of black colleges and white colleges. For example, students of both races on the same campuses are similarly academically integrated, and have similar study habits and similar satisfaction with their institution. Specifically, black and white students on white campuses have relatively low academic integration, but are more satisfied and have better study habits than students of both races at black colleges. Some negative experiences, however, are due to peculiarities of certain groups of students. The fact that white students on black campuses have relatively weak peer group relationships, for example, is most likely due to their greater likelihood of being married, their greater tendency to attend part-time and their higher age.

Based upon these comparative analyses, it appears that desegregation can thus far be characterized as having resulted in different levels of feelings of discrimination and dissatisfaction among students. Greater efforts should be made to reduce the feelings of discrimination of black and white students in the minority group on college campuses. Other factors employed in this research describing the experiences of college students of both races relate more to the type of institutions they attend, their ethnicity, and their level of personal maturity, rather than the predominant race of their institution. The next part of this analysis examines ways in which students' academic, attitudinal, and behavioral characteristics affect their college grades.

Multivariate Analyses.   Tables 9.4 through 9.7 illustrate the results of zero-order correlation analyses and regression analyses measuring the effects of several independent variables upon students' cumulative grade point average (CCGPA). A separate model is presented for each of the four student groups, but each model contains the same 17 independent variables. The purpose of these analyses is to compare and contrast the significant predictors of minority versus majority students' CCGPA on both black and white campuses. The significant predictors are the ones that should be the target of efforts to improve students' performance.

TABLE 9.4. Pearson Product-Moment Correlation and Regression of Students' College Grade Point Average on Student Academic, Personal, Attitudinal, and Behavioral Characteristics—White Students on White Campuses

	β^1	$Beta^2$	t	r	N
SAT Score	.024	.186	6.426**	.282	1042
SES	.042	.005	0.210	-.066	965
Sex (0 = female; 1 = male)	-.339	-.088	-3.232**	—	1037
High School GPA	.344	.281	9.633**	.410	—
Marital Status (0 = single; 1 = married)	-.245	-.035	-1.331	—	—
Type of High School (0 = public; 1 = private)	-.197	-.033	-1.279	—	—
Major Field of Study	.041	.059	2.362**	—	—
Transfer (0 = yes; 1 = no)	.148	.038	1.492	—	—
Miles from Permanent Home	-.029	-.018	-0.693	.009	1037
Fit between Racial Composition of High School and College	.075	.019	0.754	—	—
Highest Expected Degree (0 = Bachelor's or less; 1 = Master's or more)	.337	.085	3.190**	—	—
Academic Integration	.387	.174	5.912**	.201	1042
Feelings of Racial Discrimination	-.359	-.107	-3.541**	.025	1042
Student Satisfaction	.472	.189	5.892**	.015	1042
Peer Group Relations	.123	.052	1.809	.020	1042
Interfering Problems	-.925	-.381	-12.874**	-.380	1042
Study Habits	.391	.169	5.777**	.333	1042
Constant	5.73				
F (Equation)		42.95**			
R^2		.449			

**Significant at the .001 level.

TABLE 9.5. Pearson Product-Moment Correlation and Regression of Students' College Grade Point Average on Student Academic, Personal, Attitudinal, and Behavioral Characteristics—Black Students on White Campuses

	β^1	Beta²	t	r	N
SAT Score	.099	.078	2.22*	.153	891
SES	.082	.014	0.41	.108	732
Sex (0 = female; 1 = male)	-.131	-.039	-1.13	—	—
High School GPA	.270	.245	7.01**	.288	886
Marital Status (0 = single; 1 = married)	-.285	-.043	-1.25	—	—
Type of High School (0 = public; 1 = private)	.006	.000	0.02	—	—
Major Field of Study	.009	.014	0.43	—	—
Transfer (0 = yes; 1 = no)	.324	.093	2.82**	—	—
Miles from Permanent Home	-.052	-.034	-1.01	-.003	887
Fit between Racial Composition of High School and College	-.180	-.049	-1.48	—	—
Highest Expected Degree (0 = Bachelor's or less; 1 = Master's or more)	.487	.128	3.79**	—	—
Academic Integration	.293	.153	3.69**	.173	891
Feelings of Racial Discrimination	-.041	-.020	-0.45**	.053	891
Student Satisfaction	.317	.150	3.65**	.046	891
Peer Group Relations	.152	.083	2.29**	.110	891
Interfering Problems	.747	.376	9.90**	-.345	891
Study Habits	.120	.059	1.57	.229	891
Constant	5.89				
F (Equation)		17.20**			
R^2		.302			

*Significant at the .05 level.
**Significant at the .001 level.

TABLE 9.6. Pearson Product–Moment Correlation and Regression of Students' College Grade Point Average on Student Academic, Personal, Attitudinal, and Behavioral Characteristics—Black Students on Black Campuses

	β^1	$Beta^2$	t	r	N
SAT Score	.072	.004	0.090	.156	496
SES	.018	.028	0.604	.036	496
Sex (0 = female; 1 = male)	.219	.060	1.217	—	—
High School GPA	.331	.290	5.911**	.346	493
Marital Status (0 = single; 1 = married)	.797	.158	3.177**	—	—
Type of High School (0 = public; 1 = private)	.618	.082	1.773	—	—
Major Field of Study	.030	.044	0.976	—	—
Transfer (0 = yes; 1 = no)	.397	.104	2.275*	—	—
Miles from Permanent Home	.025	.022	0.483	-.003	491
Fit between Racial Composition of High School and College	.000	.000	0.000	—	—
Highest Expected Degree (0 = Bachelor's or less; 1 = Master's or more)	.070	.016	0.360	—	—
Academic Integration	.462	.245	4.085**	.234	496
Feelings of Racial Discrimination	-.107	-.042	-0.764	.017	496
Student Satisfaction	.292	.150	2.625**	.034	496
Peer Group Relations	.101	.050	0.970	.015	496
Interfering Problems	-.142	-.062	-1.189	.230	496
Study Habits	.574	.262	4.093**	.433	496
Constant	4.51				
F (Equation)		11.68			
R^2		.373			

*Significant at the .05 level.
**Significant at the .001 level.

TABLE 9.7. Pearson Product-Moment Correlation and Regression of Students' College Grade Point Average on Student Academic, Personal, Attitudinal, and Behavioral Characteristics—White Students on Black Campuses

	β^1	$Beta^2$	t	r	N
SAT Score	.002	.086	1.22	.190	198
SES	.092	.126	1.69	.031	165
Sex (0 = female; 1 = male)	.232	.065	0.77	—	—
High School GPA	.163	.155	1.99*	.256	198
Marital Status (0 = single; 1 = married)	.030	.008	0.12	—	—
Type of High School (0 = public; 1 = private)	.464	.096	1.27	—	—
Major Field of Study	.124	.183	2.54*	—	—
Transfer (0 = yes; 1 = no)	.659	.126	1.76	—	—
Miles from Permanent Home	-.405	-.201	-2.70**	—	—
Fit between Racial Composition of High School and College	.567	.077	1.02	.029	198
Highest Expected Degree (0 = Bachelor's or less; 1 = Master's or more)	.406	.115	1.58	—	—
Academic Integration	.837	.416	4.41**	.208	199
Feelings of Racial Discrimination	-.402	-.202	-1.85	.105	199
Student Satisfaction	.675	.321	3.04**	.109	199
Peer Group Relations	.096	.045	0.53	-.052	199
Interfering Problems	-.616	-.260	-2.89**	.191	199
Study Habits	-.055	-.025	-0.27	.273	199
Constant	7.51				
F (Equation)		5.02**			
R^2		.382			

*Significant at the .05 level.
**Significant at the .001 level.

Tables 9.4 through 9.7 illustrate a somewhat different view at the multivariate level than the bivariate analyses presented earlier. Three variables are significant predictors of CCGPA for each of four groups. The three common significant variables are high school GPA, student satisfaction, and academic integration. In other words, students with higher high-school GPAs, higher student satisfaction, and higher academic integration are likely to have higher CCGPAs regardless of their race or the predominant race of their university. Other significant predictors of CCGPA vary among the four groups.

At predominantly black universities, the variables in the model account for 38.2% of the variance in white students' CCGPA and 37.3% of the black students' CCGPA. White students on black campuses who have the highest average CCGPA (Table 9.7) exhibit, in order of importance, high academic integration, a high level of satisfaction, a low level of interfering problems, proximity to their home, and high high-school GPAs. Also, major field is significant for whites on black campuses. White students majoring in the sciences at black colleges have the highest grades. For black students on black campuses, high high-school GPAs, good study habits, high academic integration, being married, having high satisfaction with the institution, and being a transfer student are the significant predictors.

For white and black students on white campuses, the model explains 44.9 and 30.2% of the variance in CCGPA, respectively. In order of importance, the white students on white campuses with high average CCGPAs have a low number of interfering problems, high HSGPA, high satisfaction with their university, high academic integration, high SAT scores, good study habits, low feelings of discrimination, higher degree aspirations and they tend to be females. Major field is also significant. As with whites on black campuses, whites in the physical and social sciences receive the highest grades. For blacks, high high-school GPA is the most important predictor, followed by high academic integration, high student satisfaction, high degree aspirations, being a nontransfer student, high peer group relations, and high SAT scores.

In terms of unique predictors, black students on white campuses— unlike any of the other groups—are likely to benefit academically if they have high peer group relations. Feelings of discrimination have a greater effect on white students' college grades than on those of blacks. However, white students on white campuses were shown earlier to have lower feelings of racial discrimination than black students. Marital status has a unique effect upon blacks at black colleges. For white students, major field is a significant predictor on both types of campuses. For black students on black campuses, being a transfer student contributes to high CCGPA, whereas for black students on white campuses, being a transfer student has a negative effect on CCGPA.

The correlational analyses indicate that five independent variables have relatively strong relationships to the CCGPAs for all four groups. These variables and the range of their relationship with CCGPA are: high school GPA, .410 to .256; study habits, .433 to .229; interfering problems, .433 to .229; SAT scores, .282 to .153; and academic integration, .34 to .173. Thus at the bivariate level, high high-school GPA, good study habits, a low number of interfering problems, high SAT scores, and high academic integration appear to lead to relatively high CCGPAs for blacks and whites on both black and white college campuses. These findings are consistent with those of other recent studies on students' college performance (Nettles et al., 1985; Braddock, 1981).

Overall, four important observations result from the regression analyses. First, the greatest commonality exists between the two groups on the same campus; therefore, it appears that institutional type is much more of a factor than predominant race of the institution and minority or majority status of the students. This matter is also illustrative of the hazard of comparing different types of colleges and universities. The institutional differences in mission, programs, and enrollment characteristics may be far too great to permit the assumption of similarity in operation and impact.

Second, there are some very important differences between the significant predictors and the rank-order of these significant predictors of black and white students' CCGPAs on the same campuses. At black public universities, six significant variables each are found for blacks and whites, with only three of those being common to both groups. Similarly, at white institutions, 10 significant predictors were found for white students compared to eight for blacks, and only six are common to both groups.

Third, the regression models used in this paper are better suited for predicting white student CCGPAs than those for blacks. The variance explained for the whites on white campuses is 44.9%, compared to 30.2% of the blacks on the same campuses; and on black campuses, 38.2% of the variance is explained, compared to 37.3% for blacks on black campuses.

Finally, much of the cause for the lower performance of blacks on black campuses in comparison to whites on black campuses appears to be explained by lower precollege preparation and relatively poor study habits. For blacks on white campuses, lower CCGPAs appear to be a function of lower precollege preparation, lower academic integration, lower satisfaction with their university, and relatively low SAT scores compared to white students on the same campus. Efforts to improve black students' college performance should take these factors into account.

CONCLUSIONS

It is clear from the analyses presented here that desegregation progress has had an impact upon college student enrollments beyond mixing students by race. The data and analyses presented illustrate possible effects of desegregation: (1) enrollment of better-prepared black students at white institutions; (2) where quality is concerned, mixed experiences of black and white students found on a college campus to constitute the minority group; and (3) overall poorer college performance of black students.

The movement of higher-achieving black students toward white public colleges and universities appears to have the effect of placing a greater burden upon the black institutions to teach larger numbers of underprepared students. Moreover since the movement of white students toward black public universities has not been rapid, black public universities have experienced overall enrollment declines, with a little evidence of stabilization in recent years (National Center for Education Statistics, 1985). Looking toward the future, it may be more difficult for black public universities to attract the sons and daughters of today's black graduates of predominantly white universities. Greater emphasis upon enhancing black public colleges may offer the best hope for increasing their competitiveness in the future.

On the other hand, high-achieving black students who are attending white public universities are generally underperforming in comparison to their white counterparts on the same campuses, and compared to lesser prepared black students on black public college campuses. This presents a challenge for white public universities to explore methods of improving the performance of black students. It is very important in the labor market, as well as for admission to graduate and professional schools, for black undergraduates to perform at a higher level and to enjoy better academic and social experiences in college.

REFERENCES

Adams v. Richardson, 356 F. Supp. 92, (D.D.C. 1973).
Anderson, E.F., and Hrabowski, F.A. (1977 May/June). Graduate school success of black students from white colleges and black colleges. *Journal of Higher Education, 68*(3), 294–303.

Astin, A. (1982). *Minorities in American Higher Education*. San Francisco: Jossey-Bass.

Ayres, W.Q. (1983). Student achievement at predominantly white and predominantly black universities. *American Educational Research Journal, 20*(2), 291–304.

Baratz, J.C., and Ficklen, M. (1983). *Participation of Recent College Graduates in the Labor Market and in Graduate Education*. Princeton: Educational Testing Service.

Bellamy, D.D. (1982, October). *White students—Historically Black Fort Valley State College: A Study of Reverse Desegregation in Georgia. Negro Educational Review, 33*(5), 3–4.

Blumenfeld, W.S. (1968). College preferences of able Negro students: A comparison of those naming predominantly Negro institutions and those naming predominantly white institutions. *College and University, 43*, 330–341.

Braddock, J.H. (1981). Desegregation and black student attrition. *Urban Education, 15*(4), 403–418.

Braddock, J.H. and Dawkins, M. P. (1981). Predicting black academic achievement in higher education. *Journal of Negro Education, 50*(3), 319–345.

Brown, C.J., and Stein, P. (1972, October). The white student in five predominantly black universities. *Negro Educational Review, 23*(4), 148–169.

Davis, J.A., and Borders-Patterson, A. (1973). *Black students in Predominantly White North Carolina Colleges and Universities* (Research Report No. 2). New York: College Entrance Examination Board.

Geier v. Alexander, 427 Supp. 644 (M.D. Tenn. 1984).

Hills, J.R., Klock, J.A., and Lewis, S.C. (1963). *Freshman Norms for the University System of Georgia 1961–62*. Atlanta: Regents of the University System of Georgia.

Hunnicutt et al. v. Burge et al., Civil Action No. 2754, July 5, 1972.

Jaffe, A.J., Adams, W., and Meyers, S.G. (1968). *Negro Higher Education in the 1960s*. New York: Praeger.

McGrath, E. (1965). *The Predominantly Negro College in Transition*. New York: Columbia University, Institute of Higher Education.

National Advisory Committee on Black Higher Education and Black Colleges and Universities (NACBHEBCU). *Higher Education Equity: The Crisis of Appearance Versus Reality*. Washington, D.C.: GPO, 1978.

National Center for Education Statistics. (1985). *The Condition of Education*. Washington, DC: US Department of Education.

Nettles, M.T., Gosman, E.J., Thoeny, A.R., and Dandridge, B.A. (1985). *The Causes and Consequences of College Students' Performance: A Focus on Black and White Students' Attrition Rates, Progression Rates and Grade Point Averages* (final report). Nashville: The Tennessee Higher Education Commission.

Pace, C.R. (1975). *Higher Education Measurement and Evaluation Kit*. Los Angeles: University of California, Graduate School of Education, Center for Study and Evaluation.

US Department of Education, Center for Statistics. (1982). Unpublished tabulations from the 1982 Higher Education General Information Survey (HEGIS).

10
Determining Financial Inequities in Previously Segregated Public Systems of Higher Education

LARRY LESLIE
University of Arizona

JAY HEUBERT
Harvard University

This chapter examines the role of financial analysis in identifying the effects of state-imposed racial segregation in public higher education. It begins with a discussion of the legal framework within which such financial analysis takes place. It then describes a method for comparing a state's financial treatment of its historically black postsecondary institutions with that of its historically white postsecondary institutions.

THE LEGAL FRAMEWORK

Prior to May 17, 1954, the Fourteenth Amendment of the US Constitution permitted state-imposed segregation of the races in education if a state, within its borders, offered black students educational opportunities substantially equal to those offered white students (e.g., *Missouri ex rel Gaines v. Canada*, (1938). This was true for higher education institutions no less than for elementary and secondary schools.

There were some white leaders at the time prepared to swear that public higher-education institutions for black students were equal to those for white students. For example, when blacks alleged that Southern University in Baton Rouge was inferior to the nearby campus of Louisiana State University (LSU), partners in the law firm representing LSU signed a sworn affidavit stating that Southern was in every respect equal or superior to LSU. But this was obviously not the case. To cite only one of many possible facts to the contrary, until the late 1940s there were virtually no public graduate or professional schools for blacks in the South (Berman, 1966). At that time the principal purpose of public postsecondary institutions for blacks, especially in the South, was to train black teachers to serve in segregated black elementary and secondary schools. Precisely because there was no corner of American society where racial inequalities were greater or more apparent, the legal strategy of those who sought to end state-imposed segregation in the United States was to focus on inequalities in higher education.

On several occasions between 1938 and 1950 the US Supreme Court was called upon to decide whether public postsecondary institutions for blacks were equal to those for whites. The court consistently concluded that they were not. In each such case, the court's decision rested in part on financial comparisons between institutions reserved to blacks and those reserved to whites (e.g., *Missouri ex rel Gaines v. Canada,* 1938; *Sipuel v. Board of Regents of the University of Oklahoma,* 1948; *Sweatt v. Painter,* 1950; and *McLaurin v. Oklahoma State Regents,* 1950). Thus analysis of finance and other tangible factors has historically played a central role in litigation over racial discrimination in public higher education. As the discussion here will demonstrate, it continues to do so.

In *Brown v. Board of Education* (1954), the Supreme Court rejected the doctrine of "separate but equal," holding that state-imposed segregation is impermissible even where schools for black students and schools for white students are equal with respect to "physical facilities and other tangible factors. . . ." Since 1954 this principle has been applied to higher education institutions—and to public systems of higher education—no less than to elementary and secondary schools. Courts have consistently declared state-imposed segregation in higher education to be unconstitutional. Further, where states have maintained racially dual systems of public higher education, courts have uniformly recognized that it is not enough for a state to abandon its prior discriminatory purpose; each such state must, in addition, dismantle its dual system and eliminate all vestiges of state-imposed segregation.

The Supreme Court originally articulated this principle in cases involving desegregation of elementary and secondary schools (e.g., *Green v. New Kent County School Board,* 1968; *Swann v. Charlotte-Mecklenburg Board of Education,* 1971; *Milliken v. Bradley,* 1977; *Dayton Board of Education v. Brinkman,* 1979; and *Columbus Board of Education v. Penick,* 1979). This same principle has also been applied routinely in cases involving desegregation of public systems of postsecondary education (e.g., *Geier v. Dunn,* 1972; *Geier v. Blanton,* 1977; *Richardson v. Blanton,* 1979; *Hunnicutt v. Burge,* 1973; *Norris v. State Council of Higher Education,* 1971;

Board of Visitors of the College of William and Mary v. Norris, 1971; *Alabama State Teachers Association v. Alabama Public School and College Authority,* 1968; *US v. State of Louisiana,* 1981; and *US v. State of Alabama,* 1985).

In the two decades after *Brown,* federal courts invalidated most of the legal provisions that required segregation of the races in public education, and Title VI of the Civil Rights Act of 1964 gave the Department of Health, Education and Welfare (DHEW) new authority to attack racial segregation in education. Title VI empowered DHEW to withhold federal funds from racially segregated schools and postsecondary institutions. DHEW was also given authority to refer matters to the US Department of Justice, which could initiate federal lawsuits aimed at eliminating the vestiges of state-imposed segregation in education.

During this period, however, very little progress occurred in reducing the racial identifiability of public postsecondary institutions that had once been segregated by law. Moreover, the postsecondary institutions serving the vast majority of black postsecondary students remained grossly inferior to their historically white counterparts in terms of "physical facilities and other tangible factors."

To address this problem, black students and their parents initiated a lawsuit to compel DHEW to withhold federal funds from systems of public education, including those at the postsecondary level, that remained illegally segregated. This lawsuit, known colloquially as the *Adams* case (*Adams v. Richardson,* 1973; and *Adams v. Califano,* 1977), has had several ramifications relevant to this chapter.

First, DHEW began requiring states with histories of segregation under law to develop statewide plans for desegregating their public systems of postsecondary education. These states came to be known as the *Adams* states, and will be referred to here as such. Second, DHEW promulgated criteria specifying the elements of an acceptable statewide plan for desegregating a public system of higher education (*Federal Register,* 1978).

Significantly, these criteria call for the preservation and enhancement of predominantly black institutions rather than for their elimination or for merger of predominantly black institutions with predominantly white postsecondary institutions. The criteria say that states, in dismantling their racially dual systems of higher education, should among other things give priority consideration to placing at traditionally black institutions any new postbaccalaureate, undergraduate, or professional degree programs. This approach is consistent with the *Adams* decision itself, which says that "[a] predicate for minority access to quality post-graduate program is a viable, coordinated, state-wide higher education policy that takes into account the special problems of minority students and of Black colleges. . . . [T]hese Black institutions currently fulfill a crucial need and will continue to play an important role in Black higher education" (*Adams v. Richardson*, 1973). For reasons discussed below, the assumption that historically black institutions should be preserved and enhanced means that financial analysis is relevant not only to proving that there has been discrimination in the past but also to deciding what steps should be taken to remedy past unequal treatment of historically black institutions.

In this respect, the criteria take an approach different from that taken in cases involving desegregation of elementary and secondary schools. In such cases, the preferred approach has been to merge segregated schools so that what remain are neither "white" schools nor "black" schools (e.g., *Green v. New Kent County School District*, 1968). It is beyond the scope of this chapter to discuss the proper role of predominantly black institutions in efforts to eliminate the vestiges of state-imposed segregation in public higher education, but several articles address this question (e.g., Dimond, 1982; Bell, 1979; Bell, 1982; Wright, 1981).

The "revised criteria," as they later came to be known, have been used by states seeking to develop and implement higher education desegregation plans. They have also been used by DHEW and, more recently, by the Department of Education (ED), in determining whether desegregation measures undertaken by the *Adams* states satisfy Title VI.

In several instances DHEW or ED, having found state higher education systems to be in violation of Title VI, has referred matters to the Department of Justice for initiation of litigation. As a result, the Justice Department has filed lawsuits against higher education systems in three states: Louisiana, Mississippi, and Alabama.

The authors worked on these three cases, one as an attorney at the Justice Department, the other as a finance expert. The latter was asked by the Justice Department to ascertain, in each case, the extent to which predominantly black institutions had received state financial support less than that provided to predominantly white institutions.

The preceding discussion provides several reasons why it is appropriate, as part of a higher education desegregation case, to determine whether predominantly black institutions have received less financial support from the state than have predominantly white institutions.

First, against a background of state-imposed racial segregation in higher education, inferior financial treatment of predominantly black institutions amounts to inferior, illegally discriminatory treatment of black students. Thus, subject to some important qualifications discussed in the sections that follow, past or present funding discrepancies between predominantly black and predominantly white institutions constitute strong evidence of racial discrimination. Moreover, even where such discrepancies are limited to the past it is necessary to inquire whether there exist at present any unremedied vestiges of that past unequal treatment. If so, the state in question remains under a continuing legal obligation to eliminate those vestiges.

In these ways financial analysis can be and has been used to prove that a state is not in compliance with the law. For example, on December 7, 1985, the Federal District Court for the Northern District of Alabama ruled that the State of Alabama had not yet discharged its legal obligation to eliminate the vestiges of past segregation in its system of public higher education. This finding was based, in part, on comparisons between predominantly black and predominantly white institutions with respect to such financial factors as "the relative quality and quantity of [their] facilities and equipment," their "financial positions," the state appropriations they had received, and faculty salaries (*US v. State of Alabama*, 1985).

Second, where there are continuing vestiges of discriminatory treatment, financial analysis can help determine what financial resources are needed in the way of remedy. If predominantly black colleges and universities are to be preserved and enhanced through the desegregation process, as *Adams* and the revised criteria indicate, it is critical to assess just what financial and other resources the predominantly black institutions will need if they are to attain peer status among postsecondary institutions and assume a larger role within public systems of higher education.

In order to make these determinations—whether there has been unequal treatment, what the continuing vestiges of any unequal treatment are, and what financial measures are needed to eliminate those vestiges—it proved necessary to develop a somewhat specialized method of financial analysis. The remainder of this chapter attempts to describe and explain the method used to compare the financial treatment of predominantly black and white institutions in the three states the Justice Department sued. This method, we believe, can be used to analyze similar problems in other states.

THE IMPORTANCE OF FINANCIAL EVIDENCE IN HIGHER EDUCATION DESEGREGATION CASES

Financial evidence is important legally because it is important educationally. There are three reasons for this educational significance: (1) money is the most fundamental resource for providing student programs and services, (2) financial equity is important in and of itself, and (3) money is the principal public policy instrument.

Providing Programs and Services

Each new educational administrator quickly learns that it is money, not curriculum committees or faculty senates, that is the essential ingredient for new or changed educational programs and services. In the educational organization, as in any other, money is power. Without control of a budget, the educational leader is ultimately powerless to improve educational programs and services for students. This realization usually comes as a shock to neophyte administrators schooled in human relations or other concepts of leadership, but the reality soon becomes all too clear: Many concepts, strategies, and personal attributes can contribute to organizational change, but money is the only absolutely essential ingredient.

Without financial resources, the human and logistical requirements for educational change cannot be met. Old personnel can be shuffled, old curricula can be revised, and new or altered facilities can be planned; but without money, very little can be accomplished. New programs and services will require new personnel—hopefully, personnel superior to those presently at hand. They will require new equipment, enhanced facilities, and all kinds of support, each requiring financial resources.

It has been said that money is the lubricant of the educational machinery. With it, the machinery may function smoothly; without it, in time it will not function at all. The case to be made in introducing financial evidence in a higher education desegregation case, then, is that equal funding is the necessary though insufficient condition for equal educational opportunity. Money alone does not guarantee equity, but without it, equity cannot be achieved.

Financial Equity

Even if the previous section were completely fallacious, which it is not, *financial* equity would still be vital in and of itself. Even if somehow money were not necessary for equity in quality of educational services and programs provided, it would still be inequitable to provide fewer financial resources to one racial or ethnic group than to another. One should not be able, for example, to predict the racial or ethnic character of an educational institution by reference to such factors as faculty salaries, travel or research budgets, clerical support, or state appropriations per student. It is important in social legitimacy terms, as well as in legal terms, that educational institutions enrolling mostly minority students be financed at levels equal or quite similar to those enrolling predominantly majority students, taking into account other institutional differences that may affect funding requirements.

Money: The Instrument of Public Policy

The third major reason financial evidence is important to equity considerations in desegregation cases is a corollary of the first two: Money is the primary instrument of public policy. When governments attempt to remedy a problem, they usually either offer financial subsidies or invoke fiscal sanctions. Government intrusions of most other forms are politically less acceptable in most Western democracies. Since money is the principal instrument of public policy, it follows that financial equity should exist as a matter of course.

FINANCIAL ANALYSIS: CONTEXTUAL MATTERS

When speaking of equity in desegregation cases, usually we do not mean that everything must necessarily be equal. By equity we mean equality in resource availability, *all other factors being more or less equal*—which they hardly ever are. Examined in this section are the contextual factors that must be taken into account when equity is judged. Among these are institutional mission or purpose, enrollment size, and enrollment trends.

Mission

In higher education desegregation cases, which deal with equitability in treatment of black and white institutions, no issue is more critical than that of mission. Indeed, in the authors' judgment the outcome of such a case may depend to a great degree on how this issue is resolved. What is meant by the mission issue is whether only institutions of like mission may be compared—on financial or any other grounds. At first glance the issue appears very simple: Because institutional missions vary and because differences in mission mean differences in academic programs, type of faculty employed, facilities, and research equipment (to name a few key educational ingredients), it would seem that only comparisons of like institutions should be made—"like" in this case meaning similar in mission. Indeed, in almost all types of financial comparison, restrictions of mission similarity are the convention. Textbooks and other references advise that only institutions with similar missions should be compared in evaluating institutional financing. Financial comparisons are discussed in a body of literature known as "costing" or "cost analysis." In the literature the term "cost" may take on varying meanings, and surrounding issues involving the use of such definitions are complex. "Cost" as used in this chapter refers to dollars expended.

There is in this same literature, however, an even more fundamental principle, which is often expressed by finance experts in question form: Costs for what purpose? Cost comparisons depend upon what it is we are attempting to learn. If, for example—as is typically the case—our purpose is simply to determine whether equity exists in the financing of colleges with identical missions, then direct comparison is appropriate. However, suppose that mission itself is not distributed equitably. What then?

This is precisely the situation in the so-called *Adams* states. There are no predominantly black research universities and very few true predominantly black doctoral-degree-granting universities. In reality, if not in official documents, such missions were reserved for the predominantly white institutions. Some black universities, particularly the black land-grant institutions, were assigned higher-level research missions, but the means for achieving true research university status were rarely if ever provided.

Again, the question is: Cost for what purpose? If one wishes to determine equality of educational opportunity between predominantly black and white institutions or between black and white students, then mission equivalence as a precondition for comparison must be rejected or applied very cautiously. As written in a report to the court in a higher education desegregation case involving public universities in Alabama:

> In conducting financial analyses and costing comparisons, the normative approach is to compare institutions having similar missions. Typical institutional classification systems are based upon fairly simple proxies for these missions; some annual measure of research funding, number of doctorates awarded, number of graduate programs offered, or general comprehensiveness of curricula commonly are criteria for categorization. Indeed, the several Alabama institutions are classified into several different categories. The normative approach, then, is to compare institutions that are categorized together, the assumption being that institutional missions are a given. In this way some control is exercised for financial differences that may be attributable to such factors as institutional size (enrollment) and complexity of curricula.
>
> The "normative case," however, is not the issue in this litigation. Indeed, the "mission" of institutions as reflected in academic programs and

funding are fundamentally what is at issue. Institutional comparison based upon mission and size would evade, indeed pervert, the issue at hand. To argue that comparisons must be made between institutions of like mission and size is to argue that the present distribution of financial resources, students, and curricula is as it should be. That is, if one is to argue for comparisons only of similar institutions, one is to argue that there can be no comparisons of traditionally black institutions with the two largest, most prestigious, and most expensive traditionally white institutions because the state has not chosen to create a major black research university. This is tantamount to arguing that since Alabama historically has given the bulk of its resources—money, facilities, curricula—to traditionally white institutions, it is now unfair to compare the finances of these institutions to those of the less-historically-favored traditionally black institutions because the latter have not received equal resources! Through this reasoning, any college or university could be removed from financial scrutiny by heaping on it all sorts of human and financial resources. Having done so, in time the institution would have no suitable peer institution. (Leslie, 1985)

Not incidentally, enforcement of normative mission control in making financial comparisons will exclude from the analysis the more costly white institutions and large portions of state enrollments. For example, the exclusion in Alabama would have been about 40 percent of four-year enrollments; in Mississippi 80 percent would have been excluded.

Acceptance of the normative procedure of comparing only institutions of similar missions probably dooms predominantly black institutions to second- or third-class status and insures that their financial support will be commensurately less.

Enrollment and Historical Funding Patterns

All else being equal, on a per-student basis small institutions are more expensive to operate than large institutions. This principle is referred to as "returns to scale," or "economy or diseconomy of scale." Economy of scale is illustrated simply by reference to the chief executive officer (CEO) of an institution. Whether the college enrolls 3000 or 30,000 students, it will require one, but only one, CEO. Whereas the larger institution may pay its CEO considerably more, it will not pay 10 times more. Similarly, in the instructional domain there will be only one department head per area per university, and classes in larger universities on average will be notably larger than in smaller ones, assuming equality in terms of curricular breadth. (In actuality, curricular breadths usually are not equal.) It is common in the *Adams* states to find enrollments at predominantly black institutions one-third to one-fifth as great as enrollments at predominantly white institutions.

Enrollment trend is a closely related factor. During the 1970s, enrollments in many predominantly black colleges and universities in the *Adams* states declined while enrollments at predominantly white institutions grew. (Enrollments in many black colleges and universities now have stabilized or even resumed growth.) If financial resources were a direct function of enrollments per students, financing comparisons would be straightforward; however, this is not the case. Governments tend strongly to add (or, on rare occasions, to subtract) resources incrementally. That is, regardless of enrollments, public collegiate institutions, like other public agencies, almost always receive budgets amounting to the sum received in the previous year plus some modest to moderate increment, ostensibly for inflation, salary increases, and so forth. The principal reason for incrementalism is simply that governments, which typically raise more money each year, must allocate that money on some basis; politically, a flat percentage increase is most acceptable. Another reason is more rational in the traditional sense of the term: Even if enrollments change, large portions of institutional costs will be "fixed"; that is, they will not change quickly. Whether enrollments decline or increase, the CEO and the faculty still must be paid—usually, what they were paid last year plus some increment. Similarly, utility consumption will not decline unless classrooms or buildings are closed, but neither will it grow precipitously unless new facilities are opened. Also, equipment will not be sold or mothballed, nor will large new equipment purchases by made, at least until enrollment patterns are known to be long term. Such actions are themselves taken incrementally.

The result is that costs—that is, amounts expended—on a per-student basis may be deceptive in the short term where enrollment patterns vary. An institution with declining enrollments will appear to be prospering on a dollars-available-per-student basis because costs will not decline commensurate with enrollments, while a growing institution will be better off than appears from dollars per student data because commensurate costs of faculty, buildings, utilities, or administrators will not be required in the short term. Simply put, this is why institutions revel in enrollment growth and despair in enrollment decline.

Finally, historic funding patterns are important because the consequences of long-standing financial inequities cannot be corrected in a single year or even in several years. An institution that has suffered underfunding over decades will not become overnight a quality institution offering a quality education. Buildings constructed, equipment purchased, faculty hired, and, most importantly, a reputation earned persist over many years. Educational change requires enhanced funding in the long term.

THE PROCESS OF FINANCIAL ANALYSIS

What data provide the best financial evidence, and what are the most appropriate units for financial comparison? What data sources are most acceptable for financial analysis? Which data categories provide the best evidence and why? What problems of data comparability and conversion will arise? And what will be the related contentious issues? These form the outline of this section, which examines the process of composing the financial evidence.

The Financial Data and Units of Analysis

The tests applied in selecting financial data for evidence are: (1) appropriateness and (2) general availability. The data must be commonly available, while being the most germane to the legal questions involved. Since the fundamental civil rights issue concerns fairness to individuals, the financial data should be relevant to the student experience; therefore, monies received and expended directly or indirectly on students should be considered. It follows also that the most appropriate unit of analysis will be some measure of dollars per student.

To finance experts, the immediate question is how "students" shall be defined. This is a critical question because the student unit serves as the denominator of any dollar calculations. There are several student unit possibilities but only one best answer. The most appropriate unit is the full-time-equivalent (FTE) student, a standardized student unit. The most common, standard definition of FTE student used historically across the country has been the number of full-time students, as defined by the institution, plus one-third of the part-time enrollment. Thus, it has been assumed that, on average, part-time students enroll for about one-third as much coursework and represent about one-third the costs of full-time students. In recent years, many states have constructed their own definitions of FTE. Often, the Title VI states calculate FTEs by summing all the student credit hours (SCH) taken by students and dividing by a given credit hour equivalent for a full-time student. Typical full-time equivalencies are 15 credits for undergraduates and 9 credits for graduate students. Which "standard," then, should be employed?

The advantage of using the state definition is that one potentially contentious issue can be avoided. The disadvantages are that student credit hour data rarely are available over time and that state's definitions are self-serving. Regarding the standard, for the same reason historic funding patterns were shown to be important in the last section, financial evidence is far stronger if financing patterns can be demonstrated over several decades. Regarding the states' definition, division of credit hours by differing amounts for graduate and undergraduate students reflects present distributions of graduate and undergraduate programs rather than, arguably, what should exist on program equity grounds. Conceptually, this is the same issue raised in the mission section earlier in this chapter. In dividing credit hours by a smaller number for graduate students enrolled, the state implicitly is maintaining that the institution enrolling more graduate students deserves more money because graduate programs have been awarded there and because these programs historically have been funded at higher levels than have undergraduate programs.

An even more extreme illustration of this same principle is the weighted student credit hour unit, which was argued to be the most appropriate student unit in *US v. State of Alabama* (1985). The weighted student credit hour is derived from actual expenditures in the various degree programs at the different degree levels. Of course, expenditures are higher in programs and at levels found most prevalently in the predominantly white institutions, again in considerable part because the state has been more generous to these institutions. In Alabama, the state position was that revenue and expenditure figures should be divided not by simple FTEs or neutral credit hours to obtain dollars-per-student figures, but by weighted credit hours reflecting actual costs (actually, expenditures). If the court had accepted the weighted student credit hour as the appropriate divisor, it would have been accepting the existing distribution, not only of institutional missions in the state but of past funding distributions.

Data Sources and Categories

Financial officers of all stripes agree that annual institutional financial reports are the best source of institutional financial data, which in turn will be divided by the student unit to yield the basic data for comparison. Occasionally, some issue is made of whether the reports are audited or unaudited, but because the two forms of the report very rarely are substantially different, and because the audited reports typically are available much later, either is considered acceptable. Of course, the audited reports are preferable.

Other financial documents sometimes entered into evidence by the states are of little material value; indeed, usually their use would lead the courts to erroneous conclusions. Ultimately, all important financial facts must pass through the institutional financial reports; and thus other data sources normally are at best redundant and at worst misleading. For example, in related litigation against them, the states of Louisiana, Mississippi, and Alabama have variously entered documents reflecting percent of budget requests granted and percent of formula implementation in predominantly black versus predominantly white institutions. The former is poor evidence because it will reflect differences in how much was asked for rather than how much was received—which is all that matters. That budget *requests* are of doubtful value is reflected by the fact that they are known in the trade as "wish lists." They reflect the boldness of CEOs as much as anything.

"Percent of formula implementation" is the amount actually received by an institution, expressed as a percentage of the amount that would have been received if the state funding formula were funded at 100 percent. Invariably, formula implementation rates are greater for predominantly black institutions. The reason is that formula-generated amounts are direct reflections of past allocations of state (and sometimes regional) funds. Because the predominantly white colleges and universities typically have received more funds in the past, formulas typically prescribe greater amounts for them for the future. Partially in recognition of this, the states have funded black public institutions at a higher percentage of formula-specified amounts. (Another factor may be fear of federal intervention.) Thus, it appears from formula implementation data that states are more generous with funds for predominantly black institutions. The reality is usually the reverse.

Data Categories: Breaking the Evidence Down

Nearly all higher education institutions in the United States, and probably all public ones, organize their financial data into standard revenue and expenditure categories. This greatly facilitates data comparability and financial equity analysis. The standard accounting categories are contained in *College and University Business Administration (CUBA)*, published by the National Association of College and University Business Officers (1975). The *CUBA* categories are too numerous to allow easy interpretation of financial data, and many categories would be of limited relevance to equity issues; therefore, only a few categories are analyzed separately while others are combined here into aggregate categories.

Revenue categories include the following:

1. Total educational and general (E&G) income (total of 2–5 below)
2. State and local appropriations
3. Tuition and fees
4. Gifts, grants, and contracts
5. Other income

Expenditure categories include the following:

1. Total educational and general (E&G) expenditures (total of 2–5 and 8–12 below)
2. Instruction
3. Student services
4. Academic support
5. Scholarships and fellowships
6. Total categories 2–5 (categories that impact indirectly on students)
7. Total categories 8–12 (categories that impact indirectly on students)
8. Research
9. Public service
10. Operation and maintenance of physical plant
11. Institutional support
12. All others (unclassifiable expenditures, a category not included in *CUBA*)

Not all categories are equally relevant to equity considerations. Because some categories affect students more directly than others, they are ranked higher. The order adopted here is the appropriate rank ordering as judged by the authors.

Among income categories, total educational and general (E&G) income per student is judged to be of greatest significance, because this indicator reflects all income bearing directly and indirectly upon students. Second most important of the income categories is state and local appropriations: More than any other, this indicator reflects state effort to support institutions. (Local appropriations are very small in the case of four-year institutions.) The tuition and fees category ranks lower than the first two indicators because it affects students in conflicting ways: Higher tuition and fees income means more money for educating students, but also suggests a greater student financial burden. Both state and local appropriations and tuition and fees revenues commonly are used primarily to educate students, and directly or indirectly to support that education.

The gifts, grants, and contracts category bears indirectly on students and thus ranks lower. Most, though not all, income from this category gets used for restricted purposes, and government contracts largely go for research. Nevertheless, there are major spillovers of income from these sources to students: For example, not only does gifts, grants, and contracts money ultimately filter down to such expenditure categories as instruction, but generally an institution with large revenues in the gifts, grants, and contracts category attracts higher-quality faculty than an institution without significant amounts of such funds (an exception would be high-status private liberal arts colleges). The impact of other income also must be qualified. Included here are income from direct purchases of institutional goods and services, federal appropriations, and miscellaneous other sources. Although much of the income generated from this category does not affect students directly, some such income may do so.

Among expenditure categories, total E&G expenditures funds are considered most important for the same reasons that total E&G income is considered most important. Expenditures for instruction is ranked next most important because these funds affect students most directly; that is, instruction is the primary purpose for which most students attend college. Next are total expenditures for instruction, student services, academic support, and scholarships and fellowships funds. The reason for ranking these categories so highly is that collectively they represent the expenditures that bear most directly upon students. Student services funds do affect students directly, as do scholarships and fellowships. Academic support involves expenditures for libraries and for goods and services, such as audiovisual aids, that are associated closely with instruction.

The case for considering research, public service, operation and maintenance of physical plant, and institutional support monies is analogous to the case for including the income categories of government contracts and private gifts and grants: A large research effort will, for example, attract graduate students and superior faculty; public service programs will add to the visibility and prestige of the institution, thus contributing to the status of the student's degree; larger expenditures for physical plant yield more desirable student learning and leisure time environments; and greater funds to institutional support (general administration) should yield better institutional leadership for planning and decision-making; all presumably resulting in a superior learning situation for students.

Data Conversion and Additional Standardization

Problems and Solutions over Time.   Of all the tasks necessary to the comparative analysis of financial reports, experts are most skeptical about whether institutional financial data can be standardized over time. There now have been four editions of *CUBA*, each making some changes in accounting categories, with the major alterations appearing in the third edition of 1974. Further, wide-scale institutional adoption of *CUBA* guidelines did not occur until about the time of the third edition.

Our experience from analyses in three states is that the skeptics have been unduly concerned about the problems of data comparability. The ease of solving data comparability problems has been surprising, even to us. First, we have found that since about 1974, revenue and expenditure classifications have been highly consistent across institutions. Sufficient detail exists in the financial reports to gain an excellent sense of how items are classified, and only very infrequently are assignments not in accordance with *CUBA*. Only one significant deviation has been found in the three states examined to date, and that is in the classification of Pell Grants (formerly Basic Education Opportunity Grants), which between 1972 and about 1978 were variously included by institutions in institutional current operating accounts as federal grants and contracts, or were (properly) excluded as agency funds. The fourth edition requires that Pell Grants now be classified as federal grants and contracts.

Second, as one moves back in time, although some data categories have changed, most did not change, and even where other categories or definitions were used, they were usually consistent across a given state. For example, regarding consistency with *CUBA*, revenues classified as state appropriations and tuition and fees essentially always have been so classified; expenditures for instruction, research, and public service also have been treated in consistent fashion.

Where inconsistencies with *CUBA* have occurred, these discrepancies generally have been in conformity with state regulations and thus typically have been consistent among in-state institutions; therefore, for comparative purposes little if any error in drawing conclusions is made, even if the classification errors should go undetected. Two examples will be helpful to understanding this point.

Prior to the third edition of *CUBA*, administrative expenditures usually were classified as "administration" or "general institutional expenses," whereas presently administrative costs are separated into institutional support, a general administration category, and academic support, which contains expenditures for administration in direct support of instruction. The second example is capital expenditures. Presently, expenditures for capital equipment and facilities are classified into the appropriate *CUBA* functional categories or are classified as plant funds, as specified in *CUBA* guidelines; however, as recently as the early 1970s, such expenditures often were lumped together by institutions into a separate capital expenditure category. In both cases, some reclassification is necessary; however, even if some reclassification error is assumed, *comparability* will not be affected provided that the reclassification is done consistently.

Solutions to These and Other Comparability Problems. In seeking to gain maximum comparability and reduce classification errors, several steps can be taken. First, correct classification of anomalous data often will be possible from accounting detail provided in the financial reports. For example, the financial reports expenditures for "general administration" usually will be specified as "president's office," "registrar's office," or in some similar way. In keeping with approaches set forth in the fourth edition of *CUBA*, the "president's office" is properly institutional support while "registrar's office" is properly student services. Second, in the legal process of discovery there will be opportunity to inquire as to historic, institutional accounting classification practices and thus to obtain information for necessary corrections. Usually historic accounting guidelines will exist or a veteran financial officer will know of old practices. In the worst case, where such knowledge or other basis for classification is lacking, the item should be left in the category to which assigned by the institution—on the grounds that the expert should not, without basis, substitute his or her judgment for the institutional finance officer's—or if it has not already been assigned to a category, the expert's best judgment may be used.

In our experience perhaps 95 percent of revenue and expenditure items require no action by the expert. For financial reports after about 1975, the figure is closer to 99 percent. For earlier reports, easy direct translation of fourth-edition categories and direct inquiry of finance officers or finance documents will solve all but a very few remaining classification problems. Of the few remaining problems, error is by no means certain. The expert's experience will usually lead to good educated guesses, and even where errors may occur, the amounts almost certainly will be too small to affect conclusions. If amounts are large, invariably information for correct classification somehow will be available. The chance of institutional or state ignorance regarding large revenue or expenditure items is very small. We know of no such cases.

Undetected Errors.   There is, of course, always the possibility of undetected classification error. Most errors will be identified from supporting exhibits in the financial reports, but occasionally this detail may be lacking. Our experience from direct inquiries in depositions and interrogatories tells us that such undetected errors are rare, and where they do occur, often they are made consistently across all institutions, again due to some state-mandated procedure. Thus, data comparability usually is not affected.

Classification Variance by Design.   After all of the above steps and processes are taken or employed, there usually will remain one additional comparability issue. This is in the case where institutions are left some prerogative in item classification. The two cases that come to mind are intercollegiate athletics and student health. *CUBA* specifies that institutions may classify these activities under auxiliary enterprises if they are essentially self-supporting or as student services if they are not. Consistency in classification of these expenditures may be of some consequence to findings because the amounts involved may be large.

What is desired is maximum data comparability in terms of our purpose: assessment of equitability. *CUBA* permits discretion in classifying intercollegiate athletic and student health expenditures, presumably to take into account differences in institutional circumstances. For example, if such activities are financed by the state at institution A but are paid for by ticket purchases or advertisers at institution B, comparability may not be well served by classifying all athletic revenues and expenditures (or student health) in the same way. Thus, the institutional choice guideline is *CUBA*.

In our judgment, however, an even greater error is made by *disparate* classification in the special case of equity between predominantly black and predominantly white colleges, particularly for intercollegiate athletics. Invariably, major predominantly white institutions in the *Adams* states enjoy highly successful athletic programs. Examples are Louisiana State University, the University of Alabama, and Auburn University, which often earn millions annually from regularly scheduled football games, television revenue, and bowl receipts. Not only are these athletic programs self-supporting, occasionally they even provide subsidies to academic programs. Meanwhile, at the predominantly black institutions athletic programs often must be subsidized by using state and other regular revenues. It hardly seems appropriate, without adjustments, to compare revenues and expenditures per student at institutions enjoying athletic surpluses to those borrowing from academic program funds to support those same activities. The same holds, less dramatically, for student health services. Typically, predominantly white colleges and universities are able to charge their more affluent student bodies fees to cover student health costs, but predominantly black institutions may use state funds for these purposes on the assumption that their students are too poor to meet yet another cost of college attendance.

In recognition of these differing circumstances, it is our judgment that all athletic revenues and expenditures should be placed in auxiliary enterprises, which we exclude from the analysis, and that student health amounts should be assigned to student services. Although a case can be made for placing athletics in student services, the very large amounts involved at major predominantly white institutions would bias unfairly the per-student figures there; thus, we take out revenues and expenditures used to support intercollegiate athletics in both predominantly white and predominantly black institutions. We leave in (or add back in) all revenues and expenditures for student health, but would have no serious objection to their exclusion. We would object to inconsistent treatment.

Selecting Institutions for Comparison

Deciding which institutions to compare is always a challenging part of desegregation cases. Every choice made will have drawbacks, and almost every one rejected will have something to commend it. Our broad or general strategy is not to rely upon any single comparison but to construct all contrasts that make good sense. If inequities in fact exist, they should appear in all or almost all sets of comparisons. Further, a far more convincing case is made to the court when consistent equity or inequity patterns are demonstrated, and the offering of numerous comparisons is consistent with the desire for expert objectivity. Therefore, several comparison sets are offered.

State- or System-wide Comparison. First, it seems almost certain that some statewide or system-wide comparisons will be advisable. For example, in Louisiana we compared per-student financing in the LSU system to that in the Southern University system, each of which is composed of several campuses spread around the state; in Alabama we aggregated financial data at the Auburn University and University of Alabama system levels and compared these values to those for Alabama State and Alabama A&M, the two Alabama public black institutions; in Mississippi, where there were no such separate systems, we aggregated and compared all finance data for the predominantly white and black institutions.

Land-grant and Flagship Comparisons. Two other principal comparisons are of the state's land-grant and flagship campuses. Each of the three Title VI states the Justice Department has examined to date contains both predominantly white and predominantly black public land-grant institutions. Reasoning that institutions of like missions should be compared where possible, we have contrasted per-student financing of LSU-Baton Rouge with Southern-Baton Rouge, Mississippi State with Alcorn A&M, and Auburn University with Alabama A&M—the former being the white and the latter the black land-grant school in each state. In Louisiana, the two Baton Rouge campuses also are the flagship campuses of their respective systems and thus would have been compared on this basis as well. In Mississippi, three predominantly white institutions—the University of Mississippi, Mississippi State University, and the University of Southern Mississippi—all have flagship status, whereas among the public black institutions perhaps Alcorn A&M, the land-grant university, and Jackson State University, the large urban institution located in the state capital, might be considered to hold flagship status. In Alabama, Auburn's main campus at Auburn and the University of Alabama in Tuscaloosa are flagship campuses, while predominantly black Alabama State and Alabama A&M Universities might be so considered.

Comparison of Geographic Proximates.   Another, usually important comparison involves geographically proximate institutions. Such contrasts control for at least one variable, geographic location, and they may make particular sense for historic reasons. In the Title VI states, often if indeed not always both black and white institutions were established in a given population center as segregated, supposedly equal institutions. In Louisiana, for instance, the state legislature established new campuses of both LSU and of Southern University in the same locations.

Another common pattern in the *Adams* states has been to establish at some later date a new campus or "center" of a predominantly white institution in a growing city previously served exclusively or primarily by a public black college or university. Examples here are predominantly white campuses of Auburn University in Montgomery and Troy State in Montgomery, which were only relatively recently established. Prior to that time, only predominantly black Alabama State served Montgomery. Similarly the University of Alabama was organized in Huntsville to compete in an area previously served by Alabama A&M; and the predominantly white university center involving several universities in Jackson, Mississippi, began serving an area previously served only by predominantly black Jackson State University. In rural areas, it is more common to find predominantly white and predominantly black institutions only a few miles apart, and close enough to allow commuting by whites to the public white institution. An example here is Grambling University, a predominantly black institution located only a few miles from Louisiana Tech, a predominantly white one.

Other Comparison Bases.   Where mission, location, or some other obvious basis may not serve in composing institutional comparison sets, general institutional similarity may serve the purpose. In a state like Mississippi, where predominantly black and predominantly white institutions are scattered around the state, institutions may be grouped for mission and size similarity; thus, one of our comparisons in Mississippi involved the two small black institutions and an aggregation of several of the smaller white colleges. Making such comparisons may, however, result in the problems described in earlier sections on institutional mission.

Sampling.   Another issue in institutional selections may involve efficiency. In states where there are many collegiate institutions, probably as much may be learned from samples of institutions as from comparisons of all state institutions. In such cases, after the more obvious pairs for comparison are selected using the criteria described earlier, general geographic location may be a consideration. Thus, in Alabama—after comparing land-grant and flagship campuses, campuses of systems, and geographic proximates—we also compared predominantly white institutions and public black institutions with similar missions in the same geographic regions.

Supplemental Analyses

There are a few other analyses that may be useful to the court but are supplemental in nature because they are, in an important sense, redundant to the analysis of financial reports. Ultimately, almost all resources employed in a given year to support institutional programs must pass through the financial reports, and thus are accounted for. One exception is expenditures of institutional foundations, auxiliary nonprofit agencies that have been set up in recent years to raise money and fund activities unsupported by the state or other sources of regular support. Typically, these funds are separated from current funds—the regular operating budget—and may be substantial in major public white institutions. Nevertheless, certain revenue vehicles and expenditure categories warrant additional examination. Two examples are the state allocation formulas and faculty salaries.

State Formulas.   Formulas are used heavily in the *Adams* states, ostensibly as mechanisms for calculating institutional needs and allocating state resources. Such formulas employ historic cost (expenditure) data from within the state or region and expected or actual enrollment data to generate an amount to be provided for a subsequent year by the state. As a simplified illustration of how formulas work, across the entire state or category of institutions within the state, the budgets or expenditures of each academic department or departmental grouping are summed and divided by the number of full-time-equivalent students educated or student credit hours produced therein, thus yielding a dollar-per-student value for the academic unit. (These values may be calculated by student level as well—e.g., undergraduate, graduate.) This value is then multiplied by the number of student units expected or realized by the academic unit in a future year, to give a new unit budget figure for the future time period. When all such budget figures for each academic unit are summed across a given institution, plus any additional amounts for such activities as administration, libraries, and research, the institutional budget, as specified by the formula, is known. This in principle at least is the basis of the institution's state appropriations.

Clearly, the appropriation resulting from the formula is largely redundant to the category state and local appropriations, because in four-year institutions local appropriations are nonexistent or are very small. Nevertheless, examination of the formula is useful to equity issues because understanding the workings of the formula will lead to an understanding of how inequity (or equity) results.

The most vital realization is that formulas are perpetuators of the status quo because they are based upon past allocations of state revenues. If formulas are to continue to be used to allocate state funds, equity probably can be improved only if past formulas are abandoned or changed. If allocations under the formula are greater to predominantly white institutions, then the formula's unit values, the student levels represented, the academic categories employed, and other elements must favor predominantly white colleges and universities. Where this is true, remedy must involve the state formula in some way.

Faculty Salaries.   Faculty salaries may be paid out of money received from any and all revenue sources. All other factors being equal, an institution receiving greater revenues per faculty member will be able to pay an average faculty salary higher than an institution receiving lesser revenues. Salary data are redundant because all or nearly all faculty salaries paid will have been accounted for in the financial report analysis.

Yet faculty salary data are of interest to courts because equity in employee pay is considered to be an important aspect of equity in the quality of education enjoyed by students. The assumption, of course, is that salaries are related to faculty quality, which is in turn related to overall educational quality.

Faculty salary data should be aggregated by faculty rank, standardized by term of contract (10-month versus 12-month), and compared overall and by rank. Consideration should be given to highest degree held, in that one would expect salaries to be greater for those holding the Ph.D. or equivalent degrees than for those holding lesser degrees. Comparison of tenure rates may also prove useful.

Interpretation of salary and related data must be subjective. The paying of substantially higher average salaries is important information in itself. Higher salaries paid when rank, highest degree, and tenure are controlled are even more germane to equity considerations. In our experience in the three states, without exception faculty at predominantly black institutions have been paid less than faculty at public white institutions, other factors being equal. Further, the size of the salary disparity invariably seems to be greater than disparities in most other *CUBA* revenue and expenditure categories.

Much of the explanation probably lies in the fact that public black colleges and universities usually are smaller, and that economies of scale are most easily realized in administrative and support categories, leaving more dollars for faculty salaries at predominantly white institutions. Another part of the explanation probably is that public black institutions are able to pay lower salaries to attract faculty, who tend to be less highly educated and more likely to have attended less prestigious universities. Defendants' position usually is not only that they must pay more to compete successfully for research faculty but that faculty salary levels represent a choice made by predominantly black institutions: How they spend their money is up to them, according to state officials and representatives of predominantly white institutions. Obviously, there are elements of truth in both arguments. This is another reason why we consider financial reports and comparison of *CUBA* category data to be of greatest value. CUBA-based data reduce the need for subjective judgment.

SUMMARY AND CONCLUSIONS

Legally, financial comparisons between predominantly black and white institutions play an important part in both identifying unequal educational opportunity and in determining what financial resources will be necessary to address such inequities.

Money is important to the quality of education provided to both minority and majority students. Also, equity in money is important symbolically, in and of itself. Money equity is also important because money is the major vehicle by which governments intervene to achieve public ends such as educational equity by race.

In assessing financial equity among predominantly black and predominantly white institutions, consideration should be given to contextual matters: (1) mission similarity, (2) enrollment size and trend, and (3) historical funding patterns. Mission similarity is a pivotal issue and one not easily resolved. Although ideally we would wish to compare institutions of similar purpose, few public black institutions exist with high-level research and graduate missions, in considerable part because funds have not been available to them to support such missions, even where these missions were not awarded exclusively to public white institutions. To limit the analysis to comparison of institutions with similar present missions, therefore, is often to preserve the effects of past discrimination against black students and the institutions to which they have traditionally been limited.

For financial equity analysis, the most valid unit usually will be dollars per full-time-equivalent student. The superior source of financial data will be institutional financial reports, and superior data categories will be those recommended in *College and University Business Administration (NACUBO*, 1985). More important categories will be those that reflect relative overall institutional financial capability and those reflecting direct impact upon students.

The large tasks of financial analysis for equity considerations are collecting, converting, standardizing, and tabulating data for analysis. Obtaining maximum data comparability is the primary challenge; yet attaining this comparability is less troublesome than many imagine. The vast majority of data can be transformed directly from financial reports to *CUBA* categories. Where conversions must be made, ordinarily the detail provided in financial reports permits easy assignment of problem items into *CUBA* categories, even in older financial reports; in the few remaining cases, educated guesses usually will be possible from supporting schedules. These "guesses" and any still-remaining items can be verified or clarified in the discovery process, through interrogatories and depositions. For the uncertainties that cannot be removed by these steps and for undetected classification errors, there may be little reason to believe that errors will be made inconsistently across institutions, thus importantly affecting findings. Errors or vagaries involving large dollar amounts that might affect conclusions are extremely unlikely.

In deciding which predominantly white and predominantly black institutions will be compared, state- or system-wide aggregations normally are advisable. Comparisons of like missions are also a good idea, where possible, as are contrasts of the financial data of flagship predominantly white and predominantly black campuses. Other comparisons to be considered are of geographically proximate campuses and those of roughly equivalent size. Of course, it will often be necessary to choose from among comparison bases because these bases may be in conflict. Reliance on a single set of comparisons is inferior to numerous aggregations and arrangements of institutions and campuses, when possible. In some cases, efficiency may argue for samples rather than total institutional inclusiveness; here the same principles of sample selection apply. Finally, data should be aggregated across the state on a student basis, by race, because civil rights belong primarily to citizens rather than to institutions. Experience tells us, however, that the results of institutionally based comparisons likely will be very similar to student-based ones.

Useful supplemental analyses will be of the state funding formula and of faculty salaries. Although redundant of financial report analysis, these supplemental assessments will help to explain why inequities in state appropriations exist, and how resource inequities may translate into inequities in the ability to offer comparable faculty salaries and, ultimately, comparable educational environments for black and white students.

REFERENCES

Adams v. Califano, 430 F. Supp. 118 (D.D.C. 1977).

Adams v. Richardson, 480 F. 2d 1159 (D.C. Cir. 1973) (*en banc*).

Alabama State Teachers Association v. Alabama Public School and College Authority, 289 F. Supp. 784 (M.D. Al. 1968); *aff'd*, 393 U.S. 400 (1969).

Bell, Derrick. "Black Colleges and the Desegregation Dilemma," in *Emory Law School Journal* 28(949), 1979.

Bell, Derrick. "Desegregation and the Meaning of Equal Educational Opportunity in Higher Education," in *Harvard Civil Rights-Civil Liberties Law Review* 17(555), 1982.

Berman, D. *It Is So Ordered*. New York: Norton, 1966.

Board of Visitors of the College of William and Mary v. Norris, 327 F. Supp. 1368, *aff'd*, 404 U.S. 907 (1971).

Brown v. Board of Education, 347 U.S. 483 (1954).

Columbus Board of Education v. Penick, 443 U.S. 449 (1979).

Dayton Board of Education v. Brinkman, 443 U.S. 526 (1979).

Dimond, Paul. "Constitutional Requirements," in Reginald Wilson (ed.), *Race and Equity in Higher Education*. Washington, DC: American Council on Education, 1982.

Federal Register 1978, 43(32), 6658–6664.

Geier v. Blanton, 427 F. Supp. 644 (M.D. Tenn. 1977).

Geier v. Dunn, 337 F. Supp. 644 (M.D. Tenn. 1977).

Green v. New Kent County School Board, 391 U.S. 430 (1968).

Hunnicutt v. Burge, 356 F. Supp. 1227 (M.D. Ga. 1973).

Leslie, Larry. "An Analysis of the Equitability in Higher Education Financing by Race in Alabama Universities." Unpublished manuscript, April, 1985.

McLaurin v. Oklahoma State Regents, 339 U.S. 637 (1950).

Milliken v. Bradley, 433 U.S. 267, 291 (1977).

Missouri ex rel Gaines v. Canada, 305 U.S. 337, 351 (1938).

National Association of College and University Business Officers. *College and University Business Administration (CUBA)*. Washington, DC: NACUBO, 1985.

Norris v. State Council of Higher Education, 327 F. Supp. 1368 (E.D. Va. 1971).

Richardson v. Blanton, 597 F. 2d 1078 (6th Cir. 1979).

Sipuel v. Board of Regents of University of Oklahoma, 322 U.S. 631 (1948).

Swann v. Charlotte-Mecklenburg Board of Education, 402 U.S. 1 (1971).
Sweatt v. Painter, 339 U.S. 629 (1950).
US v. State of Alabama, 628 F. Supp. 1137 (N.D. Al. 1985).
US v. State of Louisiana, 527 F. Supp. 509 (E.D. La. 1981).
Wright, Stephen. "Black Higher Education in the Eighties," in *Educational Record,* Summer 1981.

11
A Research Agenda in Support of Desegregation in Higher Education

JAMES E. BLACKWELL
University of Massachusetts, Boston

Efforts to desegregate state systems of publicly supported higher education began during the 1930s. Black men and women made attempts to gain access to a graduate or professional school within their own state boundaries because of their belief in personal entitlements guaranteed under the Constitution. Pioneering black students in North Carolina, Virginia, Maryland, Tennessee, Oklahoma, and Texas challenged existing *de jure* patterns of segregation and discrimination in publicly supported higher education. As a result of their sustained attacks on the policy of segregation, aided substantially by the NAACP Legal Defense and Educational Fund (LDF) and the National Association for the Advancement of Colored People (NAACP), cracks emerged in what had been an impregnable wall of resistance (Bardolph, 1970; Blackwell, 1981, 1985).

Nevertheless, when the United States Supreme Court rendered its far-reaching decision in *Brown v. Board of Education* (1954), desegregation of higher education could be described as "token" at best. Slowly, gradually, and truly "with all deliberate speed," traditionally white institutions admitted increasingly larger numbers of black students to undergraduate, graduate, and professional degree programs. Even with the accelerated pace of desegregation at the baccalaureate level during the 1960s, the dual system of publicly supported higher education so deeply embedded in the social and educational fabric of 19 states or jurisdictions was not transforming to any appreciable degree.

In 1964, the United States Congress enacted perhaps the most sweeping piece of civil rights legislation since Reconstruction. That measure, the Civil Rights Act of 1964, became the cornerstone of subsequent political action designed to include the previously excluded from the institutional infrastructure of American society. Further, as will be noted in greater detail at a later point in this chapter, Title VI has been employed, sometimes quite effectively, by persons who wish to maintain the traditional patterns of white male privilege, dominance, and hegemony in the United States. In effect, Title VI has become a two-edged sword. It reads as follows:

> No person in the United States shall, on the ground of race, color, or national origin, be excluded from participation in, or be denied the benefits of, or be subjected to discrimination under any program or activity receiving Federal financial assistance.

Supported by Title VI and the Constitution, and invigorated by its string of victories before a sympathetic Supreme Court, the LDF pressed forward in 1970 to dismantle persisting dual systems of higher education. In 1970, on behalf of 31 students, parents, and citizens, LDF filed a class action suit in the Federal District Court of Washington, D.C. As seems customary in litigation involving multiple plaintiffs, the lead name, arranged alphabetically, became associated with the case. Hence a black man bearing the historic name of John Quincy Adams became etched in the history of litigation of higher education. Adams remains constant while the cast of defendants has changed several times by virtue of the movement of different persons into and out of the position of Secretary of Health, Education and Welfare or Secretary of the Department of Education.

Perhaps the most fundamental goal of the plaintiffs in the original *Adams v. Richardson* (1973) litigation was to eliminate all vestiges of "past policies and practices" of institutionalized segregation and discrimination in state systems of publicly supported higher education. By this expectation, institutions and all their programs should become racially neutral with respect to admissions policies; recruitment practices; staffing of faculty, executives, administrators, and managers; and selection of students to participate in specialized programs. Just as traditionally white institutions are required to eliminate all vestiges of past and present segregative and discriminatory policies and practices, historically black institutions are expected to be sufficiently "enhanced" in order to increase their attractiveness to "other-race" students.

For many this expectation connotes an explicit threat of danger to historically black colleges and universities. Should they be stripped of their historic racial identifiability, it is argued, "enhancement necessarily means a concerted effort to save and preserve historically black institutions as an integral part of our national heritage." In the period since 1972, the LDF has successfully persuaded Judge Pratt of the First Federal District Court to issue a number of orders to states deemed in violation of Title VI. The first court order encompassed 10 states. Six of these—Arkansas, Georgia, Florida, Oklahoma, Virginia, and North Carolina—became known as "first-tier states" because they did not file countersuits and were the first to file acceptable desegregation plans. Consequently they have been most consistently over the long period of time scrutinized with respect to implementation of desegregation remedies. Negotiations with the first-tier states have provided voluminous information about the processes of dismantling dual systems; the state-imposed barriers or impediments to the desegregation process; the role of civil rights organizations in maintaining pressure at the federal, state, and local levels in order to sustain the desegregation movement; the salience of local and national coalitions and support group involvement; and patterns of opposition and support regarding dismantling dual systems of publicly supported postsecondary education.

The work of two organizations has been of special importance during the past 15 years with respect to desegregation of higher education: The Southern Education Foundation (SEF) and the LDF. The Southern Education Foundation, with assistance from larger foundations, was the first to sponsor workshops in 1974 designed to scrutinize and evaluate the first system-wide state desegregation plans submitted in compliance with Judge Pratt's order. SEF has sponsored desegregation workshops, seminars, and conferences in every year since that time. These activities have involved the full range of actors who have a stake in the process and outcome of the establishment of a bona fide unitary system of higher education. Such actors have included, at varying times, representatives of the LDF, the National Association of Equal Opportunity in Higher Education, the US Office of Civil Rights, the Department of Justice including the Assistant Attorney General for Civil Rights, members of state coalitions, representatives of state systems of postsecondary education, members of boards of trustees, researchers, and many others. When SEF established its Higher Education Program in 1978, its centerpiece became research that attempts to unravel the intricacies of desegregation in the *Adams* states. Since 1978, SEF has either published or commissioned 31 pieces of higher education desegregation research.

Because LDF has been involved in the *Adams* litigation since its inception, its staff has accumulated the most complete set of untapped and unanalyzed data on this subject available in the United States (Fairfax, 1978). Systematic and rigorous analysis of its data can shed light on the history of the litigation; LDF's decisions to undertake the case and stay with it for 15 years or longer; all aspects of federal, state, and local involvement in the process of decision-making; support for the dismantling process; the philosophy of a unitary system of higher education; legal ramifications of dismantling racially identifiable systems; the social and psychological dynamics of desegregation; opposition to the process and outcomes of desegregation; spheres of progress and explanations for that progress; areas of resistance to change, both theoretical and practical; explanations for opposition; and many other aspects of the desegregation process. Researchers should make a thorough examination of the LDF data a matter of utmost priority.

Whatever progress that has been achieved toward the ultimate goal of equal educational opportunity for all Americans would not have been realized without the continued support of the SEF. It has provided a major forum for rational discussion, deliberation, and thoughtful action. Progress would not have been made without the sustained conscientiousness and determination of LDF.

A PROPOSED RESEARCH AGENDA

Proposing a research agenda in support of desegregation in higher education is risky business. There is always an explicit danger in such enterprises of assigning a higher degree of salience and priority to an issue than it actually merits based on previous research findings. The converse is equally true. It appears that the best effort one can make involves judgments informed by knowledge of gaps in the research, practical experience, and estimates of the direction in which a research agenda will lead us toward accomplishing an articulated goal.

Of primary importance is the need to face the fact that there exists a dearth of researchers in the minority group populations who have the training, skills, or interest requisite for conducting defensible, empirical research in higher education. For instance, the nation is producing only 1000 black doctorates per year, and despite the fact that 54 percent of those received doctoral degrees in education, a substantial majority of black doctorates are neither prepared for nor interested in this type of research. Hence, the need for carefully trained researchers who possess skills in survey research, statistical procedures, and data analysis techniques, and who can comprehend the short- and long-term implications of their research findings for social and public policy, is absolutely critical. Recognition of that imperative *and* a determination to eliminate such shortages, then, become the most immediate context for specifying a research agenda.

The second factor with which supporters of desegregation must deal is a new social and political context forged by the rudimentary require-

ments of social justice (Prestage, 1982) and equal opportunity ideals up-
held by every presidential administration since the 1948 election of Harry
Truman. For instance, President Truman demonstrated his commitment
to desegregation when he issued Executive Order 9981, which desegregated the military. The US Commission on Civil Rights was established
under the Eisenhower Administration, and it was Eisenhower who appointed Earl Warren Chief Justice of the US Supreme Court. It was the
Warren court that ordered school desegregation in the *Brown* case. Under the Kennedy-Johnson Administrations, the nation's commitment to
social justice got translated into an impressive array of social programs
designed to eliminate race- and gender-based structural inequalities. Furthermore, at that time measures were enacted and promulgated that resulted in the Civil Rights Act of 1964, the 1965 Voting Rights Bill, the
Equal Employment Opportunity Commission, and expanded desegregation at the college and university level.

Under the Nixon Administration affirmative action policies were
crystallized, and implemented in the public and private sectors. All of
these gains were reinforced by policies and practices observed during the
administrations of Presidents Ford and Carter.

By contrast, President Reagan has publicly announced his opposition to affirmative action and, through the Department of Justice, has
sought to dismantle even voluntary state and municipal affirmative action
programs. He opposes busing for school desegregation and has instructed
the Department of Justice to overturn busing programs in a number of
cities. Further, the Department of Justice has not vigorously enforced the
desegregation guidelines ordered by Judge Pratt in the *Adams* case. In fact,
some actions (as in the North Carolina settlement) appear to be especially
supportive of the defendants and not the plaintiffs. In brief, the Reagan
Administration has sought to overturn every civil rights program or to
make it so difficult for plaintiffs to prove "intentional discrimination" as
to undermine the entire desegregation process (Blackwell, 1985). Although 19 jurisdictions are now encompassed by the *Adams* litigation,
there exists among proponents of Title VI regulation a growing suspicion
that the Department of Education plans to totally end enforcement of Title VI, and that the Department of Justice will not be as active as it was
in previous Administrations toward facilitating compliance with court orders to dismantle dual systems. If these speculations have more than a
grain of truth to them, the implications for desegregation are enormous
and far-reaching.

One observation becomes an absolute certainty: The initial class-action dimension of the *Adams* litigation will increasingly diminish. Ultimately, this situation leads to a proliferation of suits against individual

states, with the Office of the Attorney General joining hands with recalcitrant state officials who either wish to maintain a segregative system or who believe that the advancement toward desegregation has either proceeded as far as tolerable or to an acceptable limit. One consequence of that scenario is the shift of political focus and the activities of coalitions toward the state level, where blacks are in a position to exert more direct and effective political power. Hence researchers on desegregation are more compelled than ever to remain mindful of the full range of the "politics of the desegregation process."

At least 13 areas of potential and continuing research in support of desegregation hold priority in the late 1980s. Each area is discussed separately in the paragraphs that follow.

1. *Access remains an issue of the highest priority despite the achievements made since the major court decisions of 1954 and 1972 with respect to expanded educational opportunity for blacks and other minorities.*

Bruce Hare, in a forthcoming essay, raises a thoughtful question as to whether access equals success. His response is clearly negative, in the sense that doors of opportunity may have been opened since 1954, but success as measured by equality of access and by completion of degree requirements (in the same proportion as other groups) has not been attained by black Americans. In another study, this writer measured access in terms of the relationship or ratio between enrollment within an institution or matriculation in a particular program and the proportion of blacks within the state within which the institution is located. If that ratio is 1.00, then parity of access has been attained. Relationships or ratios below that level indicate that access is either limited, restricted, or only partial. By this definition, few programs, colleges, schools, or departments within traditionally white institutions have anything more than limited access.

Obviously, access is conditioned not only by the seriousness and effectiveness of recruitment programs but by an array of cognitive, institutional, and environmental factors that affect decisions and choices made by admissions committees and students. Hence, patterns of enrollment and characteristics of students enrolled in diverse types of institutions should be continually investigated in order to strengthen the power of predictive instruments as well as to augment understanding of decision-making with respect to selection and choices made by students.

Changes in patterns of enrollment and of the factors associated with those changes over specific time-frames should be investigated in two-year institutions, four-year colleges and universities, and graduate and professional schools. One of the more salient variables in such analyses is that of institutional control. Perhaps of substantially greater importance is the variable, "the status of *Adams* litigation," and its influence on these patterns over time. Specifically, does being involved in civil rights litigation to dismantle a dual system of publicly supported education affect patterns of enrollment of black students? If so, what is the magnitude of that effect? Is that pattern determined by the degree of pressure exerted by the federal government, plaintiffs, or local influences on institutions or state systems? In what ways are private institutions affected by state and federal action with respect to implementation and compliance with such litgation? Are there particular pressure points at which accelerated compliance is likely to be observed, and what real influence do monitoring groups have on the pace of change in whatever patterns of access are revealed?

Studies of access should be mindful of the basic demographic factors influencing enrollment and the pool of possible students, not only for college admission but also for distribution within the various disciplines and specialized programs.

Despite the federal government's decision to discontinue collecting race-specific data in some essential areas, there is a growing body of evidence that points to declining access of black and other minority students to college, graduate, and professional education (Baratz, 1984; Blackwell, 1982; Darling-Hammond, 1985; Morris, 1980; Ranbom et al., 1985; Thomas, 1981). These studies demonstrate that despite declines in black high school dropout rates over the past 15 years, the disparity rate between blacks and whites entering college for the first time is widening. The result is an 11-percent decline in the college-going rate of black high school graduates within a six-year period (AASCU, 1982; ACE, 1984; Darling-Hammond, 1985).

As previously suggested, studies of access necessarily involve investigations into the degree to which determinants of access impede or accelerate the participation of black students in postsecondary education. One critically important determinant is that of the types of cognitive measures employed. Hence, in-depth research is needed in the area of testing.

2. *Testing and its impact on patterns of access for black students.*

Components of the testing issue include test bias, test abuse, and the effects of coaching on test performance. The debate over test bias, while not resolved with respect to undergraduate admissions, is now an issue at other levels of graduate and professional education. Of special interest is a determination of the degree to which the Graduate Record Examination (GRE) and similar tests employed in determining admission to schools of management (GMAT), dentistry (DAT), optometry (OCAT), and others are biased or have exclusionary outcomes. Item analysis studies as well as those that examine the basic structure of these tests should be subjected to rigorous scrutiny so as to reduce, if not totally eliminate, whatever biases may be found that impede the attainment of test scores equal to or above mean scores for the test-taking population.

Examinations of graduate enrollment among blacks show that since 1976, black participation in graduate education has declined in absolute numbers and proportionately. Among other things, it is vital to ascertain whether this decline is associated with GRE scores. By the same token, a related research issue is a determination of the power of the GRE as a sorting-out instrument. Why is that instrument more likely to sort out certain populations than others? What are the implications of this sorting-out function, whether manifest or latent, for excluded populations when undue reliance upon GRE test scores is evident by some institutions in determining access? There is also a major question of the actual predictive power of the GRE, for instance, relative to successful completion of a doctoral degree. How do we account for the fact that some blacks, as well as other individuals from other populations, who do not perform well on the GRE not only emerge as outstanding graduate students but complete doctoral degree requirements within the same or less time as high scorers on the GRE? Are such persons to be regarded as mere statistical aberrants, or does the fact of their success call into serious question unwarranted dependence on such test scores as the principal criterion for admissions?

The coaching industry is huge and exceptionally profitable. Test preparation manuals, books, and courses are available throughout the nation for anyone who is financially able to pay sometimes exorbitant costs for these aids. The fundamental principle underlying coaching—that test-takers can be taught how to execute standardized tests and thereby substantially improve test results—has been largely rejected by the testing industry. Yet some evidence demonstrates that student performance on the Scholastic Aptitude Test (SAT) can be raised by more than 100 points through systematic coaching (Johnson, 1984). In the first instance, more definitive and rigorous studies are needed to determine the impact of coaching on test performance. Does coaching have similar effects with respect to performance on tests employed as determinants for admissions to schools of medicine, dentistry, law, veterinary medicine, optometry, and management?

Further, what does improved performance through coaching suggest about the relationship between structural conditions within the black community (e.g., employment and level of income, money available for coaching) and test performance? If, indeed, coaching has a positive impact on test performance and if the economic costs of coaching are out-of-reach for low-income blacks, will not the gap between low- and high-income blacks, and between low- and high-income students generally, become broader?

3. *Basic skills and minimal competency examinations are widely used throughout the United States.*

Forty states either have installed or plan to implement some form of competency examinations for elementary, secondary, and higher education in the very near future. A basic research need is a determination of the short-term and long-term impact of the implementation of such examinations and their accompanying curriculum reforms on blacks when state and local jurisdictions have not adequately prepared for their implementation.

4. *The use of standardized tests for certification and to determine eligibility for participation in selected programs should be rigorously studied.*

The results of such research could form the basis for major policies that have an enormous impact upon the overall quality of higher education as well as provide a rational basis for the elimination of test abuse and misuse in many colleges and universities. A growing body of evidence points to the deleterious effects of many basic skills and minimal competency examinations on blacks (Smith, 1985). It may be stressed that performance on such tests reflects curriculum content and teaching methodology and not the innate ability or aptitude of test-takers. Further, there is evidence that some state education systems are required to use standardized tests as a means of determining eligibility to certain institutional programs (e.g., nursing, physical therapy, education, and others). Some institutions have requested the testing industry to suggest acceptable cut-off points for denying a teaching certificate and consequently denying that particular person his or her means of economic support.

How much predictive power do such tests have with respect to determining who will be an effective teacher? If tests are to be employed in that manner, should not all the actors involved have sufficient time to institutionalize necessary curriculum reform and obtain the human and financial resources required to assure that equal opportunity permeates the entire educational pipeline? What does the inappropriate use of such tests portend for the supply of black teachers, for instance, and for the pool of potential graduate and professional school students? What do test requirements suggest about efforts to restore widely rejected patterns of dominance in the educational community?

5. *Improving retention of black students in graduate and professional schools, as well as in some majors or disciplines at the undergraduate level, can profit from appropriate research and development efforts.*

It seems important to identify successful retention models such as the science program operated by Xavier University; models that appear to be effective in specific professions and academic disciplines, and models that are least effective; why some models work and others do not; the impact of the institutional climate on the retention of black students; and models of successful institutional learning and positive social environments that may be replicated and serve as guides for institutions experiencing retention difficulties.

In recent years, a considerable amount of publicity has been given to issues that have raised the level of consciousness about a number of areas that affect the organizational, structural, and social characteristics of institutions of higher education and desegregation within these institutions. These issues encompass an increasing tendency of state legislators to mandate policies in areas previously assumed to fall within the exclusive domains of institutions (Guthrie & Reed, 1986); the ability of black legislators to perform broker roles so as to obtain more significant enhancement of the historically black institutions (Blackwell, 1983a); the need to produce a much larger number of black doctorates and to hire blacks in much greater numbers for faculty, administrative, and managerial positions, especially in institutions covered by the Title VI litigation; the need to make academic salaries more competitive and attractive to black doctoral recipients in order to attract them to colleges and universities; and the necessity of strengthening the financial aid programs not only to enable more blacks to enter college and graduate or professional studies but to do so in a way that reduces their overall indebtedness after graduation (Blackwell, 1987, 1983; Darling-Hammond, 1985; Orlans, 1986; Thomas, 1981; Wilson, 1982).

Obviously the broad issues raised above mask a number of not-unrelated uncertainties. For instance, legislative intrusion may violate the rights of institutions to set policies concerning curriculum; admission and graduation requirements may work to the disadvantage of those students whose high school training may have occurred at schools without adequate resources for producing highly competitive students. Further, the failure of institutions to recruit, train, and graduate blacks with a doctoral degree, coupled with the implementation of more restrictive criteria for tenure in these institutions, not only reduces racial and ethnic diversity within colleges and universities but accelerates the "revolving door syndrome" by which untenured black faculty move from institution to institution without ever gaining tenure, while many students are left with few visible role models and negative stereotypes are reinforced. Research questions should focus around explanations for these situations and their impact on various population sets; they should lead to policies constructed to eliminate such barriers to equal educational opportunity.

6. *Whether greater state control over higher education results in improved access remains to be seen.*

A sixth issue warranting serious study is whether state governments are intruding into long-established prerogatives of institutions of higher education (e.g., by mandating minimal competency tests, curriculum content, and new teacher certification standards) with the payoff of increased access. What are the implications of that intrusion for issues of equity, excellence, and desegregation as they affect black and other minority students? (Blackwell, 1983a)

7. *Public policy programs for increasing the overall number of blacks with doctoral degrees deserve attention through research and inquiry.*

On an annual basis, blacks comprise less than five percent of all recipients of doctoral degrees in the United States. In several disciplines and specializations, blacks constitute less than one percent of doctoral degree recipients. The central issue is how to get more blacks into that pipeline, retain them, and graduate them as efficiently as possible. During the 1970s and 1980s, even where the pools have been sufficient, it has not been possible to increase the absolute number and distribution of blacks in faculty positions because the academic job market has been shrinking. This problem will become less of an issue during the 1990s, as more college teaching positions become available. But once blacks are hired, what professional socialization is required, and who will assume responsibility for facilitating their understanding of tenure requirements and the politics of tenure?

In many ways these problems also apply to the problem of persuading institutions to hire and promote a critical mass of black executive, managerial, and academic administrators. The number of such jobs is not, however, expected to expand much in the next several years.

8. *A research program might aim at providing a legislative strategy for black state lawmakers and other elected and appointed officials.*

As a result of the 1984 elections, there are approximately 5700 black elected officials. Significant proportions of them now are incumbents of powerful and influential positions in the state legislatures of several of states affected by Title VI (e.g., Georgia, Florida, North Carolina, Maryland, Alabama, and Virginia). A researchable question is the degree to which they are able to parlay their legislative influence in ways that facilitate desegregation goals and compliance with Title VI and the overall enhancement of the historically black institution. It may be hypothesized that, as desegregation strategies shift increasingly toward the various states, black legislators will become a major focal point of intervention and facilitation.

9. *The past and current roles played by local citizen advocacy groups deserve attention.*

During the first five or six years following the initial orders issued by Judge Pratt, several statewide coalitions of concerned black graduates of black colleges and universities were formed primarily to monitor the development of state desegregation plans. In several instances, their collective input into the deliberations was instrumental in the eventual acceptance of preliminary state plans. In recent years, these coalitions have not appeared as visible as in the past; their precise activities with respect to facilitating desegregation at all levels of the state educational enterprise are unclear. Research could be conducted that reveals essential characteristics of effective coalitions, of what strategies are required for effective functioning of state coalitions, and of other salient characteristics of such groups that facilitate the desegregation process.

10. *Salary equity studies in states affected by Title VI provide useful information for monitoring purposes.*

Other than the earlier work by Pruitt (1981, 1983), relatively little is known about employment and salary distribution or equity at the collegiate and university level in states affected by Title VI. Comparative studies are needed that focus on levels of employment, types of positions held, and salary similarities and differentials by race and gender in the 19 Title VI states.

11. *Equitable distribution and allocation of student financial aid and faculty research funds by race is another critical area of needed research.*

There is evidence that in some undergraduate colleges as many as 85 to 90 percent of all black students are compelled to rely on some form of financial assistance for college education due to the unfavorable economic condition of their parents, or because of their own inabilities to obtain sufficient work to subsidize their own education. Among the numerous researchable questions are the following: What race- and sex-based differences exist by institutions in the type of financial assistance made available to students? Are certain categories of students less likely to receive scholarships and fellowships, even though equally eligible for them, than several who receive them? Are certain categories more likely to be allocated assistance through work study programs, repayable loans, and federal funds, while others are more likely to be recipients of institutional funds? If so, what are the determinants of such arrangements? To what degree does the receipt of research fellowships facilitate the mentoring process in graduate and professional schools and beyond? What factors contribute to the racial maldistribution of research and teaching fellowships observed in graduate and professional schools? What corrective strategies can be effectively implemented regarding such maldistributions? These questions apply to both state and federal student aid sources. Further, blacks are often confronted with a limited track record for the successful attainment of research funds that may be used primarily to enhance their visibility in the profession, but that may also advance their capacity to serve as mentors for black research assistants and other students who become aware of their contributions and stature as researchers (Blackwell, 1983a).

12. *Factors underlying increased racial tension on campus might be explored by researchers.*

In view of continuing evidence of the resurgence of racial tensions on desegregated college campuses, immediate research is needed to reveal the underlying factors contributing to that situation; to suggest strategies for improving the overall institutional climate at both black and white institutions; and to create a more favorable academic and learning environment for minority students, faculty, and administrators at predominantly white institutions.

13. *Policies and procedures for enhancing traditionally black colleges will emerge from appropriate research.*

Much research is required to deal with the issue of enhancement of historically black institutions. What precisely is "enhancement"? What are its determinants? How do we measure its success? What is the relationship between enhancement and the enrollment and graduation of substantial numbers of white students at black colleges and universities? To what extent are state legislatures executing those responsibilities articulated in state desegregation plans for the enhancement of historically black institutions? How adequate are the financial and human resources made available through legislative appropriation for the realization of a successfully enhanced institution?

A related research task might involve examining the consequences of mergers between historically black institutions and newly established, predominantly white institutions that claim to be "racially neutral." The effectiveness of alternatives to mergers (e.g., relocating academic programs) and the consequences of maintaining black and white institutions in essentially the same service area should be explored as well.

This delineation of 13 areas for new research programs or the continuation of ongoing ones in support of desegregation in higher education does not exhaust the agenda. It does, however, identify some of the more urgent concerns about the full range of desegregation problems as based upon my understanding of the literature, more than a decade of personal involvement, and the wisdom of others currently involved in implementing Title VI.

REFERENCES

Adams v. Richardson, 356 F. Supp. 92, 94 (D.D.C. 1973).

American Association of State Colleges and Universities. *Student Aid and Minority Enrollment in Higher Education.* Washington, DC: AASCU, 1982.

American Council on Education. *Third Annual Status Report on Minorities in Higher Education.* Washington, DC, Nov. 1982.

Baratz, Joan C. "Black Participation in Medical Education: Holding One's Own While Falling Backward." Unpublished paper presented at the AERA/ASHE Conference on Post-Secondary Education, San Francisco, Oct. 20, 1984.

Bardolph, Richard. *The Civil Rights Record: Black Americans and 1849–1970.* New York: Crowell, 1970.

Blackwell, James E. *Mainstreaming Outsiders: The Production of Black Professionals.* New York: General Hall, 1981.

———. "Demographics of Desegregation," in Reginald Wilson (ed.), *Race and Equity in Higher Education*. Washington, DC: American Council on Education, 1982.

———. *Desegregation of State Systems of Higher Education*. Atlanta: Southern Education Foundation, 1983a.

———. *Networking and Mentoring: A Study of Cross-Generational Experiences of Blacks in Graduate and Professional Schools*. Atlanta: Southern Educational Foundation, 1983b.

———. *The Black Community: Diversity and Unity*. Second Edition. New York: Harper and Row, 1985.

———. *Mainstreaming Outsiders: The Production of Black Professionals*. (Second Edition). New York: General Hall, 1987.

Brown v. Board of Education, 347 US483 1954.

Darling-Hammond, Linda. *Equality and Excellence: The Educational Status of Black Americans*. New York: College Board, Jan. 1985.

Darling-Hammond, Linda and A.E. Wise. "Beyond Standardization: State Standards and School Improvement." *Elementary School Journal* (Jan. 1985).

Fairfax, Jean. "Current Status of the Adams Case: Implications for the Education of Blacks and Other Minorities," in *Beyond Desegregation: Urgent Issues in the Education of Minorities*. College Boards. New York: College Board, 1978.

Guthrie, James W. and Rodney J. Reed. *Educational Administration and Policy: Effective Leadership for American Education*. Englewood Cliffs, NJ: Prentice-Hall, 1986.

Johnson, Nancy. Personal correspondence with author, October, 1984.

Morris, Lorenzo. *Elusive Equality*. Washington, DC: Howard University Press, 1980.

Orlans, Harold. "On High Standards, Minority Enrollment, and Money." *The Chronicle of Higher Education* (July 25, 1986), p. 72.

Prestage, Jewel L. "A Political Taxonomy of Desegregation," in Reginald Wilson (ed.), *Race and Equity in Higher Education*. Washington, DC: American Council on Education, 1982.

Pruitt, Anne S. *Black Employees in Traditional White Institutions in the Adams States*. Atlanta: Southern Education Foundation, 1981.

———. "Does Minority Graduate Education Have a Future?" *Planning and Changing*, (Spring 1983), pp. 15–22.

Ranbom, Sheppard, et al. "Hard-Won Enrollment Gains Are Quietly Deteriorating." *Education Week* (April 17, 1985a), p. 1.

———. "Campus Tensions Flare Up Amid Charges of Racism," *Education Week* (April 17, 1985b, p. 1).

Smith, G. Pritchey. "The Impact of Competency Tests on Teacher Education: Ethical and Legal Issues in Selecting and Certifying Teachers." Unpublished manuscript. Hawkins, Texas: Jarvis Christian College, January, 1986.

Thomas, Gail. *Black Students in Higher Education*. Westport, Conn.: Greenwood Press, 1981.

Wilson, Reginald (ed.). *Race and Equity in Higher Education*. Washington, DC: American Council on Education, 1982.

12
The Future of Title VI
Regulation of Higher Education

JOHN B. WILLIAMS, III
Harvard University

The contributors to this study of Title VI regulation on the whole present a pessimistic view of progress and of measures adopted by government officials, educators, and civil rights advocacy groups to achieve progress. Contributors William Trent, Jomills Braddock, Elaine Copeland, and the editor all conclude, based upon analysis of compliance and other relevant data, that declining or steady-state enrollment and employment trends exist in almost all 19 public colleges and university systems involved. Remedial preparation, recruitment, admissions, financial aid, and employment interventions in Title VI states are simply insufficient to combat the effect of overall black declines affecting the entire nation and the residue of past discriminatory practices. Poor effort resulting in poor progress is notably troublesome, because as contributors Raymond Burse and Israel Tribble illustrate, promising approaches are possible. Edgar Epps, Kenneth Jackson, James Blackwell, and Charles Willie also imply through their research or directly argue from past experience that ways exist to improve the current direction of the nation's Title VI effort.

The current state of affairs where civil rights regulation of higher education is concerned may be understood—Blackwell, Tribble, Newell, Willie, and other knowledgeable critics imply—as an excuse to end Title VI regulation of higher education. The confluence of several complementary trends set the stage for ending system-wide civil rights regulation approaches within the public college and university arena. These include (1) accumulating evidence of a lack of progress, (2) increased reliance upon nationwide declines in black participation in higher education as a justification for no progress in Title VI states, and (3) absence of evidence of substantial effort by Title VI states to increase black participation. Even evidence of promising, albeit small-scale, desegregation approaches can

220

be used to support an unstated policy of not implementing Title VI within higher education. Arguably, desegregation approaches must remain small and locally fashioned in order for them to be successful; moreover, through incentive rather than regulatory policy approaches such efforts are more likely to emerge.

In view of the contributors' observation that the stage is now set for deregulation of public higher education systems where civil rights goals are concerned, is it likely that implementation of Title VI will continue? In the future, will Title VI be implemented in the same way, or will changes occur? Can the difficult goals of desegregation of public higher education be accomplished if Title VI regulation continues unchanged, if it continues in a revised format, or if it disappears entirely? These questions are clearly unanswerable at this time. Nonetheless, exploration of their true meaning provides insight into the future of Title VI within the college and university community.

Whether the federal government will participate in enforcing Title VI within the public college and university community may seem on the surface fairly certain. In one respect, as long as the law remains on the books, the Justice Department and the Department of Education hold responsibility of one kind or another for implementing it. But implementation can take many forms, and the responsibility of these two government agencies can be interpreted in a variety of ways. In the final analysis the federal government's policy options can be characterized in two ways: those that require states to do more and those that require them to do less than they are currently engaged in.

Aimed at requiring more or requiring less effort, Title VI implementation can vary along numerous dimensions: the extent to which the federal government shares decision-making with state and local authorities; the extent to which undesired and unanticipated outcomes from enforcing civil rights in higher education are tolerated; whether some policy options, for reasons unrelated to civil rights or higher education, meet with substantial public opposition; and whether some policy options are more expensive than others in terms of actual financial costs. Inasmuch as criteria like these will be applied to reach decisions about the future of Title VI, the emergence of more extensive requirements is perhaps not to be expected.

There exists little evidence that extensive changes in Title VI regulation will occur in the direction of requiring states to do more. It is unlikely that the current system of threatening to withdraw federal funds will be strongly supplemented by incentive policies, like offering federal funds to states that make a substantial effort to desegregate. Arguably, it was a combination of both regulatory and incentive policies that led to the accomplishment of desegregation in the primary and secondary school arenas.

On the other hand, as illustrated in my earlier chapter, evidence of less dramatic change aimed in the direction of requiring less state action and accomplishing fewer, more narrowly defined civil rights outcomes is apparent. Current Justice Department policy as described by Assistant Attorney General William Bradford Reynolds (1983) clearly indicates movement away from a strong regulatory posture toward remedies, which probably will result in even less progress. Reynolds' new policy approach is notably different from that of the Department of Education. Changes at the campus and state system levels that his department embraces in guidelines he established are inconsistent with, and arguably less substantial than, requirements the Department of Education announced in 1978 (*Federal Register*). But the Department of Education's efforts are also subsiding. Evidence of diminution in the already timid Department of Education enforcement effort occurred in response to two recent court cases, *State of North Carolina v. Department of Education* (1981) and *Grove City College v. Bell* (1982). Moreover, a court ruling against the *Adams v. Richardson* (1973) defendants' standing to bring suit will thoroughly dismantle existing Department of Education implementation.

One implication of the evidence provided in this study is that strong new Title VI policy approaches are needed if desegregation, substantially defined, is to take place. But changes in national leadership that promise major bolstering of Title VI implementation are unlikely in the near future. Where the issue of national leadership toward Title VI compliance in higher education is concerned, recall that implementation of Title VI began when Lyndon Johnson was president.

On the other hand, only small changes are needed to reduce substantially the possibility of effectiveness of Title VI implementation. Small changes already underway at the federal level are all that is needed to maintain no progress or perhaps eventually to make the situation substantially worse. Few black students enrolled today will result in fewer black enrollments in the near future. Even if the vague but certain weight of public opinion forces more attention to increased segregation in higher education, this same public opinion will undoubtedly also limit federal options and the seriousness of federal purpose. The public will risk few unplanned consequences that stem from increased black attendance; increased costs will not be approved; desegregation will once again become associated with emerging, unrelated higher education problems; and state policy-makers will insist upon making a greater share of decisions about desegregation policy. It will take a great deal of effort, in other words, to enforce Title VI; but very little is required to subvert it.

But just how important is Title VI regulation for achieving a solution to the problem of limited black participation in higher education? Arguably federal Title VI regulatory policy is only as important as several other independent factors affecting the problem. Certainly the role the federal government plays is closely tied to other important dynamics that may affect the problem.

At least three fairly significant factors along this line are notable. First of all, population demographics are shifting significantly. According to Harold Hodgkinson, an expert on this subject:

> Public school enrollments declined from 46 million in 1970 to 39 million in 1982. The lowest point on the high school graduate decline curve comes in 1994—1995 will not be a good year for higher education freshman classes, except in the 10 states, mostly "Sunbelt," that have had no youth decline at all. The high school declines suffered so far by higher education are very small. The slope of the curve steepens greatly around 1990, especially in the East and especially for white middle-class suburbanites. . . .
>
> What follows the decline is a slight turn upward in number of births since 1980. . . . But this increase in births . . . is basically not white. . . .
>
> Today we are a nation of 14.6 million Hispanics and 26.5 million Black persons. We will be a nation of 44 million Blacks and 47 million Hispanics by the year 2020. . . . As we grow to a nation of 260 million people by 2020, it is easy to see that almost all of the growth will be nonwhite and young. . . . (Harold L. Hodgkinson, "The New Demographic Realities for Education and Work." Unpublished manuscript, Institute for Educational Leadership, Washington, D.C., July, 1985, p. 2)

Many colleges and universities in Title VI states will be disproportionately affected by these important population trends. Willingness to recruit and enroll blacks may decrease or increase in response to this population change.

Whether college and university decision-makers devise new ways to rationalize excluding blacks or invent ways of successfully including them, population trends constitute a factor of consequence for achieving Title VI goals. Title VI regulation will become easier or more difficult as the proportion of minorities within the cohort of college students changes.

Hypothesizing substantial increases in black enrollment in the 19 states affected by Title VI brings up the second important factor beyond the federal role, but clearly related to the final outcome. This factor involves the induced or improved capacity of colleges and universities, particularly predominantly white ones, to educate black students. Much of public policy and policy research concerned with increasing the participation of black students assumes that black youth must be rendered better suited than they have in the past to attend college, particularly predominantly white, four-year institutions. Certainly in comparison to whites, blacks do not receive adequate primary and secondary schooling. Consequently, many actual and potential college aspirants from black families do not possess the basic academic skills and study habits to engage successfully in postsecondary education.

On the other hand notable numbers of black youth have gained the background and skills required to complete college over the past 20 years. Based upon accounts of the experiences and opinions of blacks enrolled in college and of college graduates, it is equally certain that many colleges and universities, not unlike public secondary schools, do not possess the capacity to offer an entirely suitable college experience regardless of what academic skills entering black students bring with them. This is particularly the case at four-year, predominantly white institutions, where white students are at times underprepared for participation and competition in multiracial communities.

Evidence of this problem runs the gamut from recent Ku-Klux-Klan-like aggression at the Citadel in South Carolina (*Chronicle of Higher Education*, November 5, 1986) to data measuring the relatively poor performance of qualified black students offered in the Nettles chapter and similar studies. Civil rights goals like the ones embodied in Title VI will in the future depend more than ever upon the capacity of integrated institutions to instruct all students in one setting effectively, and to provide a campus environment that supports all students' personal and vocational aspirations. Improving the capacity of colleges and universities to educate a mix of minority and nonminority students and demonstrating publicly increased capacity to do so will not be easy.

The problem of public higher education's capacity in Title VI states to educate adequately blacks and whites on the same campuses is not new, even though it is little discussed. Concern for this problem emerged with fervor during the 1970s, when black and other minority students were first being admitted to white institutions. Expanded discussions of the adequacy of higher education stemmed from sources unrelated to race, and a variety of alleged impediments emerged. But where the race issue itself was concerned, failure of faculty and others to overcome their prejudices, lack of sufficient student financial aid, and failure to place black graduates in job and postbaccalaureate training were among the many defects debated.

By 1987 many white educators seem to have overcome their prejudices; student aid exists even though reductions have occurred since 1980 and issues of delivery and substance remain unresolved, particularly for postbaccalaureate students; employment (at least outside the higher education community) and postbaccalaureate opportunities (at least for a brief period) have expanded somewhat for blacks graduating from college. But arguably one of the most salient college deficiencies that emerged in the 1970s in response to the race issue remains unresolved. This deficiency had to do with the adequacy of the American college curricula for multiracial student clienteles. The Burse chapter suggests the saliency of curriculum revision and illustrates that the current state of affairs need not continue.

Setting the stage for improved education for blacks and whites together at the college level involves a major but usually neglected undertaking: offering course materials and providing methods of instruction that facilitate learning for both black and white students. Figuring out how to undertake appropriate revisions and discovering specific ways in which such undertakings actually accomplish desegregation constitute an essential, but vexingly difficult and generally misunderstood, task. It must involve recognizing that the curriculum, particularly at prestigious institutions, is not sacred, and that changing it does not compromise tradition and status.

Since these barriers to curriculum revision exist when preparing an institution for multiracial clienteles, it should be emphasized that curriculum revision is needed at predominantly white as well as predominantly black colleges and universities in Title VI states. Moreover, approaching the problem of creating a multiracial college community and classroom environment through the medium of curriculum revision is not synonymous with decreasing the quality of a college's offerings. If the quality of the American college experience has declined in recent years, no persuasive evidence exists that enrolling blacks contributed to this trend, a commonly held but usually unstated opinion.

Focusing upon the need for improvement in the integrated college experience is not intended to dismiss the need for black students to develop better academic skills, study habits, and social maturity at the primary and secondary schooling. The issue is whether planned and ongoing public school reform programs will result in better college preparation for blacks in the 19 states involved in Title VI, many of which hold the reputation of having established some of the most far-reaching school reform legislation in the nation. Moreover, will improvements in black students' preparation for college, resulting from reforms of secondary schooling, increase blacks' college enrollment and improve their academic performance?

Barbara Newell offers insight into issues associated with emerging school reform measures where Title VI goals are concerned. Furthermore, evidence is emerging that certain reforms in teacher training and certification have already negatively affected participation of blacks in

teacher training programs (Antoine Garibaldi, 1986). Even if the full answer to this question is today uncertain, clearly the answer that later
emerges will hold implications for black participation in higher education. Whether public school reforms in Title VI states result in better
preparation of black students is an issue bearing directly upon the accomplishment of Title VI goals, but one that will have major impact independent of changes in the federal regulatory role.

This book ends by pointing out connections between various factors
other than action by the federal government and success in increasing
black participation. To that extent its contributors are perhaps willing or
unwilling participants within the political environment that has emerged
over the past several years. Since the role of federal government is likely
to be downplayed in the immediate future even if the Democrats take over
the White House, particularly where civil rights and other so-called "do-
mestic" issues are concerned, the implication of this ending is clear. Perhaps by persuading colleges to undertake the task of desegregation in a
thorough, honest, and—some would argue—courageous manner constitutes one alternative to past reliance upon federal government. Perhaps
monitoring public school reform programs to make sure that black
schoolchildren are not once again shortchanged in the primary and secondary arena constitutes another alternative. At least we have learned by
now that the problem of opening up higher education to all races of people in American society is not one that is likely to disappear. Nor will in-
sincere attempts to offer remedies or new rationalizations for failure sustain
current exclusivity for very long.

About the Editor
and the Contributors

JAMES E. BLACKWELL earned his Ph.D. at Washington State University, and is currently Professor of Sociology at the University of Massachusetts in Boston. He has also taught at Case Western Reserve University, and has lectured in East Africa, India and Nepal. His major works include: *The Black Community: Diversity and Unity*; *Mainstreaming Outsiders: The Production of Black Professionals*; and *Networking and Mentoring: A Cross-Generational Analysis of the Experiences of Blacks in Graduate and Professional Schools*.

JOMILLS H. BRADDOCK, III is Principal Research Scientist, Center for Social Organization of Schools, and Associate Professor of Sociology at Johns Hopkins University. He received his Ph.D. in Sociology from Florida State University, and has published numerous articles and chapters on inequality and social justice, and the long-term effects of school desegregation.

RAYMOND M. BURSE is President of Kentucky State University, and holds a long and impressive record of achievement in academics, athletics, and community service. A former Rhodes Scholar at Oxford University, in England, he later earned his J.D. degree from Harvard Law School, and practiced law with the firm of Wyatt, Tarrant and Combs in his native Kentucky.

ELAINE J. COPELAND is Associate Dean of the Graduate College and Assistant Professor in the Department of Educational Psychology at the University of Illinois. She received a Ph.D. in Counseling from Oregon State University, where she coordinated counseling programs for minority students. Concerned with increasing access of underrepresented minority students to graduate study, she researches cross-cultural counseling and educational policy related to minorities in higher education.

EDGAR G. EPPS has been the Marshall Field IV Professor of Urban Education at The University of Chicago since 1970. He taught previously at Tuskegee Institute and the University of Michigan. He was educated at Talladega College and Washington State University, where he earned the Ph.D. degree in Sociology. Dr.

Epps has published extensively in the fields of psychology and education. His books include: *Black Students in White Schools*; *Race Relations*; *Cultural Pluralism*; and (with Patricia Gurin) *Black Consciousness, Identity and Achievement*.

JAY HEUBERT earned his J.D. and Ed.D. degrees at Harvard University. He is Assistant Professor of Education at the Harvard Graduate School of Education, and Lecturer on Law at the Harvard Law School. Between 1980 and 1985 he was a trial attorney in the Civil Rights Division of the US Department of Justice, where he worked on desegregation cases involving public systems of higher education in Louisiana, Mississippi, and Alabama.

KENNETH W. JACKSON is Assistant Professor of Sociology at the University of Houston Downtown Campus. He received his Ph.D. in Sociology from the University of Chicago and has previously taught at Texas Southern University and Rice University. Dr. Jackson recently began a study of black faculty members at traditionally white institutions in states affected by Title VI regulation.

LARRY LESLIE received his Ed.D. at the University of California, Berkeley, and is Professor of Education and Director of the Center for the Study of Higher Education at the University of Arizona. He has worked on desegregation cases involving public systems of higher education in Louisiana, Mississippi, and Alabama, serving as the US Department of Justice's expert on issues of finance.

MICHAEL T. NETTLES is a Research Scientist in the Educational Policy Research and Services Division of the Educational Testing Service. A political scientist who specializes in policy research in higher education, Mr. Nettles was formerly Assistant Director for Academic Affairs at the Tennessee Higher Education Commission. He is currently developing an outcome assessment methodology for colleges and universities, developing models for longitudinal student research at community colleges, and assessing the effects of financial assistance upon graduate student attendance and performance.

BARBARA W. NEWELL is Regents Professor, Florida State University, and Visiting Senior Lecturer at Harvard University. Previously, she was Chancellor of the State University System of Florida, US Ambassador to UNESCO appointed by President Carter, and President of Wellesley College in Massachusetts. Her doctorate is in the field of economics, and she has held administrative and teaching posts at the University of Wisconsin, University of Michigan and the University of Pittsburgh.

WILLIAM T. TRENT is Assistant Professor in the Departments of Educational Policy Studies and Sociology at the University of Illinois, Urbana-Champaign. A former director of the Educational Opportunity Program at George Washington University, he received his Ph.D. in Sociology from the University of North Carolina at Chapel Hill. He has held research appointments with the Center for Educational Policy Studies at Duke University, and the Center for Social Organization of Schools at Johns Hopkins University. His research centers upon equity issues in higher education and the effects of school desegregation.

ISRAEL TRIBBLE, JR. is currently the Executive Director of both the McKnight Programs in Higher Education in Florida and the Florida Endowment Fund for Higher Education. He received his Ed.D. in Administration and Policy Analysis with an emphasis in Higher Education from Stanford University. Dr. Tribble has held a variety of administrative and policy-making positions in government and higher education in the State University System of Florida, US Department of Education, and other agencies.

JOHN B. WILLIAMS, III, (editor), is Associate Professor of Education and Assistant to the President at Harvard University, where he holds overall responsibility for affirmative action and equal employment opportunity programs. He teaches and conducts research on the politics of education, government regulation of higher education, public policy implementation, and urban education. Mr. Williams has taught at Vanderbilt University and has held a variety of state and federal government positions. Previously, he conducted community-based projects aimed at improving urban schools in New Jersey. Mr. Williams earned his doctorate in education administration and policy analysis at Harvard.

CHARLES V. WILLIE's Ph.D. was awarded by Syracuse University, where he served as Professor and Chair of the Department of Sociology and Vice President. Since 1974, he has been Professor of Education and Urban Studies at Harvard University's Graduate School of Education. A former president of the Eastern Sociological Society, he was appointed by President Carter to the President's Commission on Mental Health and is the author of *School Desegregation Plans That Work*, *Effective Education*, and *The Ivory and Ebony Towers*.

Index

Note: Page numbers followed by t. or f. indicate tables and figures, respectively.